T0309861

François Laruelle

STRUGGLE AND UTOPIA
AT THE END TIMES OF PHILOSOPHY

translated by Drew S. Burk and Anthony Paul Smith

La Lutte et l'Utopie à la fin des temps philosophiques by François Laruelle
© Éditions Kimé, 2004

Translated by Drew S. Burk & Anthony Paul Smith
as *Struggle and Utopia at the End Times of Philosophy*

First Edition
Minneapolis © 2012, Univocal Publishing

Published by Univocal
123 North 3rd Street, #202
Minneapolis, MN 55401

Thanks to Meredith Wagner, Christophe Wall-Romana,
John Ebert, Nicola Rubczak, Kevin Collen,
Hannah Kovacs, Taylor Adkins, Joseph Weissman,
Berit Soli-Holt, and Gina Newman.

Designed & Printed by Jason Wagner

Distributed by the University of Minnesota Press

ISBN 9781937561055
Library of Congress Control Number 2012946068

TABLE OF CONTENTS

One Foot in Struggle and the Other in Utopia:
The Vision Quest of François Laruelle

"[…] the poor is almost always seen to have a prophetic capacity: not only is the poor *in* the world, but the poor itself is the very possibility of the world. Only the poor lives radically the actual and present being, in destitution and suffering, and thus only the poor has the ability to renew being. The divinity of the multitude of the poor does not point to any transcendence. On the contrary, here and only here in this world, in the existence of the poor, is the field of immanence presented, confirmed, consolidated, and opened. The poor is god on earth."
- Michael Hardt and Antonio Negri

"Even if this relentless generation accompanies the history-world in the form of cries and despair and suffering, in the form of protests and disillusions spilling forth from Hell, even if this generation can be considered as a garbage heap through which world-history strives to provide itself with an acceptable meaning, it must be systematically adjusted with its sights set on a more sober, non-historical form in the sense where we understand this "non-" as a radical inversion of the philosophizability or world-form that structures it."
- François Laruelle

When Anthony Paul Smith and I began co-translating *Struggle and Utopia in The End Times of Philosophy* in the autumn of 2011, something was beginning to happen out in the streets. There was a cry that I had recognized from my time living in France some six years earlier. It was the cry of the disappeared. The cry of those who no longer had a voice, or never had one to begin with. In the autumn of 2005, while I was teaching in Avignon, it was a thrilling moment for the youth whom, from one day to the next, were taken seriously by the government. But the fires that burned in the streets all over France at that time were of a much greater signification than a mere acting-out or the rebelliousness of youth who were alienated from the dominant cultural narratives. There was a collective voice that could be detected within the cultural signifiers and media saturation; a familiar almost forgotten, almost stifled, cry of the disappeared. *Los desaparecidos*. There are majorities and there are minorities and then there are those who have no voice whatsoever. Those cadavers, immigrant bodies that, weeks before the French riots, were found in an all too familiar burn pyre due to the poor living conditions and unkempt housing structures. Outside the city, in shantytown suburbs with pleasant sounding vacation spot names such as *Clichy-sous-Bois*, the voices of the voiceless could be heard.

There are certain voices, singular and collective, not allowed to be heard in the city. The voices of those living in refugee camps, sitting in ICE detention centers, content to be provided with a meal and a place to sleep, and scared to death of being sent back to some geography of death and starvation. There are those silent shadows of lost families, dissolved and dispersed in camps of no-futures, living in the future of hurricanes and nuclear fall-out, earthquakes and gun-shots. You see the blind spots of the future are already amongst us.

Right before the French uprisings of 2005, 6,000 kilometers away in another francophone city, New Orleans, there were other voices being systematically stifled and put into another shantytown of the disappeared in mold-laden trailers, slowly beginning to be forgotten. Their voices sputtering out.

Six months after the first strikes in France that autumn, I was visiting Paris heading towards one of my favorite bookstores at Place de la Sorbonne, while students, taking up the lead from the frustration and disappeared voices who had lit the first spark the previous school semester, had begun to strike against new labor laws that would no longer provide protections for beginning workers in new employment. The student strike would last for months. By the time I made it to my cherished bookstore, it had been boarded up and abandoned. A year later I would stroll past Place de la Sorbonne once again, hoping that the bookstore would

X

be there again in all of its splendor. To my dismay, it had been turned into a clothing store.

And a year later in New Orleans, the disappeared were still disappeared and the gentrification had begun, the movie sets poured in and the cry from those living in abandoned trailers was no longer distinguishable from the wind. This is how it worked with the disappeared, they only rarely have their cries heard and it is usually as they are on their way to becoming disappeared, the brief faint echo or plea.

And so last autumn while plunging into the following work by François Laruelle, the cries of the disappeared once again could be heard echoing out from the abyss, but the world was only beginning to recoil in the after-shock of the nuclear fall-out from Fukushima and the real-time global hurricane of economic acceleration. The economic hurricane of the past several years didn't just hit New Orleans, it hit every territory across the western hemisphere. I had just passed through abandoned factory towns in Sweden, spoken with frustrated educators looking for those who could figure out a way to teach their 9th graders math and reading skills in a Scandinavian culture that prided itself on its techno-cultural prowess and linguistic competency. But even there, in the once seemingly utopian space I had known as a teenager, even there, I could hear the cries of the disappeared in the form of a town full of suicides and broken families.

And as I spoke with yet another colleague who was getting adjuncted to death, the low hum of the disappeared began to gain volume.

Tent cities are not new to many of those whose voices we cannot hear. And within these marginal regions, off the media and political grid, this is perhaps where we reaffirm the definition of what we can call humanity: those invisible and disappeared voices and lives, expunged from the systems and flows of the markets.

You see sometimes things emerge, accelerate, organize and form at a pace beyond any concrete understanding. The Wall St. protest is perhaps not merely a protest against Wall St. but an embodiment of the unconscious desire of a collective community that demands not to be labeled and classified and shelved into the margins of forgotten souls. The accursed share shows itself in these shadows of the future.

Collectives: networked, communal, working together, sharing, supporting, cooperating to sustain an exciting, hopeful, space of being part of an en-acting of a future-to-come which is already here. In these times of acceleration and transition into a globalized digital networked city-world (Virilio) there is an urgent call for attempting to think and creatively practice within a real-time reality where to even begin to understand a situation is to transform it, which is to say, to place oneself within it.

How does one organize within an acephalic, spherical, foamic spillage of the real-time screen word? How does one look past the surface of appearance when all that one will find beneath it is more appearance? The Occupy movement spread like a fire that, try as one might, will only remain at a level of slow burning embers. It popped up on the screen of actuality and joined the realm of the virtual where tear-gassed students and the unemployed, debt ridden future victims of the trauma of digitality were turned into images shared and cloned across screen upon screens around the world. The real didn't seem to matter as much as the image. By becoming images and being mediated around the world, a police officer macing students at UC Davis merely becomes a parody across the cybernetic invisible enclosure. And here amongst these clouds of cloned-image-streams, we already know something in our relation to the real has changed.

Photos that had been used to help liberate or bear witness to reality, entered into the realm of digitality, and within that mediated sphere, they are all swept up into the aptly named cloud. And within the cloud, the cybernetic connections were as beneficial as they were detrimental to everyone involved in the game. The public and the private is forever going away, every one of us finding ourselves in the realm of self-surveillance and immobility.

We are disappearing ourselves. As goes materiality so goes the worker. Up into the clouds.

But down on the ground, there is another Real. Another uni-version.

Some years don't last 12 months, in fact, we all know history as a temporality can be and is constructed in various ways. History is also known under the moniker of event-histories, moments where processes of duration enter into the real, out of nowhere perhaps … from the non-place, the u-topos … one possible future becomes real, what we often call the present. And so as the debt crises continue and more and more young people are left with the idea of work becoming a privilege and not a right, where we are all caught within the contradictory liberatory and enslaving relation with the digital, perhaps François Laruelle's work has found its "suspended chora" within the non-place.

Non-philosophy is a strange thought and it was precisely thought about and constructed as a science for and of, the Stranger (Stranger-subject) that we all are to ourselves and to others. For if there is one position we can see take shape to a certain degree within Laruelle's landscape it is that he is trying to engage reality from the position of the immanence of reality itself. Which is to say that, like Derrida and Deleuze before him, Laruelle understands the inherent duty of the philosopher of every generation to re-think the theory and more importantly the practice of thinking and being a friend to wisdom, of doing philosophy or "theory" *tout court*. One must engage with the present in order to understand it. One must deconstruct, one must create one's own concepts. One must re-acquaint oneself with the power of artistic theoretical practice as engagement with the real.

And so when one begins to read Laruelle's project of non-philosophy turned non-standard philosophy, what one immediately begins to notice is his perpetual engagement with writing, thinking and *seeing* the real, not merely trying to *reflect* the real, or reflect upon the real in order to get snared within a game of mirrors, but to see *the mirror without reflection* that is radical immanence and the position of philo-fiction, a philosophical poetics of seeing no longer predicated on the self-reflexive tendencies of philosophy, but on a uni-lateral duality of seeing the real like the poets, striving to take on the blind-spots of actuality, as seismographs of man's relationship with the world.

For Laruelle, ordinary man, what he names in *Struggle and Utopia* under various monikers, *Man-in-man*, *man-in-the-last-instance*, or *Humaneity*, is his continued preoccupation with trying to think and liberate humans from being subjugated to dominating conceptions of the human by philosophy and its ideal entities such as Desire, Identity, Power, etc. Philosophy should be at the service of man and not man at the service of philosophy. Laruelle's radical shift of thinking needs philosophy but no longer privileges it in the same way, in order to precisely give back to philosophy its liberatory power. For Laruelle's task in speaking of Humaneity and the subjects forced by the future, is trying as well to bring about a democratic opening in thought and philosophy in order to provide for various liberatory theoretical practices of living within a present that is weary and tired of living off its own dead limb ideologies and feeding off itself at all levels of the ecosystem.

Unlike a lot of French thinkers writing and studying immediately following the Post-68 era, Laruelle was always an outsider, not graduating from the École Normale Supérieure at the rue d'Ulm, but completing his degree at another École Normale outside Paris (École Normale St. Cloud). And yet, Laruelle was also one of the first French thinkers to grasp at the novelty and importance of the work of Gilles Deleuze and Jacques Derrida. One of the titles of his first books, *Textual Machines* [*Machines Textuelles*] says it all. As the French intellectual landscape of the 1970s gave rise to specific groups of thinkers from the Nouveaux Philosophes (whose remnants are still found in the likes of Bernard Henry-Levy) to those thinkers unwillingly inscribed into the cultural branding of French Theory (whose thought contributions were taken as models abroad as intellectual torch-bearers in the liberatory culture wars of the 70s and 80s), Laruelle was there all the while in the background sculpting his project. He was the first to show Bernard Stiegler the importance of the work of Gilbert Simondon, another thinker only now slowly beginning to be read in the Anglophone world. And Laruelle later would be one of the editors to re-issue Simondon's work in the late 80s. And it was precisely at this time, around the late 80s, that Laruelle's project slowly began to show itself to him. His attempt would be to make a science *of* and *for* philosophy, to use it as a material for a theoretical practice in order to liberate philosophy from itself providing for new democratic possibilities of expression within a world where chaos reigns and no Principle of Sufficient Philosophy, no self-reflexive vicious circles of doubled up mirroring of objects and subjects will suffice. With unilateral duality, in the landscape of uni-lation and not re-lation, there is the cut of the Real, (the One-in-One) and there is what we can do with it.

In the following book you will find yourself immersed in the universe of a rogue artist-thinker who has slowly sculpted his (-non) philosophical and theoretical work for the past 40 years. Even a reader well versed in contemporary currents of continental philosophy and theory will notice upon entering onto Laruelle's territory that it is a thought that strives to carve out its own linguistic singularity in its herculean attempt to think immanence in an immanent fashion. Laruelle's style of writing and its theoretical-science-fictional pursuits as a new genre of thought-style, what he calls philo-fiction, a poetic optics equal parts science fiction and what he now calls a generic science reliant on aspects of linear algebra and quantum physics (the imaginary number and the vector) is a linguistic universe that at times stretches the reader's ability to make the text legible.

The reader is confronted with a prose that strives to treat immanence via various new linguistic concepts such as the One-in-One or the Vision-in-One and Man-in-Man or Man-in-the-last-instance. In his attempt at achieving what he claims Spinoza and Deleuze were not capable of doing: treating immanence in an immanent manner, he strives for a thinking in-the-last-instance that verges on the edges of comprehensibility precisely because the Real or the Vision-in-One can never be fully inscribed within language as such and at best it comes in the form of what Laruelle calls a uni-lateral duality, in the form of a scientific poetic imaginary equation of the cloned subject=X.

As with the work of Deleuze and Guattari in *A Thousand Plateaus*, Laruelle's project is one that is strange in its beauty and desires of experimentation, liberation, and openness and yet it strives to go one step further in its position as theoretical science *of* and *for* philosophy. In his last book, *What is Philosophy?*, Deleuze even makes sure to note that Laruelle was one of those doing something that was interesting and of import in the aftermath of the French Theory craze. And it is perhaps from here that the new reader of Laruelle's work can gain some sort of footing to enter into his insufficient world of thought fictions. It is a new genre, a theoretical fictional practice that understands when one is within the Real, in-One, when one is trying to think a theoretical practice that strives to bring out the Humaneity in man, that this attempt must remain at the level of what he calls philo-fiction.

While Laruelle's work makes use of ways of thinking the present in a futural form of a messianism and of the cloned subject who is forced from this future and from this futural unconscious, his work is not about some sort of otherworldly salvation. Non-philosophy or non-standard philosophy is not some sort of religion or secular "non-religion." (On the contrary, non-philosophy will take as one of its main concerns to fight against any sort of re-appropriation of it as non-religion as Laruelle points out in the last sentences of *Struggle and Utopia*). Nevertheless, non-philosophy in taking seriously the religious elements and material found within philosophy will also be prudent of the pitfalls of taking on a hyper-religious position. According to Jacques Derrida, in deconstructing Christianity, Artaud became hyper-Christian, and perhaps Nietzsche as well. And so, understanding that non-philosophy is constantly on guard against the vicious circle of philosophy and its deconstruction, it pits them against each other.

Non-philosophy is still about philosophy and its history, it's still about deconstruction, desiring machines, and a myriad of theoretical inquiries, inventions and discoveries but these are merely materials amongst many others for those who are heretics *for* the World. Which is to say, those who Laruelle calls non-philosophers. Those whose theoretical practice and thinking places the human at the center of their practice. So, non-philosophy finds itself opening up mutations of these discourses. Non-marxisms, non-deconstructions, non-aesthetics, non-deleuzian readings, etc. And in this manner, there are as many non-philosophies as there are non-philosophers.

So what does non-philosophy do? How does one know if one is a non-philosopher? These are questions that perhaps are of less importance than asking more importantly what can art, music, media, and philosophy become when they are put at the service of man rather than man at the service of them. Can they become liberatory practices of self-expression and communal exchange in an age of ever more atrocities in the name of Man but which are really in the name of cannibalistic techno-excesses of an already dead age of factory production lines, junk foods, junk bots, junk democracy, and so on? As our modes of exchange and reliance on the world of the digital and the virtual continue to increase, what we need now more than ever are those who dare to think the world anew, those creators, discoverers who dare to engage in the world and know that to understand it, one must transform it.

Philosophy does not go away with the work of François Laruelle, it finds its new life. It lives as mutation, like that of non-Euclidean geometry to Euclidean geometry, providing for novel ways of moving and thinking in and about space within a world that seems on the verge of a lack of mobility at various levels. Is this a new theoretical, fictional science for the virtual? Yes. More virtual and pataphysical than Deleuze's own attempt? Perhaps. More excessive but only in its brazen attempt to be a philo-fiction and to under-determine philosophy and art in order to allow for them to be used by the man-in-the-last-instance who is perhaps the only true witness to identity. Within a position of a real-time world we urgently need an understanding and orientation in order for the man-in-man, the human within Humaneity to take up the task of allowing for liberatory theoretical fictions that can allow for a practice of expression where those lost voices, those disappeared or those struggling with philosophy and its utopias (predicated on turning its head backwards towards the past) can have the courage to take up a rigorous position of staring down the abyss of the future present with scarred eyes (Nietzsche) allowing for the scars to heal in order to put art and thought back into a democratic practice for man and for the World. Is this heretical? Is it heresy to speak the words of liberation? Neither master nor slave? Heresy is harder than it sounds. For as Laruelle reminds the reader throughout his work, "By definition no one is able to simply *snatch* his weapons from an overmaster." Philosophy needs its rebels. And so does the meat-grinder of revolution. We almost begin to laugh when we read the preciseness and bluntness of Laruelle's claim, "The Rebel is a quasi-robot or an automaton but without having the materiality of a robot." His project is a new genre akin to science fiction and from which (like philosophy and theory as well) it takes inspiration. It knows the future takes precedence over the present, indeed *is* the present and he knows like the poets and as a poetic thinker and inventor of an imaginary optics, that it is through fiction that we transform the world. It is through struggle and utopia.

Drew S. Burk
Minneapolis, September 2012

The Living and Unfinished Project of Non-Philosophy: Situating *Struggle and Utopia*

I've written at length about the experience that lead to my first translation of François Laruelle's work, *Future Christ: A Lesson in Heresy*, as well as in other essays detailing my development of a "non-theology" that builds off of and develops Laruelle's non-philosophy. So, I will not repeat here what has already been said elsewhere or add my own personal reflections to Drew's stunning placement of this book in the wider social and political struggles that mark our age. Instead, here I will only place *Struggle and Utopia at the End Times of Philosophy* within the development of non-philosophy and debates internal to that development housed under ONPHI.

Laruelle has developed his own periodization of his oeuvre, though it should be noted that this is somewhat tongue-in-cheek, and he locates *Struggle and Utopia* as part of "Philosophy IV." This period is marked by a rigorous development of non-philosophy using philosophy as a material but also alongside materials that have historically been mixed with philosophy proper, always acting as some sort of barbarian at the gate or "true philosophy's" internal enemy. I am speaking of course of religious and political materials, seemingly always mixed up with one another in human society. For non-philosophy there is no true enemy, especially not some hallucinated internal enemy like the ones central to the racist logics of 20th Century anti-Semitism and contemporary Islamophobia in both Europe and America, and so in relation to this material non-philosophy mutated itself and this in turn mutates the material, disempowering both and intensifying them in equal turns. This can be seen even in Laruelle's play on the French lyrics of the first verse of *L'Internationale* which forms the title of his fifth chapter: *Let Us Make a Tabula Rasa Out of the Future*. A literal translation of the French lyrics is "let us make a tabula rasa [or blank slate] of the past" and here the change from past to future reorients the utopian project of communism towards the undetermined immanent future rather than cleaning the slate of the past. Disempowering the vicious circle of a certain retributive justice called for in those lyrics and emotive of violent aspects of the communist project. This engagement was called for, in part, because of non-philosophy's already unexamined relationship with religious materials under the headings of gnosis and the mystical, to say nothing of the consistent political questions Laruelle has tarried with and which surround religion. Neither politics nor religion are unified wholes, but both express a certain duality as both continue to be a great source of human suffering as well as being able to be used for human liberation. As such they touch the very core of the utopian non-philosophical project.

In *Struggle and Utopia* this engagement with religion and politics is made even more explicit in relation to the specific context of the French philosophical scene generally and more specifically amongst those who developed their own theoretical work alongside of Laruelle under the auspices of ONPHI. Two of these names, and their respective philosophical systems, will likely be familiar to readers of French philosophy; namely Alain Badiou and Michel Henry. The first being the radical atheist, Communist philosopher and the other being the anti-Communist, anti-scientistic Catholic phenomenologist. But the third name will be unfamiliar to most readers, Gilles Grelet, the radical Gnostic Maoist, whose hatred of the World leads him to reject all the implicit compromises with it present in Henry's Christianity and Badiou's secular version of the Christian truth-event. A word of introduction is required because much of the last two chapters of *Struggle and Utopia* are developed specifically in relation to Grelet's work.

The critique of Grelet put forward in this book by Laruelle is certainly developed with characteristic polemical flair. But this all belies a respect for Grelet's work since Laruelle holds it up along with Badiou and Henry as one of the most creative contemporary works in philosophy and he has since 2005 edited a book series with Grelet called "Nous, les sans-philosophes." It also would cover over how much of Laruelle's critique is developed in order to sharpen the practice of his own non-philosophy. Grelet is a young theorist, and he would eschew the name philosopher calling his own work an "anti-philosophy as rigorous gnosis," who completed advanced degrees in economics and a doctorate in philosophy while working with Laruelle in the late 90s and early 2000s. After a number of years teaching in the French education system and participating with radical experimental art collectives in Paris he has now taken to the sea as a sailor, living and working on his boat which he christened *Théorème*. His work has been developed in increasingly experimental ways, mostly through short written pieces, experimental edited collections, films, and a number of short but dense books. At the time of the original French debate that *Struggle and Utopia* speaks to, that is the early 2000s, Grelet had developed a theory of "non-religion" bringing together elements of non-philosophy with elements from the work of Guy Lardreau and Christian Jambet. In the 1970s these two philosophers together attempted to develop an "ontology of revolution" by bringing together studies in political theology with their own Maoism and the anti-philosophy of Lacan.

Grelet developed this most rigorously in his 2002 work entitled *Déclarer la gnose. D'une guerre qui revient à la culture*, a possible translation of which would be *Declaring Gnosis: On a War that Falls upon Culture*. In this work Grelet lays out his own critique of philosophy in the name of an ultra-left theory of rebellion. The philosophy critiqued here is specifically Western or Occidental philosophy which is always a philosophy of murky darkness or confusion, always ending in some compromise with the World, always losing one's soul. Against this form of philosophy he looks for inspiration in "Oriental" philosophy, or really religion, which exists in purity and light. It is important to note that "the Oriental" referred to here isn't some philosophy outside of our culture, but the Oriental within Western thought, that is the Orientalism of gnosis or fanaticism. The same kind of "Orient" that Ibn-Sina looked to when he wrote of the "Oriental philosophy" of Suhrawardi, his own countryman, or Kant when he feared the *Schwärmerei*. Just as Ibn-Sina saw this as a kind of Oriental wing to his own thought, or we might even say a left-wing, Grelet begins by treating this tradition not as an other but as our own, a lesson he learned from Jambet's own masterful works in Islamic and traditional European philosophy. So this philosophy of light is a kind of anti-philosophy at war with the obscure philosophy that forms our World.

Grelet's own theory begins from an axiom that there must be a radical break or cut between the Real and reality, between the Truth and philosophy. Thus his theory is seen only in the light of a kind of violence of theoretical separation, an absolute and total cultural revolution, an eternal rebellion against all the ways of the World whose goal is to end the World. In a number of ways, this looks like the gnostic theory of heresy and rebellion developed by Laruelle in *Future Christ*, and this similarity allows Laruelle to see the possibility of certain mutations of non-philosophy that would irrevocably destroy non-philosophical practice, namely turning non-philosophy into a religious discourse. Addressing the "Grelet variant" of non-philosophy, which Laruelle calls non-religion, is a way of addressing critiques leveled at non-philosophy in general and so is an act of self-criticism and correction. Addressing the claim that non-philosophy arbitrarily engages with materials is perhaps most important for Laruelle in *Struggle and Utopia*. One must have a taste for gnosis, this critique goes, rather than gnosis being a particularly powerful form of thought. What Laruelle tries to show in this text is that the material is never arbitrary and indeed can be highly important for the development of non-philosophy. But gnosis, for Laruelle, or any other religious material, can never be sufficient regardless of how important it may be in the development of non-philosophy. And in the way that religion has historically set traps for human beings, like philosophy, it is philosophy for Laruelle that may be used as a weapon of defense against its violence, and religion used as a weapon of defense against the violence of philosophy: one must struggle on two fronts. Ultimately, Laruelle's claim is that non-philosophy, in the guise of a unified theory of philosophy and religion or revolution, will escape the violence of the vicious cycle of retributive justice by making an *a priori* defense of the human.

Anthony Paul Smith
Philadelphia, September 2012

Because of Lorraine

INTRODUCTION:
MAN AS ULTIMATUM AND AS TESTAMENT

Man, an Answer Without a Question

Non-philosophy is an attempt at a reply to perhaps the most determining if not unique question of science fiction and gnosis: *should we save humanity?* and *What do we mean by humanity?* Towards this end, it raises the generic name of man to the level of a proper noun and places it under the sign of the Name-of-Man. Despite appearances and the expected protests from the philosophers, this is no longer a question philosophy dares still pose, to say nothing of trying to answer it, having never been made for this task, man being for philosophy, a secondary or intermediary animal, and sometimes terminal, or a denatured animal one must re-establish or to which one must re-attach new chains. As for religions that make claims over him with sometimes quite hyperbolic aplomb, they are not preoccupied with Man himself, but with his being good or evil and are merely vast theodicies rather than anthropodicies. As for the manner in which one can answer, which is to say, correctly pose, the question, if not the means—the future of humanity has only a small chance to find them at the margins of certain forms of religion, science and technology, and very much at large in philosophy. This is because they have remained silent in regards to man for reasons yet to be elucidated but presumed to be arranged in the offhand manner of philosophy, the latter because their professional discourse on man has been exhausted and has been the object of disastrous "verifications" to the extent that this permanent falsification of philosophy cannot be a gauge of its capacity towards changing hypotheses. When philosophers end up posing this problem, it is as a function of other concerns, about Being, God, Thought, Reason, and other humanistic and

3

anti-humanistic fetishes, about philosophy and its narcissism and thus not with its sights set on man and not at all as a function of him. They insert man within the Whole or the horizon of the World, trying to find man a place that is generally subordinate. Philosophies and religions have developed the unfortunate confusion between Man and anthropos, an evolved animal, and they contrive to multiply the degrees of intermediaries between them, genetic and cultural transitions and displacements, going all the way to seemingly wanting to arrive at a creationist idea from the other side, the lost paradigm.

Science fiction, gnosis, and certain "spiritual" currents that are not at all spiritualistic, but quite often materialistic, better resist capture by philosophies and theologies, since they are ferments added to doctrines which, in the end, awaken human struggle from its conformist slumber and "raise" it to the level of rebellion. The fundamental problems of science fiction are "philosophical" merely by a certain vague appearance and confusion beneficial to philosophy. Wanting to recuperate gnosis via philosophy is an active illusion already in Jakob Böhme and Hegel. In reality, the problems are those of humanity's destiny within the Universe. *What is at stake is the destiny of humanity in science fiction and in gnosis,* whereas in philosophy it principally moves from a question of the history of Being to that of man in Being. In passing from the world to the Universe without horizon, and from a terrestrial technics to utopian technology, the future of humanity comes to be of the utmost importance for science fiction, which tears it away from its traditional foundational tasks in the World and consecrates it to utopia. In part, this is very similar to what gnosis produces at the edges of religion rather than science; destabilizing the traditional ground that welcomed human habitation; it unleashes a multitude of mythological creatures outside the boundaries of the World, dispersed into the universe and thirsting for salvation. They present us with another image of man; a being that does not live, which stopped living on earth or in the heavens, the nomad of the future, the universal Inhabitant. This implies another writing as a new relation to the world. Nonetheless, in the same way that science fiction is nothing more than a purely formal literary activity, philo-fiction as non-philosophy does not create a discipline, but a specific writing that engages the human as such. Hence a change in the practice of this writing of man that is inseparable from a new rigor in the pragmatics of philosophical and other codes.

That Man is not an ancient lost paradigm which we must bring back, that man is the "performed" paradigm of the future-in-person - this is not a supplementary philosophical affirmation; this is a decision that is in accord with Man and thus one must let-to-be-given. Rather than building upon it, non-philosophy makes possible an observation that is not unfair of philosophy, which knows in bad faith "what it turns around." In its highest of moments, like the *Parmenides*, it plays with quite abstract problems and with anonymous or inhuman entities, which do not concern Man but merely the Greek character of his intelligence and his rational animal language, and under repetitive and elementary forms which strived to pass as his essence. Within the same movement but at the opposite end, we find the infinite mediatic fall into gossip, into our own hell, of communication. This unique and double becoming going from one extreme to the other is necessary; this is its parallel life with the World. Necessary but uninteresting, or interesting but indifferent. As for us, we are possessed with a syndrome of religious and inhuman threat, having lost the comfort and assistance of traditional religion which seemed to be valuable to us, philosophy preferring World and Being, humanism heading off with all the others into the slums of tele-thought; what remains of humans that is worth a minute of pain, if not the humans themselves, those that are-without-being? Even the man-object or subject born prematurely and too young, ending too old and orphaned, seems out of reach. Decidedly inadequate for the World and History, the lone being threatened by solitude and condemned to look inside himself for the reasons of his abandonment. A small relief, no more, can be provided to him through one final handful of disciplines that never really abandoned him and which can be substituted for the religions and always indifferent philosophies, in the worst case scenario diverting his gaze, at best seeing through it without indeed knowing what to do with this impossible being, due to *its strangeness or irregular identity, other than calling to him and putting him into the World*. Psychoanalysis and Marxism, in part with the effects of the mutations brought about by science and rebellions that are the operations of gnosis; this is what remains of the ancient cardinal points for a being finally recognized without-world, and not merely without-a-fixed-world, a utopian subject of the Universe. Mutants, androids, eons, and clones, what else are they than the as yet undecipherable symptoms of a future, which has never abandoned us?

Specific to non-philosophy is the centering of all problems on the destination of humanity in drawing help from these supports without falling over into one specific type of imagination and science fiction writing and gnosis. From this point of view, it is philosophy despite everything that provides the indispensable conceptual technology, whereas non-philosophy is prepared to transform it into a technology of philo-fiction and gnosis-fiction that we would like to see rival or at least parallel these other disciplines. However, it is clear that philosophy will not relinquish its privileges without being forced to, and the abandonment of its authority will be an expensive price to pay. Precipitation or impatience is the specific danger of this undertaking, believing indeed that religion, art, or technology can simply substitute themselves for philosophy and that philosophy can be left on the side of the road, when philosophy is precisely the human attempt at tracing the entire possible route of the road! Non-philosophy can no doubt appear as an attempt, contradictory in its terms, of a "domestication" or "rationalization," of the reterritorialization of this free-standing new humanity, but we are counting on Man himself, Man-in-person and him alone, to keep us from this normalization which would like to fasten the new humanity to a ground, a foundation, an immobile earth and giver of the ultimate meaning.

If the conceptual tools must be forged starting from philosophy as its principle but not merely as a material, they will be such that *Man alone in his solitude can determine them, and as subject, transform them*. Non-philosophy aims overall to operate through radicality an inversion (uni-version) of this order and not a reversal, and to put philosophy in exclusive dependence on Man, in the sense that it is now him and no longer philosophy that is defined in such a manner that he can determine the possibility and meaning of this new service of philosophy. It is in this regard that non-philosophy responds to the central question of gnosis and science fiction, loyal to their spirit in affirming the primacy of the answer over the question, providing the answer that determines the form of the question. We are not, on the contrary, dealing with a vicious circle. Because this poses Man as the Answer, the X or the Unknown that *determines a subject, from which he is separate*, an operating subject of salvation for the philosophical relationship between the question and the answer. Non-philosophy also inverts the philosophical, religious, and humanist demand and, without all at once resolving the problem, provides the necessary conditions and means to solve it. This Answer is that *there is no Man but Man*, the rest is anthropology. Or more still: there is no future but the Future, the rest is present or past. Only an exclusive love of theory would be capable of seeing in this affirmation an anthropological idealism or domination of the World by Man. This would be to confuse, in the purest of philosophical styles, domination with primacy, or negative determination and determination in-the-last-instance. Man-in-person is a negative determination in terms of effectiveness and not at all a domination, and his effectiveness that leads to a "force" demands the support of the World. He does not have to be saved because it is him and him alone that is the forced necessity with the ability to save. Not that Man is the Savior, but rather the Saved-without-salvation since there are no other possible saviors before or after him. Far from promising or bringing salvation to the humanity-in-the World, it is Man that brings the World to salvation through the subject. And humanity grappling with the

World only arrives at salvation, which is to say the subject, because humanity is already given-in-Man.

Human Messianity: Inversion of Eschatology

In order to clarify this Answer = X and understand in what way the humanity-in-the-World is also already given in a completely different manner, namely in the mode of as-Man or what we will call from now on *Humaneity*, one must go to the Man beyond Man and pose an axiom that is strictly identical to the nearest language of the first, *there is no beyond-Man except Man the world over, there is no beyond the Future except the Future as it appears to the nearest Past*, and to perceive from it the grasp of the last instance the Future assumes, either as ultimatum, for our harried times and for the World in which to a certain degree we find ourselves enclosed. We understand the as-Man as the immanent utopia which arrives and which can only arrive in front-of us-the-subjects, and utopia as this ultimatum addressed to humans: to become the saved subjects from the World *for* the World. These are the *eschata*, the last things, far from merely hoping for them, we are those who have lived them for all of eternity. Suffering humanity is only introduced to salvation because the latter comes according-to-the-Future like an ultimatum demanding the act of world war.

The radical inversion of eschatology, in all its rigor, its uni-version, far from any reversal, is one of the last contributions of non-philosophy. In order to quite simply understand this gesture, one must remember philosophy and the principal gestures and variations of its subject: *to uproot* and *to displace*. The famous "changing of terrain," hardly anti-idealist. The operation of uprooting hierarchies preceded and conditioned the conquest of new terrain, the "real" is thus penetrated by an operative ideality. Uni-version is not simply the opposite of reversal, not even an inversion or version in the ordinary sense of the term, but the being-uni-versed from the World by the *Man-in-person*. The new terrain is first given, offered by kindness or provided to human subjects and cannot be by a subjective operation. This is why if it is given each time

8

without being the object of some givenness, it can only be given as the Future-in-person to the extent that it needs no operation but could itself determine one. Utopia, here, in its non-transcendental and non-imaginary concept, is not the refusal of all terrains but the permanent changing of terrain that history and philosophy seek. Man does not need to change terrain, it being given that Man is his own basis, and if as a subject he ends up changing terrain it is obviously because he is thrown by and as this Future into the World. A new slogan is revealed with a double meaning: *Let us make a tabula rasa of the future*. Either the positive future that is imposed upon us is merely the harassment of the past or the permanent Capitalist revolution (which we should get rid of), or on the contrary we use the future and Man as a new tabula rasa.

"Inversion" or even "Uni-version" is not yet adequate. What then becomes of radical immanence, which was so often a question in non-philosophy in order to characterize the Real as One? Man is *Uni-versed* where the -versed implies a (r)ejection, the Verso [*L'En-vers*], the *in*-verso, or even the Other-than ... the World, the *in*-Other-than.... Nevertheless, it is indeed as the One-in-One that Man is versed-without-version into the World, versed from oneself (in-versed to be more exact, the true sense of Verso) for the world without there having been an operation of transfer, reversal or reversion. Versed for the world for being the One-in-One rather than "inverse" as if something else versed it and its contents into the World. If we admit Man is this One-in-One, it would literally be a case of saying, like philosophers or priests, shamelessly throwing out the baby with the bathwater after having plunged him down into the water, Man is only placed into the world in a human manner for having been Man rather than anthropos inscribed within the balance sheet of the World. We distinguish the Universe that extends and prolongs the World, for whom the World is a model, and the real Uni-versed which is nothing other than Man not as micro-cosmos, but as a future-being, and as such, versed for the World.

Thus, the One-in-One is the source of the *uni*-versed, they are one and the same. Immanence is the "terrain," that which does not change, thus it is the presupposed or the without-terrain for the World. *The One is identical to in-One or in-Verso and not to the World, but for the World.* The plainly radical immanence can only be the given-in-person in the form of the future. The One-in-One is in fact separated or Other-than … the World but for the World, and this via its lone immanence, which can only act upon a mode of a (versed) thrown-being or a future-being such as Other-than … Radical immanence escapes any imaginary transcendence and it is useless or hopeless however irresistible the temptation to *represent* one final time the One as In-verso or Uni-verse and the Inverse as being for the World. There is an Inverse for the World and it is completely different than the Inverse of the World that philosophers seek in their best moments. Immanence can only be thought and spoken about as utopian and uchronic. The two terms are not opposed, uchronia is the aspect of radical immanence in material time, and in the same way utopia is its aspect relevant to that of space. But with immanent utopia as a non-representable essence of Man, we have conquered *our* conception of the unconscious, which is much more radical than that of psychoanalysis.

Philosophies as Utopias of the Past

Thus we propose the equation *Man=Real=Utopia* as the solution to the question of *what have become of our philosophies? At best utopias, nothing but utopias of the past*, and here we see what has been in reality the dominant form of the World. What was presented as anti-utopian and as a sobering thought of the real continues to turn towards a contrary state of dead suns. The soil of history is not merely filled with spiritual tombs, mummified mythologies, grand hopes become inert. Even what should be considered as the heavens of history contains a quantity of final fires, of cadaverized stars. Philosophy has always been the love of what has taken place, it tends to define existence and distribute its various modes, but are we really familiar with the manner in which philosophy itself exists? Kept in a state of survival, institutionally assisted by the State, it remains like clouds or nebulae, dreams or reveries of history, rumors or crepuscular groundwater propagating time. Philosophies do not live, they survive, are born, disappear, and are reborn in order to vanish almost at the same moment. Either philosophies die from not dying, or they do not die from continually dying, not containing a sufficient amount of reality to disappear for good. The end or death of philosophy is the greatest trap, tricking us into maintaining its will to survive. This is not an idea from today, but the phenomenon seems likely, such that a terrible rumor accompanies it, rumor against rumors that *philosophy is harassment within thought.* Harassing humans with wisdom, happiness, truth, desire, worry, or more plainly with the critique of representation, of the text, of ideology, is it that different from harassment by profit and productivity? No doubt all of this, or most of it, is necessary, and is part of, we would suppose, the resources of humanity, but why must we make it the ultimate meaning of Humaneity? Why must we make an imperative out of it? Do we really believe that to live in a world and according to a form of the world is not merely wisdom, truth, happiness, or virtue, but that from which Man can satisfy himself, that philosophy is something other than harassment by the Logos? Kant and many others are very close to addressing this problem but do not have the means to do so in a way that is more than situational. Philosophy gives us the worldly horizon for every hope, for a perspective it gives us conformism and the stupid cruelty of history, for eschatology the suicide of Logos and for apocalypse the nuclear flash that presided over its birth. There is no reply, only appeals, no decision proper to Man, a harassing appeal to conform himself to the order of production and a hesitating appeal to resist, both of which are transcendent. A survival torn between two appeals, and there is no decision, no immanent appeal that would be more than resisting or exploiting.

What is to be done? Here we decided, with good reason reflecting on the style of philosophy as a dominant form in the World, and with a decisive reason which is the Man-in-person as future identical with immanent force, to take the leap and fight general philosophical harassment in considering philosophies as *utopias of the past* alongside utopias explicitly given as such and which they often refused. It is impossible to elaborate a new practice of the future without dealing with philosophy as a whole as a failed or worldly utopia. If the Gnostics affirmed that the creation of the World was an imperfect work of an evil God, all the more reason for us to say that philosophy, which also makes a work out of the World, is the enterprise of a failed utopist and can be evil. Where does the Evil Genius hide if not in philosophy itself? Philosophical practice has become the archaeology of its own ruins, an archeology of utopias without a future. We are not saying one has to live according to a well-formed utopia, imposed and received with as much gratitude as disbelief, practically producing writings of new thinking to direct philosophy or the world-form to the state of rigorous fiction. Our solution lies within an insufficient or negative utopia. A refusal of sufficient positivity, whether a transcendental positivity of philosophies or a transcendent positivity of reigning utopias. Neither one solution nor the other. But the fabrication or production of utopias with philosophical or other material and devoid of any positive determination.

From here we get the non-philosophical style of utterances which come from both the axiom (this is its mathematical aspect) and from the oracle, this is its philosophical aspect since philosophy is born of the oracles or in any case is nourished by them and by definition leads to ambivalent interpretations. These two aspects find their identity of-the-last-instance within the force-(of)-the-Future. The style of thought and formulation (rather than expression) here is still that of man but which one? The man of-the-last-instance, not man understood as a subject but as the one who determines the subject or the thought not merely without resolving it but in not resolving it. The style is the last forced

12

decision of fidelity, the fidelity of ... and to ... the last-Humaneity; it is the respect of the processes by which the subject produces his or herself starting from his or her human identity and from a material of anonymous generalities. What, in the end, is non-philosophy? It is the style of radicality enacted against the absolute, the style of minimality against satiety, the style of uni-laterality against convertibility, the style of heresy against conformity. Radicality? Each time it poses final and minimal conditions, the least possible but essential conditions for there to be, what? Something rather than nothing? Humanism rather than barbarism? No, a rigorous and liberating knowing rather than philosophical hallucinations. Against the absolute? Its goal is not to intensify life by different drugs such as religion or art or sometimes science, or by philosophy itself, Platonism, Judaism, or even gnosis. Its goal is to save so-called "human" life itself from the survival, whether via drugs or philosophy, of superhumanity. This rigorous strictly human or heretical spirit puts something Cartesian into non-philosophy but only on the condition, as Husserl said, of getting rid of all doctrinal contents of Cartesianism. Something Platonic but only on the condition of getting rid of any Platonic contents. And in the end, there is also something a bit gnostic but only on the condition of getting rid of any mythological contents of gnosis and of religion in general. Non-philosophy's special Ockham's razor even cuts through science fiction, establishing thought in the element of a negative tabula rasa, emptied of the positivity of historical utopias. But this tabula rasa of Man, far from falling back like a full body or a transcendental capital on human life, is precisely *life offered for* ... the World.

The sufficiency of historical-all-too-historical utopias, must be eradicated and classical utopian material must be reconsidered in another manner. World-history is accompanied by a gigantic perpetual production of utopias which can obviously be considered as "scraps" but which can also assume a new destination. Let alone speaking explicitly about religions, whether it is 1. the gigantic utopist production, claimed as such, by Russia in the name of the realization of the kingdom of God on earth, by France and England in a more limited or more directly social and political manner, and in the end by America, sectarian and pioneering, literary and cinematographic; 2. the production of science fiction; 3. the production of gnosis in conceptual personae, events, and mythological becomings. Even if this relentless generation accompanies the history-world in the form of cries of despair and suffering, in the form of protests and disillusions spilling forth from Hell, even if this generation can be considered as a garbage heap through which world-history strives to provide itself with an acceptable meaning, it must be systematically adjusted with its sights set on a more sober, non-historical form in the sense where we understand this "non-" as a radical inversion of the philosophizability or world-form that structures it. Another name for this re-processing would be that of universe-utopias (uni-verse for uni-laterality and uni-version) in order to distinguish them from world-utopias. One of the possibilities of non-philosophy is to give birth to an ecology of utopias, determined by Man-in-person rather than by reasons of the management of tradition.

What we call universe-utopias are clones, unilateral by definition, produced starting from historical utopias as a material to be transformed. The Answer to the central question of science fiction and gnosis, touching on the salvation of humanity and its modality, the *Who?* and the *How?* finds here a rigorous form. The *Who?* finds its answer in the Man-in-person as bearer of a non-temporal future, *the How?* in the subject as "transcendental clone." This term denotes the limit of philosophical pertinence in general, particularly historical or historial pertinence. It is in the style of science fiction and gnosis which are themselves both preparatory forms of non-philosophy as philo-fiction. Thus we decide by default to reconstruct a historical telos that would cancel them out within a non-philosophical-becoming.

So we will have strived to focus our attention on what is generally called philosophy, but with the aim of "reversing" it, a theme that when it does not leave philosophers indifferent, too often raises utopist illusions, and religious promises when it is not just nonsense and sectarian fantasy. Is non-philosophy a new discipline to be placed next to philosophy or the humanities? a gnostic or quietist wisdom? a Greco-Judaic heresy? The final paradox, no doubt, is to try to insert it between the utopia that determines it and the struggle wherein it is resolved, finally identifying what had remained separate: struggle and utopia. This is a task for the end times of philosophy, for the most actual of times, which are by definition the last.

The End Times of Philosophy

The phrase "end times of philosophy" is not a new version of the "end of philosophy" or the "end of history," themes which have become quite vulgar and nourish all hopes of revenge and powerlessness. Moreover, philosophy itself does not stop proclaiming its own death, admitting itself to be half dead and doing nothing but providing ammunition for its adversaries. With our sights set on clearing up this nuance, we differentiate philosophy as an institutional entity, and the philosophizability of the World and History, of "thought-world," which universalizes the narrow concept of philosophy and that of "capital." We also give an eschatological and apocalyptical cause to this end, of "times" or "ages" rather than those of philosophical practice. Last but not least, it is the Future itself in the performativity of its ultimatum that determines this end times, reversing these times from the Identity the Future accorded to it, withdrawing the thought-world from the lie of its death.

Why this style of axioms and oracles, these more or less subtle distinctions, old and debased, with an appeal to the *ultimata*, to end times and last words? We fight to give, parallel to the concept of Hell, its new theoretical position, for its philosophical return and its non-philosophical transformation. No more so than any other word, Hell is not a metaphor here, just the Principle of Sufficient World. Every man, no doubt, has his "hell" readily available, connivance, control, conformism, domestication, schooling, alienation, extermination, exploitation, oppression, anxiety, etc. We have our little list that the Contemporaries established in the previous century in the same way one used to construct lists of virtues and vices or honors and wealth. They invented it for us without knowing it, for us-the-Futures who have as our responsibility to invent its use.

In the Christian and Gnostic tradition, the struggle of the End Times takes place "on earth." The most sophisticated of believers have it taking place in Heaven as well, above all in Heaven. The various kinds of gnosis imagine infinite falls and vertiginous highs, the vertigo of salvation. On Earth as in Heaven, a hell is available. The Marxists have the law of profit and the control of production, the class struggle Capital imposes on man. The Nietzscheans, the dull grumble of the struggle in the foundations of World and History, the domestication of man, the society of control. The phenomenologists, the capture of being, the most superficial amongst them, the age of suspicion.

But all of these "hells" are taken from World, History, Society, and Religion. What we call Hell is no longer of the order of these specific and total intra-worldly generalities, it is both more singular and more universal, no longer being at all of the same order, it is the determinant Identity of these small hells strung out through history but unified here in the name of the last Humaneity. It is even found within the French idiom for hell [*enfer*], en-fer literally means "in-irons." We are as much "in-irons" as we are "alive" [*en-Vie*]. We believe in Hell but as non-philosophers and it is even because we are non-philosophers that we can believe in it outside of any sort of religion. Hell is less mythological than ideological, it combines philosophizability with universal capital. Under what form? A single term could work for them without being a metaphor or something they would participate in by analogy, a more innovative and conjectural term than control, more universal than profit. It would denote the growing and permanent extortion of a surplus-value of communication, of speed and of urgency in change, in productivity and in work, in the pressure of images and slogans. It would be worse than solicitation, more tenacious than capture, more active and persecutory than control, softer and more insidious than a frontal attack, just as perverse as questioning and accusation, less brutal and offensive than extermination, less ritualized than inquisition, it would be soft and dispersed, instantaneous and vicious, it would be a crime without declared violence. Collusion and conformism, it would be afraid to show itself. Related to rumor, from which it borrows its infinite and tortuous ways. It is harassment. As a modernized form of Hell, perhaps harassment has a long future in front of it, of innocent torture, slow assassination, in short the fall, but radical with no way of recovering and which tolerates only salvation.

The Philosophical Past of Non-Philosophy

Non-philosophy is thus Man as the utopian identity of the philosophical form of the World, a utopia destined to transform it. We still have to understand these equations, in particular that of the being-uni-versed from Man, and this book adheres to this by re-exposing non-philosophy in a different way via one of its new possibilities. It uses this opportunity to once again take up formulations that lead to objections answering certain external critics, as well as revisiting diverging interpretations specific to non-philosophers. A portion of this book is devoted to going through these theories via a strict or "lengthy" presentation of non-philosophy, and its defense against more expeditious solutions. This work of rectification is the occasion, merely the occasion, for refocusing non-philosophy on Man (the "Man-in-person," "Humaneity"), and in a more innovative manner, on its utopian vocation established since the book *Future Christ*. As for this "occasion," it is quite obvious. A school of posture, not to say a school of thought, supposes a minimum of closure from the most liberating of knowledge, a heritage, its utilization, and its no less certain dispersal. Within its development, a variety of interpretations will no doubt appear, deviations that are as much normalizations, and a struggle against this multiplication of divergent tendencies.

These are perhaps not inevitable evils, especially here, merely a normal development according to the twisting paths of history. But the problem is made worse by the fact that this school of non-philosophers is that of utopia. Not the former attempts devoted to commenting on the worst authoritarian and criminal forms of the past and the present, but utopia as the determinant principle for human life, or to put it another way, of the Future as an irreducible presupposition of (for) thinking the World and History. Non-philosophers are engaged in an aleatory navigation between the respect for the most rigorous utopia, whose rules are not that of the reproductive imagination but those from the Future determining imagination itself, as well as the temptations, diversions, and remorse of history. Little by little, we will begin to understand that the Future as we understand it no longer has any temporal consistency or positive content, without being an empty form or a nothingness, but that it is foreclosed to past and present History, just as it is foreclosed to the place of places, the World, and that it is the only method for establishing the practice of thinking in a non-imaginary instance. Because it is the World and History that are imaginary and have a terrible materiality, it is not necessarily utopia. We will overlap two objectives here: the defense of non-philosophy against the (non-) philosophers that we are, only occasionally, and the introduction of philosophy to a rigorous future. Together they set out to definitively render, without any possible return to philosophical conformism or towards the facilities of the past and present, the non-philosophical enterprise understood as utopia or uchronia. Imagination and speculation, left to themselves and thus undistinguished, are quite good for participating in the grand game of History but have little value or worse for the Future which is unimaginable and unintelligible and must be maintained as such.

Man-in-Person as Suspension of the Philosophical Chora

The point where philosophical resistance is concentrated is without a doubt the invention of the Name-of-Man, first name, oracular as much as axiomatic, of the determining cause for the non-philosophical posture. And that which concentrates the differends is the style of non-philosophy as identity that possesses the dual aspect, of discipline and of the oeuvre, of the theorem and of the oracle. But the real difficulty in understanding the simplicity of non-philosophy is profoundly hidden in the depths of philosophy itself. Because philosophy, from Parmenides to Derrida, even Levinas, continues to be a divided gesture, without a veritable immanence, transforming its thematic contents of transcendence in also forgetting to transform the operative transcendence in the element from which the ontology of surface is established which we will call, in memory of Plato, the chorismos. The general effect of the chora *literally gives place* to philosophy, demanding binding and sutures to which we will once and for all "oppose" the Man-in-person, his power of cloning, and his future being. All philosophy contains a hinter-philosophy in which it deploys its operations and weaves its tradition like an understudy of a topographical nature and in the best of cases being itself topological. Philosophy as well consists of two levels, its pre-ontological operative conditions on the one hand, and its superficial theme on the other, it too has its presupposed, but is not aware of it or erases it within the unity of appearance named Logos. Rightly, the Logos, and its flash or lightning nature, possesses a "dark precursor," the chora, which is as much a virtual image, and philosophy, dazzled by its own lightning flash, seems to completely forget about it at the same time it sets itself up within it. Non-philosophy risks taking this same path, of confusing what it believes to be the real with its phantom double, contenting itself to working on the thematic level of philosophy, not its surface objects and its idle chatter (we stopped talking about this a long time ago and in any case they are merely simple materials for inducing a work of transformation), but the transcendence-form of its objects. In the end it risks, through precipitation, taking back up the heritage of philosophy, a heritage of a misunderstood presupposed, even more profound than the play of transcendences. This is what the imperative of the radicality of immanence meant, to treat immanence in an immanent manner, not to make a new object out of it. And from here we get *non-* (philosophy) and its refusal of the Platonic *chorismos*, symbol of all abstraction, and thus all transcendental appearance.

There are no illusions. The message will leave a heritage in tattered pieces and interpretations. But it was difficult not to dispute the differend to its core. There will be complete confusion of the multiple, possible, and necessary effectuations of non-philosophy with its interpretations. The non-philosophical or human freedom of philosophical effectuation and the philosophical freedom of interpretation. Effectuations demand non-philosophy to return to zero from the point of view of its philosophical material *and thus also but within these limits the formulation of its axioms*, but in no way providing from the outset divergent interpretations of the aforementioned axioms. They are divergent because they do not take into account the material from which these axioms are derived within non-philosophy, and because they do not see themselves as symptoms of another vision of the World. The utterances of non-philosophy are not mathematical theorems and pure axioms, they merely have a mathematical *aspect*. They are, by their extraction or origin, mathematical *and* transcendental. And by their determined function in-Real, within non-philosophy, they are *identically in-the-last-Humaneity* entities which have an aspect of an axiom and an aspect of interpretation (or an oracular aspect as we say) that attempts (sometimes it is ourselves who provide the occasion) to isolate and transform, in complete freedom of interpretation. There will be an opportunity to complain about the complex character of the language of non-philosophy, an idiom saturated with classical references, sophisticated in a contemporary way. Its freedom of decision up against the whole of philosophy demands these effects of "complication" and "privatization," as the saying goes. But it also demands fighting against the drift [*dérive*] of the pedagogical-all and the mediatic-all that leads philosophy into the shallow depths of opinion, which is the site of its impossible death. The noble idealism of "pop-philosophy" has been consumed into a "philo-reality;" against this we propose philo-fiction.

Parricide, which is at the bottom of these interpretations and which we can judge as being quite fertile, although it has informed tradition, only takes place once or within one lone meaning. In regards to Parmenides, it was possible; Plato introduced the Other as non-being and language, bringing into existence the philosophical system of the World, but is it possible to repeat it again with the same fecundity in regards to non-philosophy, this time in introducing (non) religion or (non) art, still mixing them without taking into account this mixture, alternatively as a philosophical or religious resentment? If philosophy begins via a crime, it is no doubt obliged to continue down similar pathways, to the effect that the crimes of philosophy, once the founding crime has been committed, are a reaction of self-defense. It is undoubtedly from this that we get Marx's declaration that history begins by tragedy and repeats itself or ends in farce.

The preservation of rigor and fecundity is, in every respect, a psychologically difficult task within a theory such as non-philosophy. Having posited an essential objective of liberation in regards to philosophy and its services, one has often understood this objective as an authorization of providing particular *interpretations* of its axioms and ends up obliterating their scope. This ends up confusing, on one hand, two kinds of freedoms in regards to non-philosophy, the freedom of its interpretations and the freedom of its effectuations. On the other hand, any defense of "principles" against precipitated interpretations is immediately taxed with a will to orthodoxy, a prohibitive objection when we are dealing with, as is the case here, a heretical theory of thought. Nevertheless, it is time to stop confusing heresy as the cause of thought with an ideology of heresies, which is certainly not at all our

21

object, but rather a form of normalization. As for the "disciplinary" aspect, which is not the only aspect, it demands something other than philosophical "answers to objections," a precision in the definition and use of its procedures in the formation of utterances, since non-philosophy is neither a supplementary doctrine interior to philosophy nor a vision of the world but one whose priority is a "vision of Man," or rather Man as "vision" that implies a theory and a practice of philosophy. In the end, struggle is only one aspect of non-philosophy, not its whole or telos, struggle coming only from its materiality. In particular, if the discipline of non-philosophy is inseparable from struggle, it is not a question of reducing the monomaniacal obsession of its "marching orders." This would reduce its complexity and kill its indivisibility, deploying it in a "long march" and a form of Maoization whose philosophical presuppositions no longer have any pertinence here, a case of the One and the Two, which are now cloned and no longer tied together. More generally, non-philosophy is *a complex thought composed of a multitude of aspects, which is to say, unilateral interpretations, of a philosophical origin but reduced by their determination in-the-last-instance*. The "liberalism" of non-philosophy is merely one of the aspects of which it is capable, not an essence. Similarly, it is only capable of having a "Maoist" aspect.

Let us generalize. The weakness of non-philosophy is due to a specific cause, the determination-in-the-last-Humaneity of a subject for the World. Everything that has a right to the philosophical city can be said about it in turn and in a retaliatory mode since Man contributes nothing of himself that Man takes from the World. We can consider non-philosophy as being pretentious, absurd, idealistic, empty, materialistic, formalistic, contradictory, modern, post-modern, Zen, Buddhist, Marxist; it endures or tolerates, perhaps "appeals" to, or at least renders possible, sarcasms, ironies, and insults without even talking about the misunderstandings, partly for the same reason as psychoanalysis. All of this goes beyond simple "deviations." They are its aspects, which is to say, its "unilateral" philosophical interpretations in both senses of the word, being either sufficient coming from the mouth of philosophers, or reduced to their absolute dimension of sufficiency and totality in the mouths of non-philosophers, and both times due to the weakness and strength of Man-in-person as their determination only in-the-last-instance. The non-philosopher is certainly not a Saint Paul fantasizing about a new Church. The non-philosopher is either a (Saint) Sebastian whose flesh is pierced with as many arrows as there are Churches, or a Christ persecuted by a Saint Paul.

What is engaged in here is the practice of retaliation. A negative rule of the non-philosophical ethics of outlawed discussion by way of argumentation (the sufficient is you, the orthodox one is always you, you are the fashionable one, and when a master you are someone else) that is founded on the confusion of effectuations of non-philosophy and of its overall interpretations. Retaliation is the law but as with any too-human law, it must acquire a dimension that displaces it, or rather emplaces it and takes away its authority but not all of its effectiveness. If the non-philosopher is only authorized by himself, which is to say by philosophy but limited by the Real-of-the-last-instance, its critique of other non-philosophers can merely be retaliatory under the same conditions, only by the Real limited in-the-last-instance.

The Tree of Philosophical Saintliness
The thematic horizon or material of these debates is in the relationships between philosophy, religion as gnosis, and non-philosophy. It is inevitable, regarding non-philosophers in general (whether they are non-philosophers by name or simply its neighbors) that we often end up evoking Marx's Holy Family and imagining, arranged on the neighboring branches of the tree of philosophy and annexed, sometimes abusively, to non-philosophy, authors who would quite evidently and quite rightly refuse this label. So it is that we find, for example, a Saint Michel, a Saint Alain, a Saint

Gilles[1] without even mentioning the youngest who aspire as well to the freedom of "saintliness" and who make their muted voices heard here. If there is a Holy Family of non-philosophers, it extends completely beyond these three, provided that the sectarian spirit can save us.

This book is organized in the following manner: To begin, in order to recall the essential part of the problematic, we have organized a *Summary of Non-Philosophy*, a vade-mecum of notions and basic problems, in a classical style. Secondly, there is *Clarifications On the Three Axioms of Non-Philosophy*, designed to posit their proper use as much as to elucidate their meaning. Thirdly, an analysis of *Philosophizability and Practicity*, both being extreme constituents of philosophical material or the contents of the third axiom. Fourthly, the heart of this work: *Let us Make a Tabula Rasa of the Future or of Utopia as Method*. Fifthly, we have a theoretical outline of a non-institutional utopia, *The International Organization of Non-Philosophy, L'Organisation Non-Philosophique Internationale, (ONPHI)* already created in practice but under the conditions of possibility and functioning from which here we put into question "de jure," thus not without a perplexity concerning "facts," in any case, without the capability of "getting to the bottom of things." Sixthly, an essay characterizing *The Right and the Left of Non-Philosophy*, a brief topology of several philosophizing and normalizing positions of proponents or tenants of this problematic. Seventhly, *Rebel in the Soul: A Theory of Future Struggle*, a systematic discussion starting from a confrontation of non-philosophical gnosis and non-religious gnosis to the extent that they pose, posed or perhaps still will pose themselves as rivals to non-philosophy in a mixture of fidelity and infidelity. Despite the fact that it can also be read as putting non-philosophy into

---

1. We will recognize allusions, and sometimes references, to closely related or distant themes, but which are related, in the work of Michel Henry, Alain Badiou and via the representative of "non-religious" gnosis of a Platonic origin, in Gilles Grelet. It goes without saying that these discussions are current and local, neither concerning the ensemble of doctrines nor prejudging the eventual evolution of certain amongst them. This concerns defining certain proximities with non-philosophy (rather than adversaries which in some sense they are) and typological and emblematic differends (rather than conflicts with a certain author).

perspective: it pits against a standard Platonism two contemporary appropriations of Gnosticism.

On the basis of the paradigm of Man who never ceases to come as the Future-in-person, each one of these moments strives to re-establish not the "true" non-philosophy and its orthodoxy, but the minimal conditions to respect in order to allow for its maximum fecundity. And in order to bring about one of the last possibilities of its development, making explicit Humaneity as a utopia-for-the-World. In introducing these considerations in the form of a "testament" and "ultimatum," we want to indicate two things: First, that this is the last time we will intervene in order to caution non-philosophers against the temptation of returning and looking backwards towards philosophy. Only a disillusioned nostalgia for the former World and its traditions barely remain permissible to us.... Secondly, that non-philosophy is also a sort of ultimatum for considering one's life and transforming one's thought from the perspective of a uni-version rather than a conversion. Man as future is this ultimatum in action, not an impatient self-proclaimed genius, and philosophy is his testament. It is obviously the ultimatum that determines this testament as "old" with a view towards a life that is, itself, non-testamentary. In and of itself, the "old" can never bear a veritable eschaton. Thus, this book intersects according to the logic of this paradigm, under the sign of the ultimate or "last" as future, philosophy as testament and cautionary note for maintaining the non-philosophical oeuvre as "future" or "utopian." We will see that between these two dimensions it cradles a theory of struggle.

In the end, this book envisions non-philosophers in multiple ways. It inevitably sees them as subjects of knowledge, most often academics insofar as life in the world demands, but above all as close relatives of three great human types. The analyst and political militant are quite obvious, for non-philosophy is close to psychoanalysis and Marxism insofar as it transforms the subject in transforming philosophy. Here again, one must have a sense not of certain nuances but of aspects (of the interpretations, albeit

unilateralized) and not in order to construct a simple proletariza-
tion or militarization of thought as theory. To be rigorous, rather
than authoritarian or spiteful, is its task. And lastly, non-philosophy is a close relative of the spiritual but definitely not the spiri-
tualist. Those who are spiritual are not at all spiritualists, for the
spiritual oscillate between fury and tranquil rage, they are great
destroyers of the forces of Philosophy and the State, which are
united under the name of Conformism. They haunt the margins
of philosophy, gnosis, mysticism, science fiction and even religions. Spiritual types are not only abstract mystics and quietists;
they are heretics for the World. The task is to bring their heresy
to the capacity of utopia, and their utopia to the capacity of the
paradigm.

SUMMARY OF NON-PHILOSOPHY

The Two Problems of Non-Philosophy

1.1 Non-philosophy is a discipline stemming from a reflection on two problems whose solutions have finally coincided. On the one hand, we have the limitrophic status of the One that, whether explicitly or not, associates by proximity with Being and the Other without either being able to grant it radical autonomy nor the ability to question its provenance and necessity. On the other hand, we have the theoretical status of philosophy, which is a theoreticist impulse without being a theory; which has practical aspects (action, affect, existence) without being a practice. It lacks a rigorous self-knowledge; it is a field of consistent and objective phenomena but one that is not yet dominated theoretically. Non-philosophy is born within this duality, and in a certain manner it will remain there.

1.2 Concerning the first point, a challenge and a proposition. The challenge: the One is a limitrophic object of philosophy, targeted by this transcendence which is not described in terms of *meta* but of *epekeina*, it is epekeinaphysical. Thus, it is just as much Other as One, divisible as indivisible, more an object of desire than effective science. It comes to thought associated with Being, convertible with it, without being thought through its essence and provenance ("How does the One come to the idea of the philosopher and with what necessity?"). Philosophy established itself in a dominant manner within the element of Being and via a certain "forgetting of the One" which it continues to prefer in favor of Being, and which it supposes as given without searching any longer for its type of reality or necessity.

1.3 The proposition: can we finally think the One "itself," as independent from Being and the Other, in-convertible with them, non-determinable by thought and language (hence, foreclosed to the Logos)? To this contradictory and at the very least paradoxical question, we must reply by inversion – to think *according* to the One rather than thinking the One as a final object or a close relative of Being, but to think this non-relation to thought with the traditional means of thinking. To separate the non-relation more so than to displace it vis-à-vis philosophy with the material help of philosophy itself, but without forming a circle with it, thus positing the non-relation as the Real or the One-in-One that itself determines this help. Thus, in order to escape its authority and its sufficiency, to unmask its transcendental appearance, but also, from then on, to transform it according to the One-in-One, such are the terms of the new problem.

1.4 Concerning the second point, a challenge and a proposition. The challenge: philosophy is governed by a principle superior to the Principle of Reason, the *Principle of Sufficient Philosophizablity*, which is specified according to its diverse goals and activities. It expresses its pretension of absolute autonomy as *auto*-position/givenness/naming/decision/foundation, etc. It assures and legitimizes its mastery over the sciences and "regional" disciplines. In the end, it articulates the idealist pretension of philosophy as being capable of co-determining the Real by confusing it with Being. The other side of this pretension, the ransom of this sufficiency, is the impossibility of philosophy being a rigorous thinking of itself, non-circular, without begging the question (*petitio principii*), a theory which is certainly transcendental but of a scientific kind. It is overall concerned with reflection and self-awareness. Philosophy thinks, or feels in the best of cases that it thinks and "is" or "exists" when it thinks. Philosophy gathers itself up within an enlarged *cogito* in the shape of the World and the *cogito* is a concentrated philosophy. It is an immanence limited to *auto*-reflection or *auto*-affectivity, at best to a fundamental affect. By this, philosophy manifests merely its *existence* and does not demonstrate that it is the Real to which it makes claim nor does it know itself as this *pretension*. Its existence contains a hallucination of the Real, which is to say, of the One, "self knowledge" being a maxim of transcendental illusion found in any philosophy.

1.5 The proposition is thus: to elaborate, with the help of philosophy and science but outside the authority of the Principle of Sufficient Philosophizability that divides and opposes them, a rigorous theoretical knowledge, but adequate or adjusted to its new object, of philosophical existence, of its style of thought and its destination as form of the World.

The Identity of the Problem of Non-Philosophy or the Solution

2.1 The principle of the solution? This is the same thing as positing the One as the radically immanent Real (One-in-One, One-in-person), not being philosophizable or autonomous in relation to philosophy, but thought with a new practical use of the means of philosophy, and forming the conditions or the real cause of a theoretical knowledge of philosophy. The solution is a new problem: how do we conceive and treat the One-in-One with the means gathered by thought and science, in such a way that it is no longer philosophizable or exchangeable with Being but at the same time is capable of determining an adequate theory of philosophy?

2.2 The style of non-philosophy? To treat everything through a duality (of problems) that does not form *a* Two as a set, and through an identity (of problems, and thus solutions) that does not form a Unity or synthesis. This style, which is generally called *uni-laterality,* opposes the ternary system of philosophy. Uni-laterality is the essence of the One-in-One that, separated from philosophy by its own immanence, is Other-than it or provides it uni-laterally. The Real is immanence-without-transcendence, simple identity and thus the *determination* of philosophy. But in saying this, philosophy also relates to itself which is not merely given by it, the determination is transcendental or *determination-in-the-last-instance.*

2.3 The resolution of this problem demands two conjoined transformations. The first, of the One as classical absolute or as the contemporary transcendental One-Other, in One-in-One or vision-in-One or One-in-person, capable of determining unilaterally a knowledge of a new type in regards to the object of "philosophy."

2.4 The second, of the *auto*-referential (with some nuances here and there) or theoreticist use of philosophical language (this is the philosophizability or invariant form of the systematic-historical structures of Logos), into a new use and *practice* in that it recognizes on the contrary an irreducible presupposed. A practice of identity and unilateral identity, which gives it an axiomatic (real) and theorematic (transcendental) aspect. The utterances deduced from the One-in-One and from its causality are no longer objects, themes, or instances of philosophy. They are formed beginning from the progressive introduction of terms and problems of philosophical extraction, and also receive a *theoretical function or position,* which is other … than the philosophical. Moreover, they refer, according to the Real, to philosophical existence and are thus transcendental in a new way that is no longer philosophical.

2.5 The One-in-One is not an object or entity in itself opposed to language, susceptible of forming a philosophical couple or dialectic of opposites. The matrix of non-philosophy is a *speaking/thinking-according-to-the-One*. It is not just a relation of synthesis, fusion or Logos, between the Real and language, the One and Being. It is a relation determined by a non-relation, a unilateral duality, and more profoundly a non-relation determined by the lack-of-relation to the Real. *There is no non-philosophical relation.* To practice non-philosophy is to think by philosophical means, or other means that are *de jure* philosophizable, and in the end determined according-to the Real.

2.6 The utterances of non-philosophy all have an axiom-aspect to the extent that they are the side of the being-determined or -real within unilateral (duality). They also have a theorem-aspect to the extent that they are being-determined in-the-last-instance or are transcendental within unilateral (duality) accompanying radical identity or that which emerges from it. Theorems can serve as axioms but only under the condition of determining-in-the-last-instance other theorems. Thus, axioms and theorems do not determine, as in science, two distinct classes of equations nor, as in philosophy, a reciprocal duality of propositions whose givenness and deduction are convertible to some operations here and there. Their "relation" or unilateral duality is that of determination and determination-in-the last instance.

From the Philosophical One to the Vision-in-One

3.1 *Immanence via immanence.* The One is the Immanent-in-person and is not thinkable on the terrain of transcendence (ecstasy, scission, nothingness, objectification, alterity, alienation, *meta-* or *epekeina*), whether we are dealing with transcendence as object or as a manner of thinking, as a thematic through which the One would be constituted or as an operative transcendence necessary for constituting it. Even the philosophies of immanence (Spinoza, Nietzsche, Deleuze) posit immanence in a transcendent or intuitive manner or render them co-extensive. Even the auto-affection of the auto-affective Ego (Michel Henry) posits in a quasi-transcendent manner inecstatic immanence, operatively objectified and still semi-intuited. The imperative of rigor is not about immanence in general, but about dealing with immanence in an immanent manner.

3.2 *Radical Immanence or the One-in-One.* The One is immanence without forming or presupposing for itself a point, plane or folding back of interiority upon itself. It is One-in-One rather than (to) itself or else is only discoverable or given within the One, and already *in-One*. It does not form a couple with Being or the Other and does not live in their proximity. It is *radical* and not *absolute* immanence. The "more" immanence is radical, the "more" it is universal or gives-in-the-last-immanence philosophy itself and philosophizability (the World, etc.).

3.3 *Identity, Ego, Man-in-person.* The first possible designations of the One-in-One, outside of this designation itself, for example, are Identity, Real, Ego, or Man, each one of them = X capable of being called *in-person or in-X, but not in-Self or in-It.* The One is Identity, Ego in flesh and blood, and it ceases being an attribute or even a subject. It is more Man-in-person or Ego-in-Ego than Subject, always unilateral and determined in-the-last-instance by the Ego. The choice of the original names is dictated by philosophical circumstances as symptoms of non-philosophy.

3.4 *The One that is not but is real.* The vision-in-One only manifests or gives the One in the mode of the One, and manifests within this mode philosophizability for which it is the necessary condition. Its being-phenomenal, however, does not come from the tradition of the commodity, from the "mode" or "manner" of the "how," of perception and the perceived, and thus from the phenomenon in the phenomenological sense. The One is the radical Real that *is* not, not because *it could have been or would still be measured by Being,* but because by its essence it is without the mixture of One-Being, and so the One affects and transforms this mixture of Logos. The *One* neither *is* nor *is there a One,* two philosophizable solutions, but the One is not in relation to its being-given or -real. Since it is neither sensible, categorial, nor intellectual, the vision-in-One is in general without intuitiveness, but it *gives*-without-givenness the phenomenon, the perceived-without-perception, the lived-without-life, etc. It eliminates from itself just as much being-there (object) as simple being (the pure mathematical multiple and its "emptiness" in terms of a set). It conditions or determines a use as an axiomatic (but transcendental) abstraction of philosophizable terms.

3.5 *(Non-) One, Uni-laterality or Other-than….* The vision-in-One is not statically enclosed "within" the One like a point, and yet it neither exceeds it nor withdraws into it. It is an immanence counter to any transcendence and not a transcendence against the grain [*à rebours*]. It inverts or uni-verts transcendence via its own immanence. The One-in-One is imparted without an operation

32

of givenness or alterity, but it is given thusly with a "(non-) One," a uni-laterality, or even an Other-than ... (Non-) One, Uni-laterality and Other-than ... are not modes, manners or accidents of the One in relation to Being, but are the essence of immanence separated from the One. Its non-intuitiveness is a radical "emptiness," via immanence rather than an absolute, as Other-than ... and not as Other-of ... transcendence.

3.6 *The being-foreclosed of the One-in-One.* The non-consistency of radical immanence implies or presupposes, these being the same thing here, the being-foreclosed of the Real to philosophical or non-philosophical thought, a thought that it can nonetheless give as being-in-One. Thus, it does not affect, it does not *receive* from the outside but *gives* it or demonstrates it and can only give it. The being-given-in-One, namely the One and the World, is without any preliminary reception. It is, in any case, the condition for it to be the true "last-instance." It is radical autonomy, the primacy of the phenomenon over phenomenology and over the philosophico-empirical mode of givenness-reception, of passivity and operative activity, etc. If there is now an explicit effectuation of the vision-in-One by philosophy then this being-foreclosed is not entirely excluded but it remains through this effectuation. The being-foreclosed suspends philosophical causality over the Real, but not all causality concerning thought itself for which philosophy is a simple effectuating occasion. In any case, the being-foreclosed is not forbidden by the One from giving (-receiving) thought, language, and more generally the World as philosophizability.

3.7 *Given-without-givenness and the givenness of the occasion.* The vision-in-One is the being-given-without-givenness (without a mixture of the given and givenness, without auto-givenness and thus also without some hinter-givenness). In this determined or real mode, it gives philosophical thought-language (Logos), but it will have reduced it to the simple state of *occasion* freed from the Principle of Sufficient Philosophy. On this real basis of the occasion, it will give or determine, but from now on in the last-instance, in the form of a clone or a subject, the thought-language of the Logos, which will be non-philosophy.

3.8 *Non-consistency*. The One-in-One not being beyond (epekeina) essence or Being but merely in-One or in-Person, it is empty, as Other-than … and without being an absolute nothingness, of all determination, even in regards to its philosophical name of "the One." Even if it is expressed with the inevitable help of the thought-language of Being, it is without-ontological, linguistic, or worldly consistency, without-being or without-essence, without-language and without-thought. This non-consistency implies its indifference or its tolerance towards any material, equivalent to the particular doctrinal position of which it can determine the use as occasion demanding nevertheless that this material has in any case the ultimate form of philosophy. It does not signify that it is in itself isolated within an absolute transcendence without relationship to thought-language, but that it is closed off to any reciprocal causality of language or thought, to any contrary effect or reaction from philosophy. If it is in no need of them, it is capable of demonstrating them or incorporating them into its own mode and obviously only *if* there is any. Under this condition of existence of philosophizability, non-consistency, or real indifference will be transcendental indifference but the latter will have no bearing on the former.

3.9 *Non-sufficiency*. Since the One-in-person is merely the being-given-without-givenness (of) the One, it in no way produces the philosophy-World (procession, emanation, ontologico-ecstatic manifestation, creation ex-nihilo, onto-theo-logical perfection). There is no real genesis of philosophy, it is given with the One which is unilaterally separated from it. The Real is the necessary but "negative" condition or the *sine qua non* for …, precisely because it is not nothingness or the negation of philosophy in itself but merely the (non-) One. A givenness of philosophy is thus required *as well* if the vision-in-One is separated from it and if it must contribute it (as occasion) in the mode of being-given.

The non-sufficiency of the One-in-One demands philosophy but undoes the Principle of Sufficient Philosophy.

3.10 *The utopian or messianic essence of the Vision-in-One.* Immanence, if it is indeed radical or in-One and not a relative-absolute, is separated from philosophy (from the form of the World), without there being a preliminary act of separation, and it has no power over it. It is Other-than … or Uni-laterality, less anonymous and more radically heterogeneous to philosophy than Other-of … and the forms of alterity that philosophy and even contemporary philosophy knows. It corresponds to an intentional originality of the immanent One. A real intentionality through and through, without transcendence, an inverted intentionality or one "against the grain" rather than reversed, the One emerges from the in-One and not from an excess of transcendence, an immanent being-separated rather than an infinite separation (Levinas). It is the immanent messianism of Man-in-person for the World, the utopian essence of the vision-in-One in the manner in which it comes to encounter the World.

3.11 *The real phase of non-philosophy.* We call the real phase the triplet of phases, rather than instances, within a unilateral two by two "without-relation:" 1. the One-in-One or radical immanence; 2. its being-separated or Other-than … this is its aspect of inverted or future "intentionality;" and finally 3. the occasion that forms the correlate or unilate of this Other-than … and whose support is in general found in philosophy. The real phase is followed by a transcendental phase controlled this time by philosophy as occasion.

The Effectuation of the Vision-in-One by Philosophy

4.1 *The existence of philosophy and its real contingency as occasion.* The vision-in-One gives (manifests) philosophy *if* there is one. And yet philosophy is itself given in the mode of auto-position/givenness/reflection/naming, in the form of an enlarged self-awareness or a universal *cogito*. It is at best existence and gives itself via the affect or feeling of its existence (I know, that I feel that I

35

am philosophizing). It nevertheless confuses its existence with the Real itself and not merely with a type of reality, because it is in any case given-in-One. Existence cannot engender its own knowledge, that which is without a vicious circle, except by means of appearance. It is a repetition of automatism which believes itself to be the Real through a well established hallucination by which only the vision-in-One can make the hallucination appear as a simple occasional [*occasionel*] cause via the Other-than….

4.2 *The effectuation of the vision-in-One by philosophy as occasion.* In virtue of its non-sufficiency, the vision-in-One in any case needs, in its real phase, and in order for non-philosophy to exist, the givenness of philosophy that becomes occasion. The latter can now *effectuate* it from its own philosophical point of view. The effectuation of the vision-in-One does not suppress its state of negative condition and does not render it sufficient but makes it assume a transcendental function, for it is neither an actualization of the virtual nor the realization of a possible. It is the consideration of philosophy as occasion, not philosophy in general itself, supposedly absolute but from then on deemed hallucinatory. It is rather the sign and witness of its relative autonomy of occasion, which applies to its specific reality and Philosophical Decision's structural consistency.

4.3 *Non-philosophy as unilateral duality.* Through its real phase, or Uni-laterality, non-philosophy is not a unitary system but a theoretical apparatus with a dual entrance or two keys, one being radically heterogeneous to the other since one of the keys is the One-in-One as Other-than…. As for its transcendental phase that supposes the second causality of philosophy's relative autonomy, it establishes the syntax of "unilateral duality" that prolongs the real Uni-laterality.

Due to its radical immanence refusing for itself any position or consistency, the vision-in-One is never present or positive, given within representation or transcendence and having the capacity of being manipulated as a key in the proper sense of the word. This duality is not that of two sides, the Real not being an assignable sign that would come into play, since all that can be found is non-philosophy produced as Stranger to (for) philosophy. Philosophy is a two sided or bilateral apparatus, that of non-philosophy or of the Stranger-subject produced as such (cloned) is *unifacial* or *unilateral*. The structure itself of the Determination-in-the-last-instance is a duality that is an identity but an identity that is not a synthesis of duality. Non-philosophy thinks without creating a system, without being either unitary or a totality. The subject according to which it is produced is not in front of me or the World but exists-unifacial-for-the-World and for this reason is a stranger to it or a future arrival but not one who is a stranger to the Real.

4.4 *Contingency and necessity of non-philosophical effectuation.* From the viewpoint of the One or the Real that is foreclosed to it, non-philosophy is overall contingent upon the material of a philosophical origin in its axioms and theorems, thus to that extent it is in general a "thought-language." As a thought determined by the Real, it acquires the real necessity of vision-in-One which would also be the transcendental necessity of this contingency. The One neither legitimizes philosophy as it is nor provides itself as absolute, but is merely transformed into an occasion as given-in-the-last-instance. From the viewpoint of maintaining philosophical sufficiency, non-philosophy is necessary but partially tautological and useless.

4.5 *The relative autonomy of philosophy.* Philosophy itself is given as having absolute autonomy or claims sufficient knowledge of the Real. Philosophy reveals itself to be a hallucination in regards to the Real, and reveals its structure of decision to be a transcendental illusion. It is indeed given *according*-to-the-One as autonomy that is relative only to the occasion. This autonomy is relative in that it is limited in its relation to spontaneous belief of philosophy and relative in a more positive manner to the extent that it is now transcendentally legitimized by the Real. The latter endorses the structural consistency of philosophy, its quasi-materiality, in order to decompose.

The Cloning of Non-Philosophy from Philosophy

5.1 Effectuation is to take the reality of philosophy into consideration, its *relative* autonomy on the basis of its being-real-in-One. It implies that the One no longer gives it as simple occasion but that it also fulfills a function alongside the occasion that intervenes in a limited but positive manner. The real One thus assumes a transcendental function, at the same time remaining the inalienable Real that it is, without changing something else or becoming some other transcendental One next to the first one. This real cloning of the transcendental subject starting from philosophical material is possible without contradicting the radical autonomy of the Real; since philosophy is already given in-One and consequently the Real does not contradict itself when it plays a transcendental role with the Real. Non-philosophy does not go from the transcendental to the Real (and from the *a-priori* to the transcendental) like philosophy, but from the Real to the transcendental (and from this to the *a-priori*), then to the occasion of philosophy.

5.2 The clone is expressed or articulates itself via non-philosophy, not via philosophy as a material for cloning, even less from the Real which, without being transformed, is made a *transcendental agent* or essence of the Stranger-subject. The non-philosophical clone is in its essence a transcendental instance, which is to say a vision-in-One expressed via a specific material representative of philosophizability. It is thus a realization of speaking/thinking-*according*-to-the-One. The transcendental is a clone because it is the One that is inalienable in the position of assuming an autonomous material and from which we take reality into account. The clone is transcendental and not real but it is real-in-the-last-instance or, more precisely, the clone is the concentrated form of the completed structure of the Determination-in-the-Last-Instance.

5.3 Unilateral being-given (the *according to*) and above all cloning appear to exceed the One-in-person, as the transcendental appears to exceed the Real. In reality, they do not exceed either, for the in-One does not supersede itself within philosophy in assuming this transcendental function. It is rather philosophy that exceeds the non-sufficiency of the in-One, but it does not exceed it in pure exteriority or in a relation (philosophical dyad) since it is already given-in-the-One. It only exceeds it via its own reality interior to its occasional or immanent-being-given. Cloning is necessary *if* there is philosophy or rather *if* philosophy is accounted for in its consistency and autonomy, and it is possible or non-contradictory from the viewpoint of the Real.

5.4 The clone is not the double of an identity given in transcendence that is in reality already a double or pair as is every philosophical concept. It is on the contrary *a philosophical double('s) real-transcendental and undivided Identity*. The Real is not a clone of itself, it is radically simple Identity. But it can thus *determine* philosophy and transform it into non-philosophy. To determine-in-the-last-instance, to supply philosophy with non-philosophy or to clone it in the guise of non-philosophy, these expressions describe the same operation but do so in a much better way than saying, "produce."

The Stranger-Subject and the Thought-World
(Essence, Existence, Assistance)

6.1 Non-philosophy is a globally transcendental discipline because it is real in any case but uses the transcendental that it transforms from philosophy in order to formulate itself. It is the unification in-the-last-instance of a theory or knowledge of its object that is distinct from it like a presupposed is (according to a model partially taken from practical science), and from a pragmatics or *usage* of philosophy (according to a model taken from philosophy). It is a practice-(of)-theory via the model of science, thus it is not a theoreticism nor an auto-positional pragmatics. Nor is it a negative theory-pragmatics, since it demands for the vision-in-One to be effectuated by invariant philosophical and scientific models or by their respective posture. In the end, it is only theoretico-pragmatic in its material and operational aspects, practical in its style of the presupposed or unilaterality, real in its determinant cause. Thus, it is not definable one way or another; it is thought = X such that it determines-in-the-last-instance the combinations of theoreticism and practice offered by the World.

6.2 The non-philosophical subject distinguishes itself from the philosophical kind but not from the radical, real, separated Man-in-person which however distinguishes itself from the non-philosophical subject. It is a transcendental subject, but real in the last-Humanity and turned-Stranger towards the World or existing-for-the-World. The unilateral duality of Man and the subject in terms of their unitary confusion, which grounds modern absolute Subjectivity. The subject does not use philosophy as if it were already constituted, but it *is* this usage on which it constitutes itself on the basis of its cloning. Not only is it pragmatic, using thought-world, but also theoretical. It does not do theory, it *is* the theoretical. The first unified theory, that of science and philosophy, is thus the subject (of) non-philosophy, but not that alone, it is also the force-(of)-thought. Ultimately, the subject's functioning varies by its material, but it is a transcendental function whose constant is the Real-in-the-Last-Instance.

6.3 The subject can be specified as Stranger-for-the-world, a transcendental organon or even still as the force-(of)-thought, but also as existence-One-in-accordance-with-the-World. Thus it only exists through ecstatic philosophizability, which transformed, gives places to the content of its structure and *a priori* contents. The complete unilateral duality of the subject thus does not in general "exist" in a unitary and vague manner but arises from a unilateral structure of thinking that we can call *assistance-for*-the-World in a theoretical and pragmatic mode.

6.4 Non-philosophy requires the radical identification of philosophizability, which only has presuppositions, and practices which only have presupposeds (science, art, ethics, technology, etc.) a unification merely in-the-last-instance, and not by some immediate confusion or a falling back of one upon the others under the law of their unitary identification where practices become "regional" and thus seize the philosophical-fundamental that always triumphs over its appearance of unity. It postulates, via cloning, the identity-in-the-last-instance of philosophical theories and practices outside the authority of the World.

The thought-world, in general a combination of philosophy and practices or forms of knowing, thereby requires two forms. It is first of all a hypothesis which has as its justification a mixture of ternary philosophical reasons (philosophy as epistemo-logical, cosmo-logical, cosmo-political, onto-cosmo-logical, etc.) and under the sole authority of philosophizability. More profoundly, non-philosophy posits the thought-world within a theorem as the identity of a clone where philosophizability and practices come together in a non-unitary manner. Thus it has the given-real status of an axiom, but the transcendental status or given-in-the-last-instance of a theorem *for* the thought-world as its object.

6.5 What does non-philosophical assistance signify? It cannot directly transform (engender, produce, create) objects of philosophy, beings of the world or the events of history. But it can *transform* (bring about in its being-determined-by-the-One-in-the-last-instance or its relative autonomy) the All of philosophy that auto-presents itself as a mixture of identity and difference. It does not intervene, as philosophy sometimes claims to do without realizing that it is an illusion, in the details of experience, nor does it give meaning to this detail. In general, it is not an operation or activity to which the subject would be exterior. The subject *is* assistance in its essence itself (an essence that is without-essence in-the-last-instance). If assistance is neither interpretation nor intervention, but effectuation, it is the practical *contribution* or the contribution determined-in-the-last-instance (in a theoretical and pragmatic mode) of the thought-world. This contribution transforms the type of autonomy of the thought-world, forming its transcendental identity or its clone. It liberates it and frees the subject from its capture by the hallucinatory belief in its own sufficiency. Non-philosophy is this transcendental identity of *the* thought-world, and it is out of proportion with "philosophy" in the philosophical sense.

41

6.6 The assistance is the without-relation of the subject to thought-world to the extent that this "relation" is determined under the condition of radicality or a unilateral ultimacy that flows from the primacy of Man over philosophy. Assistance consists in treating any sampling of the thought-world as if it no longer belongs to it, since Man-in-person is appropriating himself and tears himself away from his own transcendental appearance.

The Distinctive Criteria of Non-Philosophy

7.1 Non-philosophy has not invented the "Real," nor the One, nor Man in general (all philosophers …), nor even the ready-made idea and expression of "radical immanence" (M. Henry and perhaps others, Maine de Biran? Marx?). Not even the Idea of a tripod structure (Marx and Lacan). In contrast, non-philosophy has invented several characteristic traits that distinguish it from philosophy. They are the eight ways of reducing radicality or radicalization to the Radical, of positing *the primacy of the Radical over radicalization, or of the One over unilaterality*, what one could too quickly call the logic of radicality or Uni-laterality, but which constitute instances of its practice, its conditions of reality rather than those of existence. They are: 1. the full meaning of immanence as being only real and not transcendental yet capable of assuming a transcendental function; 2. the necessity of addressing immanence via immanence in an immanent manner, not allowing for an all-seeing purview by a philosopher, and thus the full meaning of its radical, and not absolute, nature; 3. the already-being-given of philosophy in-One, its contribution or unilation; 4. the structure of real immanence as Uni-laterality or Other-than …; 5. the couple of determination and determination-in-the-last-instance (cloning) and the identification of the latter with Marx's concept; 6. the unilateral duality of Man and subject, the dissolution of their confusion; 7. radical immanence or Uni-laterality as human messianity or immanent future, as being-turned-towards-the-World, as is the vocation of utopia and fiction; 8. the non-philosophical subject or discourse as unified theory of a mathematical (axiomatic) aspect and a philosophical or oracular aspect. All of these traits together sketch a *utopia of Man as negative tabula rasa* (in order to oppose it to utopias as positive and murderous tabula rasas) that takes the form of a *human mathematics* (in order to oppose it to a "divine mathematics" (Leibniz) and any philosophizable or Platonic mathematics). For non-philosophy, the expression "human mathematics" is a formula no more absurd than that of divine mathematics is for philosophy. If we consider these three basic axioms outside of the eight modalities and their radical usage, then above all else they will be generalities that risk being confused with philosophy.

CLARIFICATIONS ON THE THREE AXIOMS

The Three Axioms or Structural Basis of Non-Philosophy

Non-philosophy is often reduced to three fundamental axioms, which are more like matrices of axioms which simplify it, perhaps too much, but they are helpful in orientating oneself within the clutches of philosophical matter. They are as follows: 1. the Real is radically immanent; 2. its causality is unilaterality or Determination-in-the-last-instance; 3. the object of this causality is the Thought-world, or more precisely, philosophy complicated by experience. These are simple formulations of axioms capable of multiple effectuations according to the meaning given to the primary terms formulated within natural language, but also more problematic because of the multiple interpretations that, in principle, should form a "system" coherent in its own way. It still remains to be shown in what way and to what limit this could be a system.... Non-philosophy knows the insufficient exploitations of its transcendental axioms by a more or less conscious philosophical resistance, insufficiencies that should be corrected by practice if the axioms are to be recognized and essentially understood. But there are also divergent interpretations and bifurcations, or even a truncated comprehension of their non-philosophical use. For example, they could be understood in a quasi logical and formal nature, thus allowing for a return of an equality between them, authorizing an equivalence of their particular interpretations. The three axioms in this case would form a formal system in which non-philosophy would be one interpretation amongst many, a sort of axiomatic model (hence the arbitrary thesis of there being several non-philosophies). This sort of formal comprehension seems inevitable if one wants to establish a "school of non-philosophies" but is not the case if one simply wants to establish a "school of non-philosophers." Based on this, the validation of their system can be varied, operated upon by religion or any other type of knowledge. This type of formalization causes non-philosophy to lose its philosophical material and first of all its transcendental-real essence, as if the Man-in-person were a machine running on three axioms. It would no longer be a transcendental equivalence but a formal one of axioms and most likely a poor comprehension of their real indifference or equivalence. And yet, it is a "science" of objects with empirico-transcendental criteria, not a formal system; non-philosophy does not tolerate this logical exploitation and instrumentalization.

The practice of this "system" has demonstrated the difficulty of stabilizing its general interpretation and of understanding why so many realizations of non-philosophy seem possible, but also the genuine diversity which is proper to it and what the true demarcation line is between the false liberty of the surreptitious return to philosophy and the liberty which emerges within the practice of non-philosophy. Philosophically oriented tendencies can exist within non-philosophy and are thus regressive by their refusal, for example, of continuing on to *philosophizability*, and by conservation of a determinant doctrinal position within the material. How does one distinguish this regressive multiplicity and the multiplicity oriented according to the rigor that represents true liberation? Between non-philosophy as sect, circle, clique or "chapel" and non-philosophy as destructive heresy of sects? Liberty's rigor is more difficult than liberty itself....

Three conditions are necessary in order to obtain a just practice and from there the full usage, or best rendering, of non-philosophy as instrument. There must be a clear unilateral distinction of the Name-of-Man and of the subject, the comprehension of the Determination-in-the-last-Humaneity as unilateral duality, in general, the real syntax of Uni-laterality, and in the end, an analysis that we can be sure is the most complete possible of the material sphere, philosophy or thought-world. Certain non-philosophers seize upon non-philosophy's liberating principle while still not seeing that its emancipation of the subject is only within the limits of Humaneity or the Name-of-Man. Or they seize upon theory without realizing its practical and anti-theoretical aspect. Others take hold of the idea of contingent material *as such* in regards to the Real in order to conclude with the specific or generic contingency of this or that material in opposition to philosophy and which is liable to be of immediate use. These interpretations themselves are woven into philosophical appearance and cannot challenge it. In order to dissipate these appearances linked to the three axioms, we must return to the beginning and grasp the nature of its object, the "Real," its uni-lateral immanence, the nature of its uneven identity.

Against the Platonic Chorismos

What is the affect of the Real according to philosophy, or more particularly Platonism or Nietzscheanism? It is transcendence, albeit in several different forms, generally as separation or *chorismos* (meaning "to separate and to place"). It could be said that we are being too simplistic in our explanation here, but for now the simple will suffice. We are indeed distinguishing between the chorismos which demands a minimum survey of the contemplation on separation, on being-immanently-separated, or without separation. Uni-laterality is a chorismos that has become radically immanent and that demands a severe reduction of Platonism (as well as gnosis, if we want to make use of it). Moreover, the argumentative technique of philosophy is at least, without mentioning the necessity which follows from the system, that of a shared survey, of the division against the always fetishized supposed identity but a division which philosophy contemplates. In contrast, to the extent that it is merely real, the division is immanent through and through, it is a divide-without-division. In the best of contemporary philosophical cases, we are dealing with a semi-immanence. The final essence of the philosopher is recognized in that he continues, when speaking of immanence, to contemplate it in the manner of Logos instead of practicing it in a manner which is itself immanent. Hence one last exteriority of the division and a doctrine such as theory with its politics of the cutting edge, its critique of the identity of the transcendental and the subject, the multiplication of separate terms and the conception of a unilateral trinity. It is as if the philosopher had decided one last time to touch radical immanence itself and cut it into pieces in order to re-stitch it.

The affirmation of the One as "immanent division" is thus ambiguous and can secrete within it a surreptitious operation in the Hegelian sense. Non-philosophy acknowledges the One as non-separated (from) self or immanent but only as being-separated-from the World via immanence, it is immanence that separates and which is thus separated-without-an-operation-of-separation. The confusion around the "being-separated-from the One" arises from what gnosis and Platonism accentuated by passing through Hegelian and Maoist molds; the division was supposed to belong to a relative exteriority to the One itself or to be its radical "essence," while non-philosophy only attributes this to it on the basis of its radical immanence, thus as a being-separated-without-separation. It is identical to the "negative condition" or "necessary possibility," what we also call, according to the chosen vocabulary, the "Other-than" (rather than the "Other-from" …), and, in the end, the uni-lateral Future. This is the only way to speak about Immanence according to Immanence and not according to Transcendence or according to auto-immanence to the extent that it would still be the arbiter of transcendence.

Everything is illuminated in another less formal and even more Platonic manner, knowing that philosophy can be viewed as a veritable parricide that bears less on the non-philosopher "discoverer" than it bears on the Real or the One-in-One. Non-philosophy is not the philosophy of Parmenides despite radical identity, which is no longer that of the Being-One and opens itself up as Immanence of a uni-laterality. But here as well we must kill the Real in order to be able to articulate a trinity, a system or a quaternary of instances and put into immanence (which is as such misunderstood) the "life" that Plato wants to put between Forms, or better still between the blade or edge of the sword that others want to put into non-philosophy. The Real is thus fundamentally a victim of the philosophy assassin that installs itself within the timeless forgetting of the victims of humanity. When, on the contrary, radical immanence is no longer an object of contemplation, there is a strict identity between it and not its division (another property comprehended from the exterior) but the Uni-laterality that takes on its true meaning and is no longer itself contemplated. We must leave surreptitiously one last time the One and its being-separated, it is the One that is separated from it by its immanence, Other-than ... transcendence, or is no longer Uni-lateral by transcendence but by immanence. The philosophers who appeal to immanence contemplate once more, but they are still contemplating the separation they are themselves behind, being-separated as division. Hence the use of the One in Maoist formulations, often half-criticized, One splits into Two, Two unites into One. It is with this type of formulation that a certain philosophy simply opposes itself to Hegel instead of establishing itself within an immanence which could be said to be radical, which is to say, radically said, in the sense that the said itself is radically immanent while using the transcendence of Logos.

This identity (of) immanence is neither split internally nor externally, and in any case it excludes any ambiguity of the interior or exterior. It is in this way that non-philosophy, not without difficulty or hesitation, arrived at unilateral duality as immanent and not as a contemplated duality. Is this where we get the distinction? Not exactly, for we find the unilateral duality of knotting and cloning, as fundamental operators, the first being an operator of philosophy and the second, of non-philosophy. The knotting implements transcendental parts and ties them together into a knot which is itself transcendent albeit included in the binding as any other piece whatsoever. Cloning, on the other hand, is merely respect for the "law" of radical immanence for every instant in relation, or rather non-relation, with the Real. Cloning is not pasted upon two transcendental instances (in themselves and according to their relation), but is supported by instants that it has already transformed each time, thus related to the radical immanence that distributes this "each time." In turn, the unilateral duality of cloning (itself being such a duality) and of worldly-philosophico knotting is not the knot of philosophy and non-philosophy. The latter is the clone of the former since it is dedicated to producing clones in its particular way for philosophy.

Immanence Treated by Immanence

The wager of non-philosophy whose bet no one dares support or even see, is not to make a supplementary doctrine of immanence, but rather to think immanence within the mode of immanence itself. The old philosophical reflex of thinking by transcendence is also exerted upon immanence. In order to vanquish it, it is necessary to immediately give it these conditions and not to progressively attempt acquiring or achieving them. Which is only possible if this double condition depends on a lone term, only if the duality of transcendence proper to thinking is rooted within an identity that is not a Whole and leaves its autonomy relative to transcendence. It is essential then to perceive that philosophical transcendence, when it is posed with a determinant primacy, splits "into an 'object' and a 'subject,'" that philosophy is self-overseeing [*auto-survol*], and that it can only be reduced to a uni-que transcendence by a radical immanence that determines it. This is the practical character of non-philosophical theory, practical or more precisely performed, the practice being graspable as unilateral duality. The recourse to doubled philosophical language is necessary and possible if we can finally determine an immanent use of it that "simplifies" it. But this language used as such is even less adept at defining the Real than philosophical language, the Logos which is in search of it. It is not a beginning that is lost but the Real that must be definitively lost in order to act or determine in-the-last-instance this so-called "immanent" use of language (or thought). The misunderstanding of the performed and thus practical character to the extent that this performed-being, of non-philosophy, makes either a program out of it to be executed or a pure practice – here we recognize a line of philosophical resistance. Non-philosophy is a renouncement of the overseeing [*survol*] of philosophy, it is more a question of the use of a given language rather than a dismemberment and analysis of it. Wittgenstein seemingly does not escape from the limits of language but makes another transcendent use of it, securing the transcendental limits. Non-philosophy never exits the Real, but nonetheless it performs philosophical language in-the-last-instance. It is no longer a question of setting aside the intuition of the object in blinding it or in shutting its eyes from the exterior and in this way arriving at a doctrine of the invisible or ineffable Real, etc., like a philosophy of immanence or transcendence could propose. If we must think it according to its mode-in-the-last-instance, then it is non-philosophy that is responsible for the thought and the language used to express it. This is why its definition is immediately put aside since it determines as Real any attempt at a definition. Non-philosophy is amongst other things tantamount to the refusal of any worldly or philosophical use of language whatsoever, for it distinguishes the liberty of axiomatic decision from the arbitrariness of philosophical decision.

The Axiom and the Oracle,
Or How to Speak the Future: The Oraxiom

Why the transcendental axiom and its dual mathematical and philosophical aspect? The Future here is given-without-givenness. It is given in the form of a being-spoken, a pronouncement of speech, without having been previously called or questioned. It is the principle of any answer, the Answer-in-person. It is speech of an axiomatic type but without these axioms demonstrating an implied formal questioning or without them functioning within the frame of an objective type of questioning (*if* we ask …). Moreover, the oracular answer is not subject (at least here) to a question posed to the sybil as is done in philosophy and politics.

51

The oracular answer is real, it is an immanent answer about Man by Man and determines the rigorous interpretations, thus not leaving them up to the arbitrariness of the priests. In both cases the answer is necessary though its necessity does not depend on fixed or determined contents via a prior context (philosophical "vocabulary" is not a context but an occasion). The axiom and the oracle here must be *real* or immanent, for these are the characteristics that provide it with its aspect of being "primary speech," of a forced hand but one devoid of non-philosophy. It is a negative oraxiom more than an ambiguous one because it does not make a decision on the undecidable nature of the interpretations and announces nothing but that the announcement is necessary, it "makes the necessary announcement." Man is the Announced as first name, the oracle of an ultimatum.

The real (-transcendental) axiom is even devoid of any formal form, its abstraction exceeds that of the mathematical axiom but it still should be called an axiom for practical scientific reasons. And the equally real (-transcendental) oracle is an answer, empty of any particular decision. We should be careful to note that "empty" in both cases does not mean absolutely empty but radically empty or undetermined by the concrete contents of the primary speech the oraxiom conveys. What perhaps distinguishes the oracle is having the characteristics of the Answer that the axiom does not spontaneously appear to have, being rather a condition or hypothesis, having no preliminary question on the horizon. The utterances of non-philosophy are Answers-without-questions or non-questioning-Oracles (Man is the radical answer). And they are hypotheses-without-deduction, axioms indeed having a hypothetical nature when they only tell of truth but as being without-truth, in the sense that a deduction is possible but is without a formal type of continuity or necessity. The separated-being deprives the axiom of any continuing deduction or analytic or synthetic inference, it is *hypothetico-non-deductive*. And it deprives the oracle of any answer whatsoever to any question, or query, for it is the *non-questioning-oracular* style.

Thus we will distinguish as two aspects the oracular Response and the Hypothesis or axiom that is itself not without an answer but without deduction or inference. Earlier, we characterized in too simple a manner the axiom as answer and insisted upon Man as answer while he is also a hypothesis, a true-without-truth, but from which nothing can deduce itself in *any formally continuous manner*. In both science and philosophy, there is a certain analytic and synthetic continuity, the inference, between the premises and the consequences. Contemporary philosophy has substituted dis-ference or difference for inference and others have added reference, but non-philosophy adds to the mix uni-ference and its unilateral duality between the Real (or premises) and that which uni-fers from it. Uni-ference or uni-lation is not the input of an object, reference for a language or experiment for induction or deduction. It is the input of a transcendental theorem as subject for the contingency and relative autonomy of the World. Non-deductive-hypothetico can be stated in a more positive manner as the *uniference hypothesis* and the non-questioning oracular can be called oracular uniference (uni-questioning). The uni-ference that follows from the oraxiom has, necessarily, a theoretical aspect and an interpretive aspect, since it is the input of both the interpretations and theorems together, of intelligence and comprehension identical in the last-in-Humaneity.

The Future has two manners of being non-philosophically given or expressed. It speaks in the axiom as the theorems' hypothesis or provides the necessary conditions for the hypothesis. The axiom is merely the true, the real possibility of demonstrated truth; it is the scientific side of utterances. But it also speaks within the oracle that announces the future and does nothing but announce it, and acts by this ambivalent announcement. The difference between these two non-separated modes of speaking language in the mode of the Future of a City of heretics is that the axiom is as separate as a presupposition can be, quite radically but incompletely because it is nothing, if not real, without the theorem. But the oracle is an implied or committed future within the interpretation, and we need a priest-subject to untangle the meaning. He argues for a more concrete and fundamentally ambivalent future, which is a transcendental circle. Non-philosophy is a language as identity of-the-last-instance of these two aspects.

What is a Non-Philosophical Rule?

Supposing that non-philosophy is capable of forming a school, would it be a school of non-philosopher subjects in their arbitrariness or that of non-philosophy as anonymous discipline? A dubious alternative. Its body of utterable rules gives the impression that we are dealing sometimes with a rigid science that restrains subjects and sometimes with a "doctrine" that provides them with all the possibilities of free interpretation. How does one conceive the principles of liberation without immediately unleashing fantasies of total freedom and anything goes?

We do not believe in the sharp distinction between a doctrine whose rigidity renders it communicable, and works supplied for "personal" arbitrariness. This distinction can exist but here it cannot be made into a law. Non-philosophy is the unification in-the-last-instance of a discipline and a work, and first of all, a theory and practice, not an ever-contemplative doctrine. It has its type of rules, neither rigid nor ludic nor "blended" but rigorous or "mixed" in a unilateral mode. What is rigid are those rules that derive from mathematics or logic, or some other science, whose invariance with positive content has a unilateral primacy over the contingent variation of the case or application, and at best they are invariants to transformation. What is ludic are the doctrines or philosophies that combine a double primacy, of invariance over variation and the opposite primacy, *de jure* of reversibles, which at least contain their auto-affection or auto-application which in its own manner conditions their self-critique and permanent displacements. From here we see the arbitrariness of the decisions and doctrines which are elsewhere considered coherent, a mixture which rightly impresses upon everyone its family resemblance with philosophy. What is rigorous are those rules that have neither the invariant rigidness of the first, nor the variance-invariance of the second, but a negative invariance without an empirical content but unilaterally determinant, from then on in-the-last-instance of the contingent contents formed from the rules of the two preceding types. The rules of this type take after the rigidity of scientific invariance, but do not retain a positive content and "lucidity" proper to philosophical style in the larger sense. Understood correctly, this distinction should put an end to conflicts of interpretations that beset non-philosophers and distributes them between discipline and work, theory and practice, between the unicity and multiplicity of non-philosophy provided they secretly refuse to submit themselves to this type of necessity and surreptitiously project content upon it. This discipline is negative from the single point of view of the Real, but not of reality. We would be tempted to say that the obedience (not to rules in general but to the unilaterality of rules or the rule of unilaterality) is enough for non-philosophically steering oneself in relation to the World.

The Problem of Meta-Language for Non-Philosophy

There is no meta-language for saying what non-philosophy is or is capable of doing, if it is not philosophy itself but precisely under the conditions of dualysis or of its immanent use in-the-last-instance, because by itself philosophy does not know any veritable meta-language. We will not even claim, like deconstruction, that there are *effects* of meta-language, but that this meta-language of a philosophical origin is the material determined and transformed in-the-last-instance by the first Name of Man. This is the same principle as the one for rules, in which meta-language and rules auto-affect themselves with the *proximate determining Real* that unifies them. Provided that one understands the equation correctly, philosophy is the meta-language determined in-the-last-instance for non-philosophy.

This quasi definition matters for "defining" the evaluation of criteria and the establishment of non-philosophy. If it is not the fullest or best rendering of non-philosophy, in less economic terms than that of maximum and minimum, it is at least the most just usage of non-philosophy. In the absence of economic or quantitative criteria, which would already only partially count for philosophy and which would only be introduced here by this bias, the evaluation of the practices of non-philosophy can be done in several ways. In terms of True-without-truth as for its real principles and its nature of pre-supposed-thought [*pensée-à-presuposée*], and of truth of-the-last-instance in regard to the determination of its effects. But also in terms of justice, of the Just-without-justification, Man-in-person, adjusting his effects according to their determining cause, and from the relation of the subject to this cause according to the theoretical and practical aspects of this subject. Adjusting according to the material-philosophy, and from the articulation of its axioms. An adjustment according to a work of precision and demarcation, of miniaturization and connection performed on each piece of the puzzle. These final forms of criteria are only artisanal in so much as they are of philosophical extraction but they can receive more technological and computational data-based interpretations, the "hard" and "soft" technological sides of non-philosophy.

Moreover, it is better to think the constitution of non-philosophy (above all starting from Philosophy II), using the same principle of a meta-language derived from material. Immediate *interpretations* founded upon the historical and philosophical can obviously be given in this process of constitution. They are generally of a hermeneutic style, with a retrospective auto-interpretation such as is found in Heidegger. Another distinct mode but which is related to the preceding one is the deconstructive style, by capitalization and unpacking, pieces of memory, anamnesis of utterances, auto-hetero-references, "already treated" themes, "already deconstructed" words. And yet still more modes? Why not add the "dogmatic catholic development" of Cardinal Newman? Intended to assure the authority of the Roman Church (against heresies). And the theory of the three sources of Marxism and its constitution as theoretical tradition at the heart of proletarian struggles, etc. All these styles are of interest to the constitution of non-philosophy, which follows alongside them or from afar, mentioning them and making reference to them, but using them as material for its own intelligence and strictly to the extent that it is *separated from them in an ultimate manner*. Even Catholic dogma can be interesting for it, which might be quite humorous but not without some truth, and to the extent that a theological doctrine (or Marxist thesis) can resemble an anaxiomatic axiom in-the-last-instance. All of these styles depend on occasional material and moreover must be unified with the style of constitution of the scientific type of knowledge. Even if this scientific type of knowledge remains at the level of a vague and schematic reference, it plays a necessary role in the production of unified theories in progress and obviously in non-philosophy itself.

This internal criterion *of auto-affection of material to its limit-determination-in-the-last-instance* is consistent with the style of non-philosophy and is preferable to any opposition and in particular that of the "edge of the blade," which it is by default or that of "liberalism" of which it would be an excess. Save for clarifying that the true edge is that of the uni-lateral weapon of the "single-edged blade," the double-edged blade being capable of being used against its user. Moreover, in pursuing a goal of liberation, it is indeed "liberalism" that non-philosophy mocks, or determines and dualizes, in the same way that its equality-in-the-last-instance mocks all egalitarianism. As for rigor, for rules that are more fertile and less authoritarian or at least less violent than the cutting-edge, we will come back to it later, but this rigor must be a means and an effect of justice, of Man as unilateral cause rather than a rational and empty form.

Discipline, Interpretation, Effectuation

When the interpretation of non-philosophy prevails over its effectuation, it gives rise to a particular contradiction which would be that of a discipline, a unique body of relatively coherent rules, applicable to all, but a discipline that is by definition multiple, non-philosophy expressing itself in the plural from its aspects, and demanding invention. We have seen that non-philosophy resolves this paradox itself, by a new division between a body of rules defined by Identity or the transcendental uni-city of their unilateral duality, and a field of auto-affecting proprieties providing their materiality to rules and objects. A body of rules supposed to be fixed but in themselves, along with the notion of a plurality of non-philosophies, would be either too obvious or too contradictory. Internal identity and the plurality of effectuations according to the philosophical material are internal and transcendental concepts of non-philosophy. Now is not the moment to confuse its effectuations and the unicity of its concept with the interpretations that just broke it. Non-philosophy is not itself subject to interpretation and invention, even for its "inventor," or "discoverer," it is the condition allowing for non-philosophy to invent without once again regressing back into philosophy. This consideration, which seems to shut down any perspective, is no doubt difficult to accept even if it is better for the opening up of its possibilities.

Naturally, at best, we should ourselves admit the idea of a plurality of "non-philosophies" (or rather non-religions, non-aesthetics, non-epistemologies, etc.) under the hypothesis of the most extreme philosophical resistance and in the manner in which we theorize it. The paramount problem here is that the tenants of a plurality of non-philosophies linked to the interpretations of its axioms most often leads them to believe that their solution better combats philosophical resistance by religion, art, or science than non-philosophy itself because of the priority it gives to philosophy….

Without a doubt, the effectuation of axioms as theses by this or that philosophical sequence implies a part of the interpretation. But if the unified theory always contains a transcendental-philosophical ingredient, it is enveloped in and mixed with a scientific ingredient, thus limited and dualyzed in its interpretative grasp of the axioms. In other words, we refuse an absolute and overall *a priori* interpretation of the axioms. This gives way rather to the practice of a unified theory in which it is no longer the philosophical or religious or aesthetic subject that decides axioms and their meaning, but in which it is the specific subject of the unified theory that practices them in a non-decisional manner (of) itself. And the non-philosophical subject is neither the subject of philosophy nor the subject of science in the Lacanian sense, but the subject of the unified theory that effectuates these axioms in a "mixed" [*mixte*] and not "blended" [*mélangée*] manner.

The Two Ends of Philosophy:
The Name-of-Man as Ultimatum

In a manner this time misleading for philosophy, non-philosophy seems to define itself via a unique adversary, "philosophy," that can take hold of it, transforming in this assumption one of the masks that are as numerous as doctrinal systems, suitors (Plato), pretension and appearance (Kant), the gregarious (Nietzsche), semblance and the specular (Lacan), logocentrism and representation (deconstruction), mastery (the neo-gnostics), profit and surplus value (Marx), etc. Philosophies seem to converge upon a common adversary, even if there is not a homogeneous and singular concept of all these notions, just an evil genius who is a bit confused. But defining a common adversary always makes for an attacker who is just as common and for a crowd welded together by generality and hatred. The primary means for not demonstrating the same resentment philosophy conveys towards itself is to determine it as unique or indivisible, which means not as a generality. Because then nothing in and of itself could spontaneously or without addressing itself operate an auto- or hetero-critique, and in one sense it will remain in that state. And yet, this is an impossible task with philosophical means, except in so far as it poses an empty and verbal generality of systems. Philosophy and its adversary are so protean, the "representation" so multiple in its definitions, that we should in any case invent a new form of struggle that is both unique in its practice (it can no longer be "philosophical" nor scientifico-positivist) and its object (philosophy

… and every possible philosophy) and that admits *de jure* this multiplicity of its local adversaries, without obviously justifiably totalizing them in a philosophical manner.

The wager of non-philosophy is to simultaneously pose and resolve these problems, obviously in displacing them onto another terrain, namely *the Real as Man or Future-for-philosophy*. The Name-of-Man here is, first as much as last, radical threshold, the ultimatum or oraxiom from which philosophy is forced to gather itself up in a singular appearance that will prepare for other designations (philosophizability, thought-world). Such a forced-being (without being forced) of the gathering up of philosophy operated upon by a foreign cause but which can only be external by way of radical immanence. Such an identity *for* philosophy is thus completely distinct from philosophical identities, of "ends" or metaphysical self-assemblies, self-turnings of its possibilities by one of them (Nietzsche, according to Heidegger). It is the end times of philosophy. There are, for philosophy, two types of ends that are unilaterally embedded. If its contents and form are its power to surround oneself like a self-engulfment, then we still have not yet arrived at the veritable ultimatum for philosophy. The *end* or death is in effect taken from philosophy or orients itself in philosophy's margins, implying a new beginning of the same type of thinking, with the same but softened or altered pretensions. The ultimatum, on the other hand, is the imperative of having to renounce its pretensions but to continue under another form, under the condition of available materiality and *definitive peacefulness*. If its end leads to the continuation of the civil war of philosophy under another form, the ultimatum forces it to sign a peace treaty with itself and other disciplines. This forced identity of philosophical appearance (still named philosophizability; then, when it has become empirically concrete, a thought-world), is merely the effect of the Real or the Name-of-Man on philosophy and must be specified as unidentity, unilaterality, and universality of (for) philosophy. We should be careful to note that these three components of the effect of the Name-of-Man on philosophy do not yet equate to a material transformation of philosophy but merely its being-given-in-One, thus in abeyance of the belief that accompanies philosophical appearance, the Principle of Sufficient Philosophy. It is with the help or the arrival of this material that will constitute the *a priori* side of the Stranger-subject *for* philosophy.

Thus there are two types of heterogeneous ends of philosophy which are each one in their own manner causes of change within thought. If the end taken by philosophy implies a re-activation that is a continuation, the ultimatum of the Name-of-Man as inversion-transformation of philosophy reduced to this peaceful materiality forces thought to take up a radical or primary beginning. It is thought as an arrival-without-arriving, the un-hoped for (non-hoped for) *eschaton* of the end times of philosophy. Against the semi-suicidal narcissism of philosophy, we propose a grace that determines the subject as a struggle, which it has its sights set on transforming. But what is most bizarre is that the two ends are unilaterally intertwined, the philosophical end becoming material for the non-philosophical ultimatum.

First Axiom: There is no Man but Man

Let it be uttered, *there is no Man but Man*. We put forth his apparently dogmatic character of affirmation against the philosophically undecideable Kantian question, *what is man?* Perhaps it would be enough to say that it determines a "mono-humanism" or better still a heno-humanism in order to begin to understand the equation. And in order to derive the conclusion of humanoclastic posture or stance. But this utterance has two identical aspects in-the-last-Humaneity which help in understanding the scope of it.

This is a hypothesis from which we can derive no definitive conclusion by formal necessity, except that the man-in-the-World, the famous "subject," is suspended by Man as uni-versed or Other-than ..., but this is not a conclusion or inference in the form of a theorem, just a negative and real uniference that prepares a theorem. In order for it to become a transcendental uniference or a theorem, we must write it in the following way: there is no Man except in view of the science of man. Which implies that the intelligence of the rest to which man belongs, not at all the rest but the Whole still called "Remainder," is deduced from it.

But *there is no Man but Man* is also an oracular answer that has primacy over all questions posed to the subject or the philosopher, an answer which did not wait for its question and has no need for it. A real Oracle that will give rise to an answer or a transcendental oracle jeopardizing the World, and that will formulate itself thusly: *there is no Man except for a human subject of the human sciences.*

Theory of the Dual Symptom (the Symptom and its Identity)
Is the first axiom in the name of the Real, "of matter or of man?" In the name of the anthropological man, which is to say, very close to chimpanzees, or indeed in the name of Man-in-Man? Of humanism or indeed the Name-of-Man? Were we obliged to name the Real as "man?" And how do we avoid for example the risk of a humanism? Concerning this latter point, obviously all we need to do is perform a unilateralization or dualysis of the images of man rather than claiming simply to reject them, in order to transform this humanistic material into a function of the Name-of-Man. The first point is much more delicate and appears to engage in a traditional "metaphysical" choice and precisely prepares the return of humanism. The symbolization of the Real by the name of the Man-in-person is not a recent operation within a non-philosophy that would have taken back up the great anonymous and anti-subjectivist tradition of ontology. The theme of man has been introduced in a primary and definitive manner with "human theorems" from *Une biographie de l'homme ordinaire*. It is possible that the formulations with a scientific emphasis of the intermediary period obscured it. Still, it hardly seems the case and this would not be a way of understanding the development of non-philosophy but would fix its focus on local formulations that respond to the logic of the occasionality of the material.

Is there now a sufficient reason for the introduction of the Name-of-Man at the helm of a thought taking philosophy for an object? There is sufficient reason for the materialist reversal of humanism, but there is none for the inversion or the putting down of the authority of philosophical Reason itself. Nevertheless there is a necessary cause. From its beginnings non-philosophy continues to fight against the Principle of Sufficient Reason, against the sufficiency of philosophy. The great confusion here is between necessity and sufficiency, which together in varying degrees form a circle. For this mixture of sufficient-and-necessary reason, non-philosophy substitutes an empty necessity, without object or objective, not even a form, still less an anthropological theme. This unilateral necessity is the Real-in-Person in which the last possible thought operates. Its effect is a radical reversal, of a uni-version of the whole of philosophy and no longer a reversal of a part of it by another. But why choose the Name-of-Man in order to re-name (since it is already there) the Real and grant this term a certain primacy over others against any simply formal indifference?

It is still possible to loosely sketch the arguments put forth by humanism if they are not treated according to our criteria: *sufficiency and auto-affection proper to philosophical material are determinable in-the-last-instance by the Name-of-Man*. Thus, for example, all knowledge ultimately passes through a living human being, man possesses a special dignity that is rightly repressed, even foreclosed, from philosophy that rejects it as the image of the One or of God, the least intelligible being of philosophy, the last to be understood, or strictly speaking an intermediary stage in the intelligence of the World (the *cogito*). There is necessarily an ultimate reduction of knowledge more profound than the awareness of an object as the teaching of phenomenology and mysticism. All these reasons exploit the classic privileges of consciousness and advocate for a reversal of the authority of philosophy by the man of humanism. They are not illegitimate but to go from there all the way to philosophy's inversion via the Man-in-Man and to be treated as a symptom of Man, is a big step.

But on the basis of what right are these argument-occasions transformed into symptoms of a non-philosophical discourse?

Scientific practice, which is also an aspect of non-philosophy, can encourage and enlighten us (as we will clarify) as any practice has a presupposed irreducible to philosophical presupposition, and in this case it is the Man-in-Person. But this is still not enough. Rightly, there is no reason whatsoever that is sufficient for positing man as presupposition of the knowledge of the World but *everything* enforces upon him as occasion. It is philosophy itself that gives man this *symptomatic importance*, correlative of the One in the manner he understands it and that one must now read as primary name for the axioms. An instance called "man" is twice a symptom, first within philosophy and in relation to its One, a second time outside of philosophy as a relation of philosophy to non-philosophy, the One of consciousness to One-in-One or of the *cogito* to unlearned [*indocte*] Knowledge. The first symptomatic status of man is necessarily the material of the second symptomatic status which binds philosophy to non-philosophy and which is itself of another nature than the first. The appeal to man-material is not a smuggled philosophical thesis that some deconstruction could have quickly tracked down, for it is reworked as a symptom and a symbol, as a simple occasion, with the intention and the task of positing the intelligence of science and philosophy. Such is the minimum of constraints that we conserve from philosophy which one must recognize nonetheless as having some right in this affair.

As primary Name or symbol, it no longer imposes itself in *any case*, in *all* cases, nor even once and for *all*, in the manner of a universally valid *cogito* under all conditions, which is to say, if we understand the whole we are dealing with, under each of the conditions taken one by one indefinitely in its supposed power of determining the *cogito*. This belief in an already supposed whole which one must re-create anew, this vicious circle of philosophy, is at the origin of the objection of humanism and is the result of the confusion of the material-occasion of the primary Name. It only imposes itself in a single manner, in a single case, one time every time, under the condition of the Whole which is itself, this time, the contingent occasion. Thus Man-in-Person is neither a way, nor a figure, nor even an occasion. Accordingly, if the subject-in-the-world is a symptom that makes an occasion, the Name-of-Man is not an occasion but is what makes for occasions, ways, figures, etc. and determines them. The Man-in-Man is the envelope of necessity but empty of *cogito*, free of thought and existence, the radical I separated from the *sum* and *existo*.

Non-philosophy obeys a sort of Precaution Principle. But this too is a formulation of a philosophical and critical spirit, called into consciousness as judging instance. In reality it's a principle of fidelity, yes, fidelity, but to whom or what? To the Man-in-Person or the Name-of-Man. Thus it is a fidelity of the last-instance or still the last fidelity, the fidelity to Man as ultimatum addressed to philosophy. If "man" is time and again also a concept of philosophy, then one must speak of "non-humanism" and put the non-man at the head of thought. Non-philosophy concentrates on or can be summarized in its fidelity to the primary term of "Name-of-Man" or the "In-manned."

The Argument of the Third Man

The auto-dissolution of human reality – and that of the World – is programmed within philosophy in the form of a process of the One, by consequence, and from its entanglement with Being, of a birth of the One becoming One, or of the constitution of Man becoming Man, reforming the dyad then triad and supposes a third One or a third Man, etc. Taken literally, the argument of the third man refutes the authority of philosophy or demands its dualysis. It is more profound than philosophy, which makes a negative use of it or imagines it to be for its own benefit. Its competence is the performed (or "performative") fitness of its logical form and its semantic contents once we have perceived that it is precisely Man that should be "one" or uni-que. In the sense that he is even less than "one," merely One-in-One, Man-in-Man, or One separated from the World and thus assuring man his relative autonomy. This argument presupposes strictly speaking, if not a performative act, then at least a being-given or performed-without-performance (of the name) of Man. If we want to treat it seriously and not with the usual scholarly carelessness of a Greek game, one that acknowledges the auto-dissolution of the human within the philosophical apparatus and argues for the uni-city or *identity of Man as in-Man suspending philosophical sufficiency*. The starting point he uses is not exactly that of the *cogito* against universal doubt, a self-reflexive starting point, or feelings of consciousness or transcendence but that of the being-performed of Man by the primary name of "Man." To avoid the multiplication and auto-dissolution of the One within the One-etc. of the Man in man, etc., they must be given as primary names.

How does thought radically begin if not by a term that is unique because it is identical, as in for example the mystical ejaculation, "God!" or "Jesus!", as we have here with "Man-in-Man!". Why must one repeat it with a slight difference if not in order to comply with grammatical conformity or logically conform to the principle of identity, "man humanizes," "the world worlds," "nothingness nothings," "redemption to the redeemer?" Why a third man or the ternary of the *cogito* as philosophy would have it? A beginning of thought radical-in-the-last-instance must be given, but given as non-existent. Obviously not a philosophical or absolute beginning that in effect does not exist (Hegel), but rather a beginning of the axiomatic type, a primary thought that merits its "scientific" name and does not shy away from science as is still the case with Husserl.

If Being has become the center of contemporary philosophy in accessing the status of *a priori* and categorical intuition, the axiomatization un-intuits it in the-last-identity with the other transcendentals. The overtaking of the empty concept and judgment via pure intuitive sensation and categorical intuition must prolong itself until this threshold, this decision of a completely new type that formalizes not the One but thought according to the One and that can in some way empty it of any ontological determination, even of form, thus without rendering it formal.

Heidegger led Being towards the earth of pure intuition and time, and we must steer it back towards the heresy and utopia that is Humaneity. The mysticism born from philosophy never exceeds intellectual, emotional, or even affective intuition, but the mysticism born from non-philosophy, without "exceeding" intuition, but in inverting it, finds in the Man-in-person an "office" freed of any intuitive support whatsoever. The One in its heretical or separated-being is neither pure matter nor form in which the God of the Christian mystics and the subject of the philosophical humanists always risk dogmatically sinking into. We thus believe in God and the *cogito* but only to the extent that we no longer believe in the monad and Unicity, but that we perform the One-in-One or the Identity determining God as God-world and the *cogito* as *cogito*-world. The heno-humaneity is the real content and critique of this symptom, the monotheistic mixture. For example, the in-One only has its hallucinatory image in the monad whose being is the expression of the World. It does not itself go all the way to the monad and is not endowed with a sufficient appetite, perception and consciousness, but is merely endowed with that which makes identity rather than unicity. Unlearned knowledge or vision-in-One avoids the labyrinth of the One-and-the-Multiple in which philosophy and mysticism get lost.

Real and Thought-Language Are Not in and of Themselves
Matter can be addressed, not as being the Real in the radical sense in the way we talk about it in regard to the Man-in-person and destined to substitute itself for him, but as one of the symptoms of immanence that philosophy produces in its task of ontological generalization and anonymization. From our point of view a crude return to the materialism of Marxism, even ameliorated by contemporary philosophy, is excluded. But nowhere do we see a treatment of materialism that would pass by its reduction prior to the invariants of the most fundamental philosophical Decision, the inverse reduction of this decision to the primacy of materialism having no more value than its reduction to the idealist position.

Not only is materialism nothing without practice, even if it has primacy over it, but it is doubtful that matter can immediately give-in-One thought-language of philosophy and transform it. Already philosophy completes or else Decision admits that this givenness of thought by matter is only possible if the latter contains ideality, any other conception being itself unthinkable like a primary or crude unconscious. The same can be said for a materialism that goes by the letter in the Lacanian sense and which can at best, like any transcendental materialism, merely lead to a topological mathematization and a transcendental binding. Should we do as Marx sometimes does in making productive forces out of science, etc., the Real, only assigning to man the role of the conscious support of the structures? That would be giving a transcendental and worldly positivity to the Real and the Determination-in-the-last-instance, finally repeating the anti-humanist gesture of a reduction of man to the state of a scientific object. Matter as "last instance" can be called "immanent," but the problem for non-philosophy will always be knowing whether this immanence is thought or formulated from immanent matter (despite the evident appeal to the transcendence of thought-language that names the Real, but a transcendence according to immanence or one that is non-positional (of) itself). In short, we must not confuse a materialist position within philosophy and the thesis according to which philosophy is materiality through and through.

If the Real and thought-language should not be in and of themselves (in and of themselves what?) (that is to say objects of philosophy, even called "immanent," or simply philosophizable) of which materialism is a good example, is the solution then to look to the side of the signifier and the signified? Is the void as "formal" or structural, the Real as a non-philosophical element of abstraction? But it possesses as well the positivity and transcendence of form, if not the mathematical set. If we are only dealing with pushing abstraction to the maximum, then "radical void" or the "in-void" would be better suited for the Real. No doubt, but this ideal of the maximum of abstraction is not the only case because it is still an abstraction within the symbolic order, which is to say, of thought-language (which is the matter of Logos). And yet the apparent omnipotence of symbolic abstraction is still impotent for the Real=X and its power, even if this power of the Real=X at minimum demands and remembers from philosophy this quasi-formalization and symbolization. The "immanence" of language is not alone, it is just as much a transcendence, and it is determined by the transcendence of the Real which accomplishes pulling non-philosophy away from the in itself of language. Language continues in any case albeit without having an effect on the Real. It is not enough to say that the Real and language are generally inseparable because in the Real the latter is separate (without being in and of itself) albeit nonetheless still named with the help of speech [*la langue*].

Thus this X=Man-in-person is not a *pure* symbol or signifier in the linguistic sense, no more so than a "transcendental signifier," it is, rather, a *name or a transcendental term, which is to say real* in-the-last-instance, the "letter" if you will, but specific to non-philosophy rather than psychoanalysis. The *Name-of-Man* is a concentrated form of non-philosophy, or thought-language; that is, a philosophical language by its origin but one already determined in-the-last-Humaneity. We must exclude formalism as realism in itself or materialism. Despite the fact that it is inseparable from language in the non-philosophical exercise of practice, X is never the object of a discourse on its supposed being-in-itself, which would be a contradiction, but on the other hand one can say that it is what determines a subject for the relationship of two signifiers-signifieds of this discourse.

Idealism will perhaps object that this Real, capable of giving in an appropriately immanent manner transcendence itself, must be "ideal," at least partially. In order to avoid this idealistic objection, as the fall into a transcendental materialism incapable of tolerating the thought-language of philosophy (the twin dangers of consciousness and the material subconscious), we had to invent, starting from philosophical symptoms, the oraxiom in general and the concepts of the vision-in-One, of the manifest-without-manifestation, of giving-without-givenness or of unlearned knowledge, which is to say a third type of knowledge or phenomenon separated by its immanence itself from consciousness and matter. This is perhaps problematic from the point of view of philosophical and psychoanalytic authority, but it is the only chance of never entering into philosophy, of not being definitively alienated from the World while at the same time being "turned" towards it.

Non-Philosophical Re-Naming

It is within this context of uni-laterality that philosophy functions as symptom or language *forced* by the Real. The name "Real" is itself also a symbol coming from philosophy like the others and thus the others can be substituted for it in its place and within this function of symptom in order to denote the cause. If one admits this functioning of the symptom of philosophy, a symptom of a structure that by its very nature is separated from the action of thought-language necessary for its effectuation, then non-philosophy has reasons for re-naming the Real "Man-in-person" or the One-in-One. Most of the discussions on this presuppose, without recognizing it, that the Real and thought-language are distinct as given in themselves, when in reality the latter is given in-Real, the Real being nevertheless separate from thought-language. It is within the element of this unilateral duality that one must examine the possibility of naming the cause, and it is a process of re-naming *that is always also a transformation of the philosophical use* of language. And yet, within this framework of non-philosophy, and not the Real in itself, we have seen that there is some necessity of positing the equivalence of this term with others such as the One-in-One or the Real and even to give preference to the "Man-in-Person" over others. The Man-in-Man is not an exception to philosophy or science; it is separated from them and determines a subject for the relations of these opposites of the thought-world. We must abandon thinking in the form of "either this … or that …," for non-philosophy knows no alternative, as it undoes amphibologies via its unilateral style and not via an antithetical style.

As for the subject who prefers the designation "Man" to that of "matter," the same goes for him and his responsibility because from the beginning he obviously has intentions or motifs of a philosophical, sentimental, or even (why not?) religious order. But as non-philosophical subject or determined by the Man-in-person, he struggles in a permanent manner against his reduction to the state of a philosophico-humanist subject. His freedom only challenges him as a subject, but it is true that the subject decides between two dissimilar forcings [*forcages*], the real or human forcing and the philosophical, humanist forcing. In any case, one should not forget the *practice* or conditions of the struggle that resolves problems created by theoretical contemplation and interpretation. We will also strive to resolve, via the same path, the other amphibologies that nourish the interpretations of non-philosophy.

Man as Paradigm of Uni-Laterality or Ultimatum

Let us now penetrate into the heart of immanence, of the Man-in-person. The in-Man is the presupposition not of all thought (which has natural, worldly social aspects in general) but the final thought, the thought-ultimatum. How does a "thought" present itself when it is defined by a presupposition and no longer has the philosophical form of a presupposition, which is to say of reciprocity or convertibility? The novelty of non-philosophy, that which focuses on what we called its eight principles of the radical functioning of immanence, can be summarized within the paradigm of Unilaterality. We should nevertheless distinguish (we will not yet do it here) its real form (uni-laterality) from its transcendental or subjective form (unilateral duality). We will have to content ourselves with a description that is in some ways of an essence or phenomenon.

1. Non-philosophy is unilateral, which is to say that it has no assignable point of departure and goes only in one direction and in one single burst towards its point of arrival, its "object" neither being that from which it came nor that to which it returns but towards which it goes. Unilateral is expressed out of a thought in which only the object is identifiable, without a localizable or determinable initial instance of arrival, the identity of the Real or thought not capable of being identifiable in itself according to the ordinary sense of the term. Generally, a direction, from the simple fact of the duality of di-rection, has a point of arrival and a point of departure towards which it either returns or departs, for it is bilateral and travels in both directions, in any case, and inscribes itself within an operatory space that is pre-given and capable of being summarized. In general, it only needs to be assigned a point of departure in order for the trajectory to "make" a direction. This is the case of presupposition or of a condition that is itself unconditional or absolute. Conversely, the presupposition, in the rigorous and not philosophical or confused sense of the term, is not a di-rection. Such a uni-rectional thought, which obviously risks passing as dogmatism, is non-reflexive, and it prepares the possibility for a quasi-unconscious instance (to make a comparison with the unconscious). But it possesses a force that is irreducible to philosophy and cannot be appropriated by it, and which has been repressed more, certainly, than it has been used. *(From) Out of Nowhere* is one possible name for this force that never comes to the future.

2. The great insufficiency of philosophy was to have refused the premise for the benefit of the presupposition and its programmed replacement, of having confused under the name of the "Real" necessity as force with transcendence, of having made of the Real an originary transcending and sometimes a simple transcendent entity that necessarily split between an initial subject and a terminal object, which are sometimes one and the same. Radical immanence is not a substantial point, it is by definition and origin a utopian force destined for the Whole or that of which the Whole reveals itself to be the symptom, the subject. We will not stop distinguishing between thinking by transcendence and the force-(of)-thought that the Greeks naturalized and reified in a demonic manner. In a different way than Bergson, we distinguish the force-trajectory or the traced transcendence of an existing space, and the emergence-force that is indivisible and that, without leaving a trajectory in which it would unwind itself, invents a throw-without-trajectory that modifies any trajectory into a subject.

3. The premise, when it is not reduced to a disguised presupposition, destroys the dualities that are consumed into a synthesis or system, for example, the bottom and form, object and World, transcendence into *meta* and *epekeina*, being and Being, etc. Without a hinter-world, no less than without departure, it is definitively turned-thrown once and for all towards the World or better still, *one time every time for the Whole*. For the first time it is the concept of an emergence or a *rection* that does not emerge from a bottom, from predisposed universality or a poor generality and which thus does not aim for a form at the heart of a whole, no more a form than a part, nor being than Being. Coming from nowhere as coherence of a lone and unique thrownness, it cannot help aiming for the Whole itself, or rather see it as an object, transforming it into this determining vision and giving it as a subject. It is therefore not only necessary to deprive it of the terminals of the subject and object, but to give it primacy (not priority) over these two entities, putting the subject and object together in one, the one side that exists. So thoroughly, indeed, that this indivisible intention or whole of identity is doubly intentional. The first time it is a real or noetic intention that gives the material object in-Real as we already know, noetic in that the Real has primacy over the material-object. A second time it is still the same intention but transcendental or "noematic" that gives the material-object itself as subject. Hence the unilateral dissociation of the noematic real and the noematic subjective, of the Man-in-person and the subject, a radical inversion of the noetico-noematic correlation.

4. Thus, it is an intentionality decapitated of any subject or will, of any empirical or transcendental consciousness, of any ego, generally in the form of transcendence. But also of another unilaterality that will serve as a point of departure for it after having served as a point of arrival in the manner of desiring machines (Deleuze) that have two heads or two functions and that already represent a certain incomplete simplification of the classical philosophical system. It is an acephalic intentionality, a force, so profoundly idiotic, like the future itself, that it is not even intelligent or unintelligent like forces sometimes are. It distinguishes itself as simpler than the Nietzschean "perspectives," Spinozist attributes, partial objects, and in general any forms of three-headed consciousness or two-headed or bipolar unconsciousness which merely endorse philosophy and content themselves with dissolving or *molecularizing* it. The opposition of molar and molecular, of the general and the specific and partial, is inoperable here and sinks into the di-rectional and bi-lateral. One would say that these real or human entities are uni-rectional or uni-lateral. Rather than relation, we will obviously speak of uni-lation, etc.

5. These entities will be realized by non-philosophy which will radicalize this dimension of "arrival for …" or of intention without-subject but of-subject in the form of the "future" or even the immanent and necessary messianism. Hence the non-phenomenological axiom, that any future is future of (for) a subject, force-being is forced-being of a subject. The Real and the thought that forces it are such phenomena of messianism. It is nevertheless not about falling into some sort of dogmatism in order to avoid the risks of mechanism and all-automatism of a thought that wants to be non-reflexive and non-conscious. Uni-lateral intention (One-tention) is the ether of the future coming into the World and into the totalities of this type. Its utopian as much as heretical interest is not to be closed and situated by an assignable departure point, as was Nietzsche's intention in his dissolution of the subject and the object, although he conserved the World and the Whole as the Eternal Return that envelops all directions and encloses them into a single direction. He is caught up with the last philosophical fetishism, that of the One-All rather than hinter-worlds, which is the transcendental form of the knotting. Forbidding the future from presenting itself as the force-(of)-freedom that has never taken place, that arrives, and does not stop arriving from out of *No Where*. In other words, we will keep ourselves from casting the Real and the thought forced by it into a couple like that of unbinding and suturing or the knot that witnesses the state of alienation and transcendent fragmentation of thought.

6. We will call "practical thought" or "practicity," any knowledge that has the presupposed-form, in priority the minimum syntax or "logic" of uni-laterality thus understood in a definitively non-dialectical manner. We would have to add its substantial double nature of language and reality. We will examine how the two sides of the presupposition, language and object, are distributed in the chapter called *Philosophizability and Practicity*.

7. The symbol by which we can write Uni-laterality and uni-lateral identity naturally seems to be the game of parenthesis around the (of). But in all strictness one must write the "of" according to a unilateral parenthesis because it is unique and non-divisible, it cannot be split or redoubled, it should be written in the following way: the thought-world and its utterances are generally put between parentheses as the *entre-deux* par excellence, as with deconstruction, but which we would say to put "in-parenthesis." It is not about putting the thought-world once and for all between two parentheses, but into one unique parenthesis coming from the Real and which *re-moves* the thought-world rather than *revives it* as philosophy claims. The in-parenthesis is the immanent identity that unilaterally re-moves the weight of the sufficiency of the World.

The Forced Hand or the Ultimatum of the Real

The Man-in-Man is the "forced hand," the last straw or ultimatum of philosophy. It is the forced hand that forces the subject and its force-(of)-thought rather than the inverse. This original organization in the subject of the negative or non-sufficient necessity and positive but determined freedom, such are the real contents for us of this otherwise authoritarian equation of Rousseau, "we will force them to be free," which in our language will either be stated as "we will force them to be heretical" or "non-philosophers." If Humaneity is a completely "negative" force, a forced-without-forcing, it clones or forces a subject, it is the immanent cloning of the subject that is itself in its essence "force." We call the subject the "force-(of)-thought" as it comes from the immanent forcing in-the-last-Humaneity.

Non-philosophy always risks letting a fragment of appearance pass from the World or philosophy into the Real. And there is a refusal of philosophy for the benefit of nothingness or something else, another substitute, which is another manner of retaining philosophy within the Real. Necessity then once again becomes authority, the liberty of the subject becomes alienation in a fetish. The Real is the forced hand of non-philosophy but rightly a forced hand without an external operation of forcing, a card hand present in givenness but which has not been given. The philosophical game of appearance knows as well the forced hand to be positive, whether out of nothingness, forcing the subject by its positivity itself. And it is this fold of the forced and the forcing called "force" in philosophy. In order to ward off any simply dogmatic constraint, it is necessary to conceive the forced-being of the Man-in-person as immanent and, from there, as forcing from its void, the subject making World. One sees how Rousseau's formula swerves into an authoritarian style. What is it that forces in Rousseau, what is this "one" if not the "general will" that substitutes its formalism for the real void of the Man-in-person, the sovereign in the Name-of-Man, a philosophical and anonymous abstraction to the abstract real? The radical autonomy of the Man-in-Man is the phenomenal real content of this absolute autonomy. Reason can be sufficient, it is never last-instance or ultimatum.

Non-philosophy begins as an appeal to let the dead bury the dead and to invent the future. But it is the Future that forces us to invent the present as transformation of the past. It is the force-(of)-thought that from its void of being and nothingness proceeds as force of invention even to the World. Is this force then an empty form, are we returning to Kantian formalism? A completely negative force, without philosophizable or wordly contents, even without contents of form, cannot give way to a transcendental formalism. To force the decision of non-decisionality avoids the will of liberation like that of consent. We know contemporary philosophers of difference made fun of the neither … nor … as a facile solution and diversely distributed it with the and … and … which either follows (Derrida) or precedes (Deleuze). But the problem is this combination itself and the highest philosophical positivity it conserves.

Rather than even force (of) thought, we can call it *force (of) letting* this force that can let the World be-given-in-One. Such a force does not suppose a substrate and an attribute, namely forcing or letting according to a preliminary form as force or as letting and abandon as well as an attribute of letting or force. It is the radical identity of letting, consent through an immanence that has already forced the will of renouncement. Forced abandon by force? A forcing of the abandoning of abandonment or renouncement? These formulations are of a necessarily philosophical extraction but are transformable and escape the antimonies still present in Rousseau and Heidegger, and others that tried to scare them away.

The Beginning or the Unilateral Leap

Man is not a leap, but a leap('s) identity or a future('s) identity from which the World is "versed."

The Man-in-Man as vision-in-One is not attained by a leap but renders a uni-lateral one necessary, a unilateral duality of the leap rather than the classical leap, which is necessarily bi-lateral and self-sufficient. Rightly so, we do not leap towards or within the Real (which is already given and which itself verses philosophy, given with it without being it) into non-philosophy (but not into Reality). We must not confuse the primacy of the Real which does not show or discuss itself, and the radical beginning of thought-according-to-this-Real that is made as an identity of a unilateral leap.

Thought is a problem whose solution is given with the Real without being the Real.

From the point of view of supposedly sufficient and pertinent philosophy, the Name-of-Man would be a pure and simple leap, an arbitrary decision, not into the absolute as Kierkegaard would have said, but into the radical. From the point of view of this latter position however, it is no longer, it never has been a leap outside of philosophy, the latter being accompanied by the Name-of-Man, with which it is given, by definition, we could say, since the name of "man" is philosophizable and from then on arrives as symptom. The problem is posed in the form of its solution, somewhat in the same way as the *cogito*, but within a performativity without idealism, that of non-philosophy as it speaks and thinks. The same goes for the previously sketched arguments that somehow call for an irrational leap. Whoever believes in philosophical sufficiency has no reason to exit it even to the point that non-philosophy offers no motive whatsoever for appearing even if only as a chimera. Outside of spontaneous philosophy and its contemporary complications, absolute nihilism seems to reign and one needs skepticism and other limitations in order for philosophy itself to perceive that an Other is possible, but this Other cannot go beyond it. In order to perceive sufficiency, one already has to be there "halfway out" or, more precisely, has to put philosophical language in the mouth of the Man-in-person and listen to what he does with it. In short, there is no possible genesis of non-philosophy starting from philosophy alone and its limits.

The Second Axiom or the Subject:
The Multiplicity of Effectuations

With the second axiom we are already obligated to take back up problems we have already examined from a different angle. It is their transcendental repetition.

How can we explain that non-philosophy is singular as a school but that it is also compatible with a multiplicity of existing-non-philosopher-subjects that effectuate it, and even insists on them?

It is about explaining this overdetermination of the principle not of non-philosophy as uni-que organon, always identical to its essence, but of its effectuations and their subjects, and to thus prevent non-philosophy from returning to philosophy. We will first of all use an approach via a hypothesis of the Duhem-Quine type, then we will return once again to the subject, unilaterality and determination-in-the-last-instance, namely, to the second of the axioms of our tripod as Lacan would have called it (Real, Subject and Philosophy, or thought-world).

Concerning this first argument, by its scientific aspect, non-philosophy is a theory and is thus under-determined by the experience corresponding to it and which is philosophy as material. More precisely, the conditions not exactly being those of science in the empirical sense, the non-philosophical theoretical apparatus is too universal for the always singular material but it also has its own particular manner of exceeding non-philosophical univocity. What matters here, in terms of uni-city or the theoretical identity of non-philosophy, is that the material is always too singular for determining it and verifying it by exhaustion. Whatever the pretensions of singular effectuations of non-philosophy, they are incapable of exhausting Identity of the this-here, which is to say, the universal power (albeit negative) of the Real.

The Real is underdetermined by philosophy and probably by all activity. We can be sure that religion as material underdetermines it even more than philosophy, however without being sure that the former is equal to the latter in furnishing essence and the whole of appearances. The necessity of giving form to non-philosophy in exercising this power comes from, amongst other things, the universality of philosophy-material in the field of knowledge and the World, but even this necessity enveloping philosophy cannot determine the Real and, in this regard, non-philosophy itself or the "logic" of unilaterality that this cause implies. A quasi-infinite multiplicity of effectuations is possible, to the extent that the contents of philosophy permits it and not its form which is also unique but divisible. We will conclude in a general manner that by its real cause, non-philosophy radicalizes, which is to say universalizes, the thesis of Duhem-Quine, ripping it away from its positivistic-scientific limits. Nevertheless, without canceling out what was just said, this radicalization of Duhem-Quine's thesis provides a phenomenon that is unacceptable by the essence of a subject, but is receivable by the transformed contents of experience and provides it from the point of view of philosophy or the material that non-philosophy claims to measure in terms of totality. The thesis of a multiplicity of non-philosophies, apart from what we strategically believe, does not have a theoretical rigor and hides its true contents, which are the multiplicity of effectuations. Furthermore, it covers over intentions of philosophical and religious subversions (amongst others) of non-philosophy.

The Confusion of the Name-of-Man and the Subject

Posed from the viewpoint of the Real, the problem is now that of the subject, the subject of unilaterality or the subject of determination-in-the-last-instance, three things that are really one and which provide the practical framework for the generalization of Quine's thesis. Why this stubbornness of division as duality, to the conflicts of interpretation that would make one believe there are as many non-philosophies as non-philosophers? It is because the practice of non-philosophy happens on the plane of the isolated subject, who is halfway-engaged within philosophy and its contrary decisions. The confusion of the Name-of-Man and the subject, their unilateral non-distinction, the reduction of the former to the latter, implies the confusion of real or indivisible Identity and division (difference, duality, etc.). And yet *Identity, in order to be indivisible, is nevertheless uni-lateral or separate-without-division (Other-than …) and its effectuation gives way to a philosophically unheard-of duality*. And to put it in an inverse way, for it to be a duality it is nevertheless a radically undivided identity. *The duality of the subject is thus identity not simultaneously but in-the-last-instance*. The deployment of this logic implies a flawless rigor (because there are no flaws where everything happens without fault albeit without positive necessity). One is obviously tempted to give equal weight to Identity and Duality on the balance scale, but the former cannot be placed on any scale and the latter bears all the possible weight of reality but a weight that is radically light. Thus thinking with the help of philosophy each time one time or according to Identity. To think the Real without error, the One without the Two, is also to think the Two in-One, but certainly not the "Two fuses into One." Any position of the Real within transcendence or implicitly with it, any tension or attention brought upon the One is excessive and erroneous, and engages with thought within the error of philosophical sufficiency.

Within this order of problems touching the subject, we will avoid the chorismos of a thought-without-subject *and* of a subject-without-thought, or more still a rebellion-without-subject and of the subject-without-rebellion, which only come together by a theoretical act of force. The subject is the clone or the in-One of the thought-world (amongst which, there is the possibility, but an historical contingency, of a thought-rebellion or "people"), which is to say the One, assuming as transcendental identity or essence of the subject that which is given as the subject to-world-form. Cloning is the operated upon or the oeuvre-without-operation that puts an end to the "future" or "ultimatum," to the operation demanded by the chorismos and logical pathos of Plato and all philosophy. The theory of the subject cannot once again be determined within a trinity albeit unilateral. Unilateral precisely when it is no longer confused with a form of the chorismos or a transcendental treatment of immanence, calls for duality and nothing else. We will definitively oppose pure theory and the immanent arrival of Man in the World and the thought within the cloned person of the subject to Platonic philosophy with its transcendence and the chance arrival, for example, of the people for the transcendental or an Angel miraculously rising. Finally, the determination-in-the-last instance is also equivocal and can be interpreted by exteriority, binding, and transcendence (its Platonizing recuperation), while its rigorous conception, without interruption, requires cloning.

The subject exists concretely as transformation of the bilateral or common division into a unilateral duality. It is thus in the subject that we see the risk of confusion being prolonged or reborn in its order of philosophical appearance, annihilated or otherwise transformed. If there is a site for the *de jure* multiplicity of non-philosophers, it is the subject rather than the Name-of-Man. But it is also in the practice of the subject that the mixture of philosophical appearance and the destruction of this appearance can be evaluated. The thesis of a multiplicity of non-philosophies under the pretext of the freedom of invention (everyone with his/her own non-philosophy …) supposes a reduction of the Real to the subject, an idealistic and activist vision of non-philosophy. And more profoundly, it is a return to the pretensions of a worldly subjectivity of the non-philosopher.

From Knotting to Cloning

What we name "cloning," the essence of the determination-in-the-last-instance and which ends the transcendental phase, is not the operation of knotting two instances but of its real or phenomenal contents. There is nothing between Man and philosophy to tie together the Real (or Being) and thinking, even if Parmenides decided it once and for all, for all philosophies. The knot is the system par excellence of relative-absolute instances, the essence of the philosophical ternary or quaternary, it is why Lacan's psychoanalysis is a theory fettered by a system. Every philosopher has wanted to link, to assemble the degrees and forms of heterogeneous reality, the most classical of philosophers by the *vinculum substantiale*, the most contemporary by knotting and suture. The principle is that of the knotting or binding instant or the instant which creates the knot itself being knotted and is the binding object and ties itself to all the others. The knot can be dialectical, structural, or topological, witnessing a certain condition of exteriority and transcendence of the operation. The efforts of contemporary thinkers (who believe they have made progress in substituting knotting for System) are the result of the use of a material, topological, opaque, ensemblist, temporal, signifying or linguistic substrate. This recourse to a substrate is a disregarded minor form for the third term of philosophical ternaries. The problem becomes clear with the Borromean knot of the Lacanian RSI. Before giving way to such a knot, this structure is in reality that of philosophy itself as metaphysical double of transcendence, from the I to the S., but which is also the epikeina-physics of the I. and S. to the R. But the knotting of the three strands, in order to be topological, is nonetheless their "flattening" of the principle or their equalization within a non-hierarchizing operatory space, and it is thus also a scientific enterprise that violates the transcendental essence of philosophy be it Western or Eastern, violating it because it is unable to unite itself in a radical manner with philosophy like non-philosophy strives to do.

Nevertheless, cloning is not a simple and unique operation in opposition to the complexity of knottings, it is not an operation but a cloned-without-cloning, a unilateral duality of phases. On one hand, philosophy is effectively not supposedly given, not acquired, in the mode of the One or determination, and thus without the metaphysical operation of givenness that would from then on pose the problem of the relationship to the World as insolvable. On the other hand, on this base another transcendental phase simultaneously grafts itself continuously but nevertheless takes into account the material, which is the determination-in-last instance or cloning as solicitation of the determination by the already given occasion.

The Real as simple is always uni-lateral, precisely to the extent that it is simple: because it does not have to exit-itself in order to act on an exterior material. So immanent is the knotting that it is still operation *ex machina*. And so immanent is cloning, it is not without a certain duality or semi-duality. There is no totality of the foreground or background to absorb the One, but the One or the Man-in-Person is radically necessary for philosophy to *leave to be discovered* the "invisible" that demarcates its pretensions. If there is nothing to bind together in order to make a

World, for reduplicating philosophy and for re-inscribing it within Man, there is everything available for cloning, but this cloning of the Whole excludes the self-engulfment of the Whole that the knotting seeks and is merely a theory of the *one-dividual*. Knotting aspires to the world as philosophy, whereas cloning is the thought and practice of the radical individual *for* the World. But in order to remain loyal to the spirit of cloning, one must admit that cloning and knotting rightly form an indivi-dual structure, while the spirit of knotting is the denegation of cloning. Cloning is apparently infinitely "weaker" than knotting, but it is cloning that transforms and explains knotting. We will avoid returning to philosophy, simply pitting them against each other one more time. From this point of view, we could "correlate" within a new unilateral duality a transcendent practice of knotting of the terms or signifiers in Lacan and Derrida and the immanent practice of their cloning and find there a distinction and correlation (unilation) of two different styles of writing. Hence, the complexity or apparent sophistication of non-philosophical writing whose only equal is found within the simplicity of its schema. To maintain cloning and unilateral duality rather than knottings of transcendent identities is a principle of caution or accuracy [*justesse*], that requires vigilance as much as effective practice. If the principle is to be something other than the internal movement guiding non-philosophy, or to be at each instant contemplated in a theoretical manner as completed, non-philosophy would be supposedly realized within the philosophical mode.

Non-Philosophy and Non-Philosophers

We will put forth the principle contesting any transcendental splitting, via a "unilateral" division and choice but without *duality*, thus in fact via a unity, in order to characterize non-philosophy, as an end or even as a means, a public or even private language, as theoretical or practical, as program or indeed as a realization. Conversely, a danger threatens all uses of non-philosophy, once more dividing what is uni-by-immanence [uni-par-immanence].

From here we get dualities where non-philosophy hardly recognizes itself despite the prudence consisting of returning to these divisions in order to correct them in the manner of repentance. This division cancels out the uni-lateral dualities and recreates bi-lateral ones. Several examples of these semi-solutions are woven within philosophical appearance. Non-philosophy will have as its objective to work with and on philosophy rather than creating some sort of institution of new humanity, it will be a discipline rather than a new examination of life. Or more still a theoretical discipline that is valuable and useful for a community of researchers rather than an oeuvre marked by a fashionable particularity and subjective choices. Or it is a theoretical discipline rather than a practical one, or one could say it is a forgetful practice of theory. Or a program for a machine rather than its execution still to come. Or a mysticism rather than a philosophical doctrine. Or an immanence without alterity, a metaphysical rewind vis-à-vis the philosophers of the 20th century, or on the contrary it is a theory of the Other that prolongs those of the 20th century philosophers.

All these interpretations no doubt have their occasion at some point within the inevitable hesitations of research and its work of adjustments. But it is one thing to identify them as simple aspects and another thing to let them develop into doctrines and interpretations that are sometimes antithetical and continuously circular and dialectical, giving the impression of a contestable choice to which one could properly pose another interpretation. From here we ultimately find philosophical and doctrinal conflicts of interest traversing all the groups working under this label of non-philosophy (including even its inventor if we take into account each book on non-philosophy separately) and which are the annunciators of future divides. The divides always have a theoretically objective appearance within the proposed reasoning, but there is always a more complex cause. The divisions of non-philosophy also have this appearance but they have a specifically philosophical cause. These conflicts are not like those that on a much more modest scale traverse the school of phenomenology and psychoanalytic associations. There is no point in saying that a conflict of interpretations of non-philosophy cannot give way to a hermeneutic interpretation by a subject even if the status of the subject is directly engaged within this appearance. These immediate bifurcations of meaning are obviously worrisome for the consistency and theoretical solidity of non-philosophy that seems to be plagued by this richness of interpretations and overdetermined in its concept.

Non-philosophy distinguishes a cause (the Real), an essence (the transcendental identity of the subject as clone), and in the end aspects that are the contents of the *a priori* transformed subject from the material of the World (on the theory of sources and aspects of non-philosophy, the *Introduction to Non-Marxism* is theoretically fundamental for the consistency of non-philosophy and in order to learn to distinguish between the cause, essence, and aspect whose non-distinction leads to confusions spoken of here). Non-philosophy possesses both an aspect of science and an aspect of philosophy, and it is what we could call a unified theory or a united-in-the-last-instance whose less self-conscious sketches can be found achieved in the work of Marx (the duality and unity of the two materialisms, historical and dialectical, or more still the infra- and the superstructure), Freud perhaps, and above all Lacan (the topological or Borromean knotting of the three instances, and the combination of science and philosophy that renders psychoanalysis undeterminable as a genre, and in its own way Marxism as well). It is these aspects that make possible the multiplicity of the principle of effectuations and that, when poorly understood, turns into a multiplicity of philosophical choices, even interpretations and non-philosophies. Non-philosophy is expressed in the singular and even towards identity, it is indivisible, non-philosophers can be expressed in the plural in terms of the *aspects* that they choose but not in terms of the philosophical decisions into which they turn these simple aspects.

The Indifference of-the-last-instance Towards Language

One cannot reduce non-philosophy, in a contemplative or theoretical manner, to an abstract schema or diagram, to a pure logical thought without its concrete language of philosophical origin or even more complex, that language in which we bathe in this actual moment itself. In the relation between the Real and language, we will avoid any spontaneous or naive position of the two terms one in front of the other, as two in themselves or at best as a philosophical dyad. The lone transcendental philosophy would have already demanded, though not without trouble it is true, a transcendental determination of the required language, but the introduction of the Real as non-transcendental displaces the givens of the problem without eliminating it. Rather than speaking about the general indifference of the Real towards language, we could say that its indifference is of-the-last-instance. To put it differently, this indifference can be examined in two phases, real and transcendental. We will remember that non-philosophy conjugates two philosophically and traditionally antithetical characteristics: the notion of a presupposition of thought, and that of a transcendental conditioning. It is completely contained within the notion of a *presupposed transcendental-Real*. Non-philosophy is the transcendental language, presumed to be Real, for philosophy or the thought-world.

In the first of the two phases, we must suppose language to already be given in-One and thus nowhere created by it nor connected or introduced from the outside to the Real by a primary and contradictory act. The Real imparts the Real *and* language not at the same time or *simultaneously* but uni-laterally and as devoid of sufficiency. More precisely, the formulas "at the same time" and "uni-laterally" would not be contradictory if at the least, the first term was understood as "within an identity of time" or radical inimmanence since uni-lateral Identity will, for its part, give way to a (unilateral) duality. We can say, in order to summarize, that the Real uni-laterally gives and we will speak of the *uni-lateral being-given*. It is in this manner that we should suppose language to be already given, and thus already reduced, and this, naturally, in the mode of the future. Nevertheless, it is still not yet a question of nomination of the Real (by the subject) but just of the presupposition of this nomination. And the state of the presupposition as far as language is concerned excludes that it be examined in itself or as the interior of a relation. We could say that language is given or determined, every determination being uni-lateral identity.

The second phase, that of cloning, is the phase that sees a practical utilization of language thus manifest in a still negative manner. Uni-laterally referred to, or mentioned, it is taken into account as referred or reference. Real uni-laterality is invested and repeated within cloning and in the transcendental mode under the solicitation of this given language that is philosophy. We are entering into the sphere of actuality of non-philosophy, which is to say, the sphere of an identically presupposed and transcendental language for language-material.

It is clear within the interior of this transcendental phase of the presupposition that language is used in order to name the Real in a pertinent manner, because the "Real" must not become a term of the philosophical or language in itself but of "non-language" or the "tongue" of non-philosophy. The Real, One-in-One, Man-in-Man, etc., are the primary names of this language. These terms are obviously subject to immediate philosophical appearance while for us they only have a meaning within the practice of how they are used. Non-philosophy only knows language within the limits of its use as a presupposed-transcendental real for common-and-philosophical use. To such an extent that the non-philosophical axioms must not be understood in a spontaneous philosophical manner, as if we surreptitiously distinguished the thing "non-philosophy" from what we say of this thing. This is often the case in the naive "discussions" about non-philosophy which are of a theoretical and contemplative spirit, outside practice, and which take place within a discourse and ontology, a meta-language, woven within philosophical appearance. Hence, for example, the antinomies between non-philosophy as thing (the Real, etc.) and as discourse about this thing, their impossible connections, etc.…. The proper discourse on non-philosophy is already this one here in its practical effectivity.

Materials: Allusion, Mention, Reference

The order of the moments of the abstract material is important. We will distinguish philosophy or the World as (Platonic) *allusion*, as occasional *mention* and as *reference* or cause of the transcendental. The initial situation, that of radical immanence or of the given in-One, that signifies that philosophy as well is given in-One. As everything takes place within non-philosophy and the One can only be posed in a dogmatic manner or in itself, everything said about it already supposes that philosophy is given but simply *mentioned* without being taken into account *for itself* within the analysis. Thus, the in-One is already the necessary or determining cause and thus the struggle or Other-than … but real (-transcendental). As philosophy is already given in-One, the struggle is necessarily real, albeit not already transcendental, the Other-than is no more a problem than the state of philosophy already given in-One. Language does not fall outside the One, which nonetheless does not mix with language holding it at a distance from itself. It is within non-religious gnosis that language, Platonic or otherwise, falls outside of the One and leads an independent life. But the mention of philosophy is not yet its being taken into account, its givenness in-One is not yet its effectuation of the One, whereby the transcendental will recover the whole. To make mention of philosophy as given in-One does not seem to implicate the transcendental (as the thesis of gnosis would like to have it) or perhaps then it is because the Real is incapable of giving it in-One and that there is an exterior construction. Gnosis knows mention in the form of the first occasion but understands it as already supposing the transcendental. It is the philosophical Real still as yet opposed to the reception of a given, incapable of giving it itself. The spirit of struggle is not transcendental but real, it is a real "property" which does not here mean "transcendental," or else then we must understand it in the classical sense of a property that adds nothing to the Real, which is the case. We can indeed speak of a transcendental Rebel, comprised of struggle, but this conception of the transcendental supposes a transcendent Real, in a philosophical manner, thus a being of ontology. It is useful to make the link between the transcendent and the empirical as it is confirmed in gnosis with the simple allusion to the sensible. Does radical immanence need and tolerate a transcendental of this nature since it is not a being? No, because radical immanence, *which has nothing transcendent about it, is independent of the "sensible" or of the World that is mentioned*. The properties of the immanent Real are strictly real and cannot be said to be about it in terms of an empiricism which would be constitutive. Nevertheless, the whole of non-philosophy will obviously be claimed to be "transcendental" or claiming the reality of the World and not of the Real (confusion of the philosophical One and the real One), and secondly on the basis of the taking into account of philosophy as an object of experience and not as a simple Platonic allusion to the World. Philosophy is now a point of view, but this time as coming from the in-One, it is not the point of view for itself as the Principle of sufficiency would have it, but it is offered up to itself to the nearest-One [*à L'un près*], thus to the limit-struggle. It is experience that becomes the point of reference, it ceases being a simple mention in order to become reference. Material signifies two things: 1. mention or the passage of the support to the state of occasion; 2. occasion (the preceding one) as reference. Allusion really claims to be from the material but still supposes philosophy in and for itself.

The Third Axiom: Philosophical Language as Symptom

If the Real is indifferent ("separated") to its naming, to language-material (philosophy, contingent for this lone point of view, not for its own or of Logos), the problem becomes that of the status of this language, then of recourse, whether necessary or not to philosophy as principle material. A quite general reply fixes the problem: any "vocabulary" would be possible, religious, materialistic, artistic, and could be directly confronted with the Real and with the subject. From here we get doctrines that can no longer be called non-philosophy in a rigorous way but "non-religion," "non-materialism," "non-art," etc. and merely have a family resemblance with non-philosophy.

The non-absolute and radical indifference which we have spoken about is uni-lateral and it is this indifference that paradoxically gives (imparts) all language from which it is itself separated, being Other-than … language, which it nevertheless makes manifest. This structure of "giving" indifference does not seem to make an appeal to this or that language of preference. But this is only true as long as we treat this structure of indifference in itself. And yet, in whatever manner it speaks of the Real, a determined vocabulary is already engaged with (and it is either *de jure* or implicitly philosophical).

Why must this language be a symptom of the Real? It is the reverse side or inverse of the uni-lateral indifference of the Real. Here the symptom cannot result from an exterior connection of the Real and language in the mode of a symbolic alterity, but from a determination-in-the-last-instance of the one by the other but which is not aware of itself. It is not a symptom in the analytical or immediate sense, where the Other is simultaneously interior and exterior to language, there is indeed the Other but it is the Real which announces itself as immanent determination in regard to this mode of alterity. In other words, we do not consider the language-material as symptom via an arbitrary decision. The language-material in its order can always be taken in its spontaneous and intuitive sense, which it is in any case, and in any case, it already contains the idea of the symptom. *But the non-philosophical work of the determination is already by definition or axiomatization at work*, it has primacy over the infra-philosophical symptom itself that it determines as such in a more profound sense than it has already been observed. This remains to be demonstrated and there is a long path ahead.

The Election of Philosophical Language as Rival

The third axiom could prove fundamental to our task of the delineation of the concept of non-philosophy. The radical Real "calls for" or tolerates that it make use in any case of all discourses, even generic ones which we will see have something in particular that helps in fighting against fundamental philosophical appearance. We must decide what is the "closest" discourse to the Real (and thus also the most illusory and deceptive) and put it at the forefront as the front on which to fight. Here the Platonic problem of suitors can be rediscovered but displaced. It is no longer a question of which discourse is the most true between sophistry and philosophy, but the most illusory, indeed the most hallucinatory discourse between philosophy and generic discourses.

The matter of the primacy of philosophy over other forms of knowledge in the principal position of discourse to the symptom can be posed in this way. If the Real seems indifferent to such discourse, the other forms of knowledge, as soon as we invoke them, recognize (whether we like it or not) the domination of philosophy which philosophy itself elsewhere affirms. Can we refuse the traditional connection of philosophy with the other forms of knowledge in the manner that it organizes the world? Regardless of the reality or effectiveness of this domination, it is a symptom and it is this connection which we must undo. But the problem is that of the nature of this connection. First, does the Real liberate us from this domination of philosophy, or does it confirm it in a new manner? That it liberates us immediately would be to suppose that it does so by an *absolute* indifference in general in regard to any language, which would allow it to oppose any vocabulary whatsoever to the Real. And yet, radical indifference cannot be of this type, as has been said. And if the Real effectively liberates us from this domination of philosophical appearance, it will be after the task of a confrontation between these two types of operated knowledge under its primacy.

This being granted, why have philosophy as principal adversary, if not because it is the title holder of transcendental appearance, as opposed to thought by the "presupposed real-transcendental," and because any formulation of non-philosophy in any case begins *de jure* and *de facto*, within philosophical language, which is to say, within philosophizability? "Principal adversary," what does this formula mean? The third axiom is not determined axiomatically via a universal language but by a language as a universal object, be it principle or dominant, it is completely different. The axiom does not at all posit itself as common to all the varying forms of knowledge, as certain non-philosophers would have it. The All is not immediately totalizing, it is opposed to what it *claims* to totalize, the totalization is thus an objective appearance, not a natural law. Thus we are not talking about presuming a supposedly general or common object, "philosophy," that would assume all others. Transcendental appearance in its greatest universality and pretension, philosophizability, other forms of knowledge voluntarily participate or are forced to do so, but they have their relative autonomy, and it is these forms of knowledge that will be required (art, religion, science, and technology) in order to undo this universal appearance. We have to understand that there exists within philosophy a duality of philosophizability and practices, that the radical critique of philosophical appearance is not at all that of practices.

It is possible to determine the *ultimate* (but not genetic) cause of this elevation of philosophy to the level of universal appearance to undo and as principle object to conserve as transcendental posture, it is the structure of the real that uni-laterally gives the form of a language-system and that requires loosening the knot of philosophy and other forms of knowledge. How would it not give, would it not first insist on the philosophical as principle rather than the other? We can only reply to the question of the rival-language by the fact, itself of a symptom of philosophy that auto-elects itself as a domination over the discourses. But, as we have said, this primary form of symptom is determined by the Real without being generated by it.

Philosophizability as Cogitative Structure

What is it that we first mean by "philosophy" since it is not a position that is interior to philosophizability? It is the passage from particular doctrines or systems to the universal philosophizability of the World, into the form of the thought-world. It cannot be a question of conserving, even within the auto-description of philosophy, the least trace of an object or an ontic or empirical reference, just that of the inevitable system or systems in their most formalized and all-encompassing "axioms," and considered universal *par excellence*. We could say that the form-system is itself particular in its realizations but that it is a dominant and normative form, Parmenides with the sameness of Being and Thinking, Plato with the double transcendence of the *meta* and *epekeina*, Aristotle with the convertibility of the One and Being, Hegel with the identity of difference and identity, etc. In truth, there is always a decision of the Philosophical Decision, but it is philosophically absorbable and is no longer arbitrary, subjective or a matter of perspective or character, a matter of Greek philosophemes and irreducible semantism, or at the least, we conceive of it in complete rigor and in its greatest most powerful extension as auto/(hetero)-decision. We do not have a more enveloping definition of philosophy than auto-definitional, auto-positional, auto-decisional, than its auto-encompassing style that puts into action the reduction of the attempts of metaphilosophy. We will say that philosophy possesses a universal *cogitative* structure. Naturally, this auto-encompassing nature, always at the limit of itself, can also, in the work of certain contemporaries, also transgress this limit without actually leaving it, and posit itself as outer-limit (Heidegger and the inverse of the world or horizon, Derrida and the beyond closure [*outre-clôture*]) or as the boundlessness of Deleuze [*il-limitation*] who leaves it even less. This movement of transgression or of infinitization obviously modifies the general "cogitative" structure of philosophy, slowing it down, or anticipating it, spoiling it, tampering with it, *but in no way destroys it whatsoever*. The deconstruction or intensification of the *cogito* is not the suspense of the universal cogitative

94

power, the historical *cogito* being merely a particular of a more universal axiomatic of philosophy, a particular effectuation of the Same that are Being and Thinking or the structure mentioned earlier.

We call this universal structure *philosophizability*, distinguishing it from philosophies in the same way calculability is distinguished from concrete calculations. It is of an auto-specular nature (and not merely specular which would still presuppose an object to reflect), it is the form of the thought-world (that presupposes a particular ontic fulfillment) such as we constitute it as the principal object of non-philosophy. The problem will be that of a more forceful analysis of philosophizability that will impose the consideration of a necessary meta-language and will show that the idealism of the definition as auto-encompassing denies or conceals a radical presupposed more than a condition.

The Name-of-Man as
Negative Meta-Language for Philosophy

The enlarged cogitative structure can no doubt be considered momentary, fixed and immobilized as a transcendent invariant, as a set of objective presuppositions, but this set in its turn will be reabsorbed in the auto-encompassing or absolute-idealist gesture of philosophizability Philosophy turns around an abyssal labyrinth of a new nothingness. It is an invariant to transformations or variations. Better still, in its perfect form, which we should also consider rather than thinking of average forms mixed with the dross of common thought to in the end define the object as clearly as possible, it is a dynamic structure or a historico-systematic entity that programs and thus includes its variations. It is an invariance of the variance and of invariance, finally the immanence of a nothingness that has dissolved all its objects but which is not nothing. Philosophizability is the Real, or gives it, presents it, and re-includes its auto-presentation; this is at the least its pretension.

But it is already an absolute-idealist interpretation of philosophy, thus an intra-philosophical definition and vicious as the circle from which it benefits. Philosophizability is ready to state (like Lacan and others) that there is no meta-language, which supposes an infinite virtual or even actual of the philosophical decision or the decision of language.

What can we do in the face of this absolute idealism? Either we no longer accept that the philosopher lives within a transcendental hallucination as within the Real, which merges with belief in the Real, this is the idealism of auto-decision, etc., or we posit that there must be a positive meta-language, or at least, like the more Kantian than Hegelian contemporaries, that there are objective effects of meta-language brought into their effectiveness by the Other of philosophy, in the manner of Heidegger and Derrida. We will admit that despite its immanence an "exterior" point of view is necessary in order to define philosophizability, either a support that is operative and opaque, geometrical or topological, or an Other of the Levinasian or Derridean type and which is a manner of refining or making the "material" support more subtle, and of "deconstructing" Logos.

Non-philosophy obviously endorses the contemporary solution rather than the solution of metaphysical idealism. But it radicalizes the thesis of a necessary meta-language against the auto-positional idealism of philosophizability. In order to do this, it has a completely different conception of the Real than metaphysics and that of its deconstruction – as Uni-lateral, Other-than … or Future – and it has the help of practices that are not spontaneously philosophizable. The Name-of-Man is the primary term of this future and necessary meta-language in order to speak philosophy, a *completely negative meta-language*, necessary but non-sufficient. A meta-language that must include both a philosophical and scientific aspect precisely to the extent that one is in need of a language of this kind in order to procure an intelligence from philosophy. In this negative and philosophico-scientific (or transcendental) form, the Name-of-Man has all the opportunities to no longer be absorbable into philosophizability, in the same way a positive or directly determined meta-language has all the opportunities to return to philosophy. Meta-language is of the order of an ultimatum, not of a description of a statement of fact.

Recapitulation: The Relative Power of Philosophy.
It is through comparison with other "vocabularies" that it deems "regional" that the power of philosophy brands itself. Firstly by its auto/hetero-analytical superiority and power which make it destined to serve as a critical entry point for other forms of knowledge. An example of this pretension can be found in its relation to religion. The religious is perhaps more alienating than the philosophical, in any case more criminal, conjuncture proves that religion is a great threat for humans and that one should start by transforming it into a non-religion. But delivered from itself and face to face with the Real, it limits its auto/hetero-critique, and in reality, does not even achieve this ideal, which remains foreign to it and that it leaves without ideal means for critique or deconstruction and their non-philosophical transmutation. Despite the regular return to the religious in philosophy, philosophy has always also been a critique of these religious fantasies. Only the philosophical can also allow us to judge them and help to liberate itself from the inhumane pretensions of religion while at the same time allowing it to return to Man. Then by its proximity and distance the set of its practices, by its "fundamental" or foundational pretensions in regard to specific forms of knowledge, pretensions which we will see whether they are founded or not, but which are so well known that it is useless to return to them, if only to consider the damages of the structure that the operation of philosophical division and synthesis make within the specific identity of its practices and their object.

In one sense, we are right to want to take down these types of pretensions but only non-philosophically speaking and not philosophically. Nevertheless non-philosophy is already a symptom of a more vast pretension of philosophy in regard to the whole of experience as such, thus also in regard to what philosophy itself names the "real." But there is nothing of the philosophical that allows us to justify a continuous passage from this real-All to the Real in the manner that we understand it in its radicality. The non-philosophical critique is made by including itself starting from the critical-material in the opposite direction, from the Real-One to the (for the) real-All, for example from the One-in-One to (for) the metaphysical One. It is under this condition that the pretension of the Real is a symptom and conveys the symptom-material of the pretension of philosophy to other forms of knowledge. The Real can only be put into parenthesis in a provisional way because it is from the point of view of the Real that the status of philosophy is evaluated, not from itself or sciences or religion. Non-philosophy conveys the auto/hetero-analytical power of philosophy in transforming it without prolonging it as a critical or even deconstructive ideal; non-philosophy has already transmuted this ideal.

What we call philosophizability is thus established *in-the-last-instance* of the Real and it alone allows for finally determining a scale of philosophical pretensions or appearances, bearing in mind the relative-absolute or double appearance of philosophy over forms of knowledge and over itself, right up to appearances which share in philosophico-regional blends. It seems justifiable to us to establish as a matter of priority a non-philosophy that will be the means of a non-religion, a non-aesthetics, etc. This problem is just as important, or in any case of the same kind as that of the order in which categories are uttered and classified, rather than simply "finding" them in a more or less empirical manner.

The problem of the contents of the third axiom and of philosophical material is systematically and incessantly taken back up under the section titled *Philosophizability and Practicity*.

PHILOSOPHIZABILITY AND PRACTICITY

Non-philosophy has three axiom matrices (the *Real* as radical Immanent or Uni-laterality, *Determination-in-the-last-instance* as cloning, *Philosophizability* of every object as materials). It is the third which poses a delicate problem, since there is a part of philosophy's variable empirical determination and consequently a problem of limitation and extricating from it the kernel of philosophizability. This analysis will end up tracing a new demarcation line within *Philosophy*. It will no longer pass between an object and a thought, between two regions, between the fundamental and the regional, not even between Being and Thinking. Instead it will pass between Philosophizability and Practice, what we will come to call Practicity, or still between thought-with-presupposition and thought-with-the-presupposed. Following this analysis we will settle the problem of its relation to non-philosophy, at the same time as its autonomy and its determination by the Real.

Ecce Homo Philosophicus

The most visible principle within the discrimination of the conceptions of non-philosophy is the concept that gives itself as the object or materials ("*Philosophy*"). The importance accorded to the third axiom can be understood by the fact that the first is, as decisive as it is, ontologically non-sufficient or does not bring itself any object or content, any empirical determination but takes them from philosophy and practices. Every misinterpretation of the third (an incomplete analysis or one that ends too quickly with philosophy, a conservation of a doctrinal position under the term of "philosophy," in the end a primacy accorded to another type of thought or experience over philosophy, such as religion or art or politics) leads to a deviation from non-philosophy's destination (which is to be a *unified theory of philosophizability and a practice* = *X*), a deviation that is a lack of liberty, the closing down of a field of possibilities.

In order to open this field to its greatest extent and not to, in our turn, reconstitute an authoritarian stranglehold that would exclude certain realizations for fear of deviations, we will push as far as possible the possibilities of opening up the concept of philosophy, an examination that, so that it does not let itself affirm itself by itself, demands a prior objectification of philosophical narcissism independently from the *explicit* intervention of non-philosophy. This examination must go all the way to the point beyond which the lack of respect for axioms turns into regression, which means that it turns to *philosophical re-normalization*. Since the lack of rigor in general defends itself through the easy reproach of *orthodoxy*, the intellectual situation being a double *correction*, *that of left-wing haste* or to the contrary *that of right-wing intellectual conformism*, it does not address this problem at its source in a radical manner.

Speaking here about the third axiom, two problems present themselves. Firstly, why philosophy rather than religion or art if the Real is as devoid of religion or art as it is of philosophy? And if philosophy is the material, what is its ultimate constitution between dominant philosophizability and its practical contents, which is their relation, undoubtedly a relation of domination, but must not the response be more nuanced? On the one hand the Real-in-person is devoid of all language and practice, of every determination, but a practice or a language are necessarily found there. It is from the pure future but necessary and foreclosed to … and … for a reality that fulfills it. On the other hand, as we have already said, by whatever name we call it, we use philosophical language and its logic with a priority or in a dominant way, even if it axiomatically "retreats." Non-philosophy's contingency, which is incomplete in spite of this response, is that of (non-) philosophy and not at first non-science or non-art. It is bound in a dominant way to that constitution of philosophy in a *cogito*-form. This *cogito* of philosophy, sometimes infinitely enlarged, assures us that it exists once its presuppositions are given. Can we imagine a non-art (or a non-science) in the sense where artistic practice without its theory would be directly plugged in to the Real, which would have none of the characteristics of art or of this practice? There have been several attempts at this but which are no longer being pursued. We will return at greater length to the topics concerning non-philosophy's "neighbors" or "relatives" via this basis of philosophy.

Opinion of the System of Opinions

Philosophy is a kind of thought that brings out the symptom of two correlative traits. On the one hand it has always been threatened by a becoming-opinion, contaminated from inside and outside by the traps of language and so therefore by the sophistical and more recently by communication or the "media-complex" where communication continues to wallow. On the one hand it has always been divided by particular conflictual systems and never reached the identity that it claims, though only in a form of multiple unity. We formulate the hypothesis that these two traits only make one, that philosophy is an opinion set in form, the rigor that it gains by that form does not abolish its nature as opinion. There are different ways of saying the same thing. As an opinion it claims an absolute validity and divides itself (it is its opinion and divides it …), this is a historico-systematic formation of knowledge, it is a traditional blending where the law of composition auto-affects itself, etc. More profoundly this structure of partition or opinion finds its origin in the determined priority of division over identity reduced to unity, and explains itself as a structure of an *undecidable decision* in 2/3 or 3/2 terms. Its conjuncture demonstrates a little further this congenital vice of being a well established opinion and not being an understanding as we go further into its forecasted immersion along the lines of universal communication. But it is necessary to admit that it is not fundamentally a practice but a theoreticism (which includes practices) and detects within

Philosophical Decision the philosophizability of principle and the principle of philosophizability.

Philosophy Stripped Bare by Itself

Philosophical dialectic is a principle of the World's auto-dissolution. This is not bad, it may be good, if this auto-dissolution of reality is seized as the World's normal process that frees itself little by little (but never radically) from its belief that it is, even in the form of nothingness, only what it hallucinates of the Real in the dissolution of its own reality. It dissolves the World's reality *such that it posits itself for the first time in a transcendental hallucination and a transcendental illusion.* The World does not know the Real and dissolves itself by virtue of desiring it.

The mechanism of auto-dissolution may be broadly called the dialectic, for example, in the form of (Hegelian) phantoms and (Nietzschean) simulacra. The most general invariant of its syntax is in effect that the two and the One are reciprocally determined. There are several versions of this logic. For example, the Two, while remaining Two in this way, affects the One which becomes One for the One and expands as becoming on its own plane. The One is therefore "born" as One; this is the hallucinated thesis of philosophical idealism and "its" mystique, for example. It is born as One through a double negation by annihilating the Two through which it nevertheless conserves the terms at the heart of their relation. It births itself by generating specters. This juxtaposition of the logical plane of the One and the empirical plane of the Two is typical of philosophy and the dialectic that wants to conserve everything by way of ontological hierarchies and continuous processes without being able to transform the World practically. Idealism still reinforces itself with the other interiorization, namely Nietzschean through immanence without a double negation, of the dialectic in "becoming." The terms of the Two, and the Two and the One merge themselves within a unique becoming that reduces the planes and hierarchies a little more, concluding by turning Hegelian phantoms into Nietzschean simulacra.

Reality's auto-dissolution as a philosophical machine, meaning what philosophy believes to be the Real, is consummated. This is not to confuse this auto-nihilism with an absolute nihilism, meaning of course a counter-nihilism.

This double dissolution is as much the cause as the effect of philosophy. Of course philosophy has means for limiting this dissolution, it mobilizes counter-attacks against this idealist and theoreticist process, in the form of materialisms and various realisms. But in an immanent way an auto-dissolving drive brings together philosophy on the whole within its own abyss, a kind of super-nihilism the exterior signs of which were formerly sophism and now mediatic communication.

What does it matter if we replace, for example, the couple of *meta* and *epekeina* with other decisions of duality, otherwise disposed but which always go with the already-worn grooves in the substance of the World? What this substitution gains over positivity is largely lost by the conservation of the same traditional, invariant structure. With this structural displacement and the reversals that come with it and give it a completely apparent life, philosophy thinks it changes the World but it does so by making itself more and more the "World." In reality it strips itself bare without knowing it. Philosophy has always confused its own immanent becoming with a real immanence. The dialectic is structured *as* a metaphysics and what it brings forth is the disappearance in itself of the World. This is a ruse or magic, nothing less than understanding an object in a theoretical mode. How can some form of knowledge, a theoretical or even experimental "science" like the one philosophy wants to be, let itself stray for so long through theoreticist idealism and admit to being a science of specters or simulacra without which there is no real object? Knowledge is not a discourse of appearances and still less one of phantoms, it must be able to distinguish a real-objective object within the appearances of knowledge and is in this way not only a science of appearances, a science of being- and becoming-phantom or simulacra. More generally, philosophy is a vast *cogito* structure in the dimensions of the World which is constantly proving its existence without ever proving its Real efficacy [*teneur en Réel*].

Against this autophagic enterprise as a hallucinated logic, and without completely abandoning philosophy, only the Real as radical immanence can still save the reality of man and the World *if only as a simulacrum, by recognizing in the World the possibility of a Real efficacy in-the-last-instance*. This is not about denying this benevolent auto-dissolution of philosophy or of the World that it forms, but only the belief that it engenders in the real character of this becoming. The immanence of the Real, when it is devoid of all traces of transcendence, of course affects the terms but not in an ideal or idealizing manner, it conserves them in the state of relative autonomy without "vampirizing" the vampires or "ghosting" the ghosts. It gives its own Real efficacy to the vanished ghost of reality as soon as it recognizes it. Left to itself the World contains many specters and many simulacra and it becomes both one and the other. The salvation of this reality is now a task that must set out on paths that are no longer merely, nor principally, those of philosophy.

Thought-World, Philosophizability, Practicity

What calls itself or auto-designates itself as "philosophy," or even as "*Philosophy*" is likely to be a nest of amphibologies and must be first analyzed under the conditions that remain themselves "philosophical." However the self-proclamation "I am a philosopher," "here is philosophy" is not a guarantee of precision and still less of reality. At the very most this statement contains an affirmation of existence, a *cogito* of philosophy and not only of the philosopher, but such a position of existence no longer assures non-philosophy of a real determination and knowledge of the philosopher. Let us remain for a moment at the level of this proclamation.

Thus we analyze philosophically the vague concept of philosophy using several operations.

1. A material [*matérielle*] extension of philosophy's contents causes it to become a thought-world but also forces it to an internal distinction that is more precise than that of the ideal of empirical real. Beyond objects that are reputedly traditionally empirical, the thing, beings, sensation, and even art or science as objects assuming them also to be "empiricities," which (to various degrees of idealization) are all intra-philosophical objects or at least the correlates of an idealist position, we are still forced to introduce objects of the highest "regional" or "generic" level, which are forms of knowledge sometimes supposedly free of philosophy, sometimes rescued by philosophy as a meta-ontology, and sometimes dominated philosophically and submitted to its meaning, to truth, value, foundation. Throughout these various conceptions where each can recognize their child, there is again and again a great deal of doctrinal idealism in the state of denial. With its extension and its intensifications, the concept of philosophy is little by little abandoned for that of a more complex and more adequate *thought-world.*

2. But why a "world" and how does one make a "world?" Not only through a material extension. There must be a formal condition. How does this vague thing, too rich and yet also too simple, the "World," become "*the-World*" and acquire a conceptual consistency? By philosophy, this or that philosophy, and only by philosophy, it is the World's philosophizability in principle. Suppose that we add to things not a particular philosophy as its conditions, not this or that philosophical postulate, but *Philosophy* itself supposed in its invariant essence. The World then truly becomes universal (in the philosophical *sense* that is a self-reflection of *Philosophy*) and no longer a particular doctrine, such that it is included in a mysticism or art or science, which still cannot determine the World, critique it or explain it in this form. Like philosophy, with some different accents, the disciplines or forms of knowledge aim to reject the representative diversity, the World as representation. But here we have a definition of the World that is too narrow and too partial; rather the concept of the World must include the totality of philosophical conditions of its thought and not only a part of philosophy's structure or a particular doctrine.

For example, Christianity does not fundamentally modify the concept of the World from this perspective even if Christianity enriches its experience with new affects. The World always has the interior form of the philosophical apparatus, enriched with a supplement of Christic experience assumed to bring forth or reinforce the dimension of the Real. This combination is for us, here and now, an integral whole, the lone concrete where philosophy, theory, predication, theology, and desire for unitedness [*unition*] are inseparable moments. The World is, for example, now a *mystique-world*, the ontological knot, theological and mystical, obviously in its still sufficient form, such that it can be naively accepted or on the contrary suspended and made intelligible.

3. But this idealist concept of the thought-world remains naive and spontaneous, internal to philosophy's absolute idealism. So, a more precise understanding of the thought-world puts forward a new distinction, that of "philosophizability," an abstraction devoid of objects, and non fundamental forms of knowledge whose essential trait we have freed under the name of "practice," or still (parallel to "empiricities") preferably as "practicities." This is preferable to: 1. the "practical," a too simple and brutal term owing to its lack of ideality and its often primarily empirical usage, and 2. "regional" or "generic," which bears witness to their justifiably intra-philosophical interpretation. We will later unpack a practicity that runs parallel to philosophizabilty and within it forms a new relation to it. In Platonic terms, there are two heterogeneous essences: the essence of philosophizability and the essence of practicity. The thought-world (of which concrete philosophy will no longer be more than a particular form) is thus a duality of essences that it will have to put back into play, since the relations split the beautiful sphere of philosophy in two and only let it subsist as a unity constitutive of transcendental appearance. We are already within non-philosophy without knowing it.

The Transcendental Identity of the System (of) Opinion

Let us examine the properly non-philosophical second phase of the concept of thought-world, no longer in its intrinsic formation, in its matter and its form, but in its determination by the Real in the form of a theorem.

It is important to point out that the thought-world's transcendental Identity is not at all a kind of philosophical identity like a unity, its Identity does not contradict philosophical identity, but transforms it. In effect this is not like a knot which is always re-divisible and interpretable from one of its parts, as an Idea of the all susceptible to a particular interpretation, as an All integrating a multiplicity of moments, but as *this knot('s) undivided Identity, or for this All* which reveals the new conjuncture that only the human vision-in-One can catch sight of. The subject elaborated by non-philosophy is nothing other than the real-transcendental Identity, the philosophical blending('s) clone. If these are defined within their absolute autoposition as *unitary,* then the non-philosophical Word [*verbe*] is what we call *the unified theory of philosophy and a knowledge or practice* = X. And a *unified theory* in general turns away from a combination that claims to think itself sufficiently by itself and turns instead to a cause of-the-last-identity that determines its theory practically.

Qualitatively theoretical conditions are necessary in order to explain the World as thus "enlarged" and "complicated," universals (by their real determination) other than philosophy itself. The *uni-versality of Identity* is necessary, in so far as it does not result in a complement or extension of philosophical universality but has a completely other origin, coming from the uni-versal Identity capable of determining (*for …*) philosophy's transcendent universality. The set of particular philosophical postulates, with the general postulate of the Real's autoposition, that gathers together philosophy's essence and forms of knowing, must desert "regional" forms of knowing or the practicities for which it is confused, and moves over to the side of the "object" or field of properties that non-philosophy utilizes as symptoms and models. Hence it is more than an extension or universalization of the World, which was philosophy's object.

Primacy of Philosophizability over Philosophy

Beyond doctrinal distinctions and completely side-stepping them, it is necessary to first distinguish philosophizability and philosophical effectivity. Philosophizability designates the *well-grounded, but only grounded, pretension* of philosophy in every thinking of reality, in thinking the All, thus capable of thinking itself. Universal philosophizability *de jure* and not only *de facto*, a pretension that is the same thing as the auto-encompassing of reality and itself.

The abstraction of philosophizability is itself philosophical rather than formal. It designates an auto-encompassing or absolute ability to which every object would have its sense renewed or to which it would finally be reduced. Every definition of philosophy remains in every way affected by an operation that is itself philosophical. It is by definition impossible to posit it in the form of a scientific type of object because it is auto-affected within its same definition. It is therefore a limit-concept, fundamentally "hermeneutic," whose defining and act of definition vary one according to the other. There is also a relative-absolute definition of philosophy, but not a "radical" definition or one via its immanent identity, simply presupposed and inaccessible. The best definition among all the relative-absolute definitions we have been given is the one that posits the primacy of the absolute over the relative or defines philosophy according to philosophizability. This is why there is no definition of philosophizability that is "absolute" in the definitive sense, fixed and arrested. But on the contrary (by way of an objective local appearance, of philosophy by itself) philosophizability tends towards a relative-absolute limit, and it is necessary to understand philosophizability in this way (not even as a Platonic Idea or in-itself) but as an auto-encompassing universal.

Since we are condemned to the giving of this object in a partially but nonetheless empirical way, through a definition that mobilizes material elements and not only by an *a priori* procedure or even an auto-deductive one, a margin of choice remains possible within its delimitation and its usage, which brings us the plurality of definitions of what is meant by "philosophy." However, this multiplicity is not indifference, there is already a traditional ontological semantics limiting choice, and that indicates the Greco-historical contingency that defines philosophy or systems and doctrines by "proper names." Amongst these empirically designated and tributary definitions, in the sense of a signifier, some (Hegel, Nietzsche) pose just a univocal philosophizability, a unique voice of philosophy where the significant determination is reduced and internalized (with some differences in degree and of blending, or even of degree but which constitute a nature irreducible to the scale of degrees). This univocity proper to the philosophizable is varied, at times even undermined, pushed down as a horizon but not destroyed, by way of an equivocity irreducible to an empirical origin and that can be of concern to a body of knowledge assumed to be regional. It is necessary to take into account this duality in order to define the object or philosophical materials, inseparable from this tension and complementarity between idealist univocity and the equivocity of a non philosophical origin. But because of its pretension maintained towards the Real and according to its symptom, we will take the form of the univocity of the philosophizable as philosophy's essence, a kernel more or less altered by "transcendence" proper to some other knowledge, such as science. In the end philosophizability is not the empirical whole of *Philosophy* or a philosophy but the whole of its formal kernel, which adds to itself annexed pieces that "critique" it or that more or less vary. The specificity of *Philosophy* is auto-specularity or auto-encompassing, and tolerates empirical references that define philosophies but not philosophizability. It is necessary to account for this *inequality in the relation of philosophizability and philosophy*, an inequality between the kernel and modes that are not simply reducible to the kernel of philosophizability, and that serve as symptoms of practicity for us. There is no external and

109

specific usage, properly speaking, of philosophizability that would be the *element* of a certain kind of thought, but there is an internal usage according to its bearings, buttresses, and empirical obstacles, but philosophizability possesses a primacy over them.

The third axiom must be thought in any case according to the inequality within the materials, from the primacy of philosophizability over philosophy. This primacy defines non-philosophical rigor as "non-philosophizability," while the inverse primacy within the materials defines a possible empiricism within non-philosophy, as "determined non-philosophy" (non-Platonism, non-Nietzscheanism, etc.). There is of course already philosophy in art, religion, science, etc., but the primacy of these over philosophy and above all over philosophizability bears witness (supposing that the second is only glimpsed) to a constitutive or ultimate empiricism. So this is no longer a simple opposition between an assumedly "orthodox" non-philosophy and its "deviations." This opposition is more delicate, also more tolerant, since it is an inequality. There is no pure or orthodox non-philosophy and there are no deviations, but only a non-philosophy that is a non-philosophizability or approaches non-philosophizability, and a non-philosophy that remains a (non-)"philosophy."

We then accept that the implementation of axioms tolerates, while remaining non-philosophical, a margin of negotiation within the definition of the object. In particular the third axiom (relating in any case every material whatsoever to philosophizability), then the two others that will undergo its effects, tolerate a hesitation linked to this inequality of possibilities of its contents. Already within the carrying out of these effects, the third has already supported several *interpretations,* but we will now try to explain and limit this play of possibilities. The three axioms form a coherent, rigorous system: the usage of one of them must lead to consequences that are not contradictory with the consequences of the others. But in order to avoid a premature sterilization and formalism of non-philosophy we are *de facto* condemned to accept a game ruled by the usage and comprehension of the primacy of *philosophizability*. So it is that we distinguish a lengthy non-philosophy, strict or universal (not wanting to say purely deductive) and alternatively a provisional non-philosophy, but such that it inscribes, by way of concern with fidelity to "*Philosophy*," spontaneous doctrinal positions or ones not reduced from the outset to the primacy of philosophizability. From these three axioms the enterprise would appear either to be like a closed orthodoxy, or to be like a completed dualysis, in the manner of an analysis assumed to be over. One cannot ignore these ways of moving faster, having borrowed them ourselves in the past before the optimal rigor of its concept was posited, and so we must, despite ourselves, borrow again. The first non-philosophers came from a particular doctrinal position that continues to impregnate their non-philosophical work; this is the eternal problem of self-analysis that new data has transformed and complicated. Elsewhere it is possible to re-thematize non-philosophy on the basis of this multiplicity of philosophical hypotheses at the source, while knowing that the problem of optimal rigor is not thereby resolved.

Philosophizability and Practice

Philosophy, having become an object of non-philosophy, reveals its ambiguous nature. Non-philosophy, in its first constitution was easily and too immediately contrasted with regional materials that were not strictly based on philosophy. But the more precise analysis of philosophy points out some hesitations, not so much in the possibility of thematizing them as in philosophy's essence and hierarchical structure. This is not a homogeneous environment, but it possesses a homogenous limit that is its auto-encompassing or auto-specular drive: philosophizability. This drive reaches its end on the one hand via transcendental structures, and on the other hand via the reference to "empiricities" that are *practices* and not just *objects*. In general, this reference defines the singular types and cases of philosophy at the point where the concrete doctrinal decisions stand firmly behind the forgetting of philosophizability as their essence. In particular, the great example of Platonism,

111

so destined to form a tradition, merely thematizes philosophizability by its interior fringe turned towards science and ethics. The ascending and descending dialectic, even in the *Parmenides*, is turned towards the thematic contents of genres rather than towards the elucidation of its operative possibility. However, this forgetting does not do justice to "regional" reality, and philosophizability ends by undifferentiating the practical references as simply empirical. Even Plato could no longer make an allusion to the experience of practice, in order to "overcome" and subsume it in his way, or even in order to plunge the philosopher back into a symmetrical cave. Finally, philosophizability would remain strictly blended and confused with practices that it absorbs or that it rejects all at once as "empirical." Hegel and Nietzsche also tried to simultaneously exert it on a determined content and flaunt it as an ultimate law of philosophy (the circle of circles, the eternal return). So either tradition thematizes philosophizability but in an idealist way without realizing its duality with an empirico-practical world and its autonomy, or it thematizes this world as determining of the philosophical and forgets through an excess of empiricism its other side, which is philosophizability. *Within these two cases it is the duality or "contradiction" of the sides, of auto-specular philosophizability and non specular practices, that is forgotten.* Under the pretext of the forgetting of Being or the Other, local and artifactual forgetting, we have forgotten not only the essence of philosophizability, but more seriously, the essence of practicity and of science in particular, suddenly reduced to the production line of knowledges [*connaissances*] immediately captured by philosophy. It is therefore of supreme importance to give non-philosophy its complete extension, giving it the material of philosophy as a duality or two-sided structure.

Practicity as Thought-with-the-Presupposed

Practice understood as practicity is a form or a type of thought alongside philosophizability, a thought-with-the-presupposed which differs entirely from a thought-with-presupposition like

112

philosophy. Instead of taking philosophy as a model of every possible thought, or even those degraded or deficient in "*Practice*" or *praxis*, we will posit that philosophical thought, for reasons anticipated by Kant but radicalized here, is an appearance or an objective transcendental illusion, and that the only *effective* thought, *without appearance* or without unity (but not without identity), is thought-with-the-presupposed. There is a *practical thought* which is not the know-how of technique, but merely *practice as a duality of dimensions, of language and the real, the one irreducible to the other within a Logos, and that surrounds a kernel of technical procedures.* We cannot believe that a thought which is an effect of practice is the only one, because this is still an idealist thesis, either surreptitious or simply reversed, which makes practice an effect on philosophical thought. In the same way no thought that does not have a philosophical form can accompany practice as its structure rather than as its shadow. There is a second thought that is a "true thought," but that has never been philosophical and on the other hand has been partially usurped by philosophy, which is itself *a particular practice with a transcendental appearance.* Our thesis is that determining thought on the side of philosophizability is practice as presupposed-without-presupposition, and that philosophical thought, in order to be unquestionably dominant, is not the determining or real thought.

The ultimate structure and, above all, the signification that philosophy *attributes to itself* is here shattered as soon as practice as thought-with-the-presupposed is introduced on the side of philosophizability. The practical presupposed is itself distributed as a "thought" or "language" side and a "being" or "real" side; these are its two irreducible faces which cannot form a system even though it makes reference to the unique and vague term of "practice." Practice is not the synthesis or the system that would unify these two sides since it is concerned with them as its means, *destined to remain as such and for that reason not adjustable and synthesizable.* Practice as presupposed remains definitively in the state of an *irreducible duality*, if not division, and never reshapes (except as philosophical appearance) a unique Logos or a "Same." Object and Language form a duality which has shattered the form of the Same and seems initially closer to an Unconscious than to a Logos. Strictly speaking it should have been written *Practice = Thinking/Being*.

A Non-Parmenidean Equation: Practice = Thought

Let us provisionally posit the equation *practice = thought* under the heading of a hypothesis of the non philosophical *type* in anticipation of giving it its true sense or a plain non-philosophical use. It is in any case an indication of a change of venue, at least changing thought's center of gravity. It is philosophically absurd, since philosophy only accords to practice a minimum of thought or merely a driving or motivating function; at best it accords it the status of an adjustable presupposition. Furthermore, thus simplified, it is certainly imprecise and subject to blunders, only philosophy may be able to posit and verify an equation whose terms will be equal or the same as a becoming. It is more a *non-equation*, practice and thought not being inevitably opposed as they are in philosophy, but at least unequal, a special inequality that is no longer a difference (a concept of differential practices). One must certainly understand the inequality of this equality via non-philosophy, not as a reversal of philosophy but as its *radical inversion*. Instead of being a philosophical equality, meaning at once conditional (according to the definition of basic terms) and absolute (the same), it is a radical equality or a necessary one (by practice) but empty, and thus conditional (by the provision of thought). *Non-equation* or *non-Parmenidean equation* will be the name of this kind of radical or unilateral transformation of the equation-form. It is of little importance, just useful, to modify the meaning of the terms themselves which form the dyad of the base of the Parmenidean equation. Instead, it concerns questioning this "Same," a unifying entity or invariant system but with possible distortions according to the comprehension of the terms. The non-equation *practice = thought* does not have the same format since, having only two

114

terms, it contains its own solution as unknown and not as a third term given analytically or synthetically. The first names the "utopian" place or origin of every possible *determining* thought (i.e. not apparent), the second names this thought (i.e. what has been transformed by this practice). In order to clearly distinguish philosophy, we will say that *practice and thought are identical in-the-last-instance*, or even that *practice is the presupposed that determines thought*. This is the non-Parmenidean paradigm and it must put an end to theoreticism and idealism, which are both the effect of philosophizability. In each case it contains a refutation of transcendental appearance proper to the Parmenidean founding of philosophy, that *being and thinking are the same*, and it is destined to receive a "utopian" and critical function. Remember that this general form of practicity will also apply to non-philosophy itself except that there it will be a transformed aspect, hence its current ambiguity.

Structure of Practicity (OK, ML, RO)

A practice in this larger but precise sense is not divided, it is dual, for it possesses two sides that surround its operative content. This content is itself complex and constitutes something of a ternary (matter of reality, technical and theoretical means, knowledge or produced work), and is known as the object-of-knowledge (OK). We will not confuse this technical, theoretical and material aspect (extremely diversified as it is by the transformation of a first material, and so invested within the OK) with the entire complex of practice as a mode of thought constituted by its structure as presupposed meta-language (ML) and the real object (RO) as well as by the ternary of knowledge. Altogether this is a quaternary and even pentadal structure.

Language, such as it is carried or "animated" by intention or by the function of a unilateral constitution that it fulfills, is called "meta-language" (ML) when it is concerned with a description and constitution of another "language," of a natural or formal language-object (OK). In general it consists of postulates and axioms that are intuitive and natural *for* practice and what it is destined for. It is a way of positing the theoretico-technical ternary and conditioning it.

But any practice whatsoever in its full meaning also has a real object (RO) that does not belong to the first worked matter and *in view* of which it destines this transformation. The simple transformation is an idealist act and in a sense does not have a real object by itself but merely a reality or materiality. But practicity is not exhausted in these operations and idealized materiality, so we must assume that idealized materiality has a supplementary relationship to a real that determines in its aspect of materiality the transformation of idealized reality. Every practice, even an ideal one, is a *real practice*. We will return later to this problem.

Philosophical Practice and Practice with the Presupposed

Practice as division in general is its highest philosophical concept, a Hegelian concept. Immanent in its way, it forms a system with contemplative Identity, and it is a theoreticist concept of practice. Against this we put forward a completely different concept of practicity, for which science has a privileged place. It is a presupposed activity that is double or "divided" (in effect as in philosophy) but where what is "divided" in an irreducible way and concerns the presupposed and is never presupposition itself. In other words, the practical division is not by nature theoreticist or transcendental but is rather a type of Uni-laterality or Uni-alterity in general which arises from immanence or at least has an affinity with its radical form.

Speaking of "immanent practice" in general for non-philosophy, the formula, without being false, is still vague and subject to confusion, and it assimilates the Real's immanence and division. So on the one hand we know that the Real, without being divided, is Other-than … or that Uni-laterality, Uni-alterity should not be confused with a division, and on the other hand the concept of practice must be extracted from its philosophical element and adjusted as opposable to philosophizability or theoreticism and

116

not only to "theory" in the limited meaning it has for philosophy. It is within this larger framework of theoreticist philosophizability and practice (for which science is the model *par excellence*, but not of theory in the positivist scientific sense) that these distinctions must be replaced by forming a Unified Theory. Non-philosophy in effect fuses together practicity and philosophizability in-the-last-instance by way of the Real. It possesses two initial aspects, a practical aspect in a theoretical or scientific mode and a theoreticist aspect in a philosophical or transcendental mode. These aspects cannot be made absolute in the unitary way without damage being done.

The Non-Equation Practice = Ontology

Let us formalize the preceding thesis. It is a hypothesis *concerning the Real that the practices postulate*. We posit that each practice ordinarily called "regional" possesses a specific quasi-ontology, an original conception of the real and procedures for appropriating it itself. Let us suppose for a moment that epistemology or aesthetics are transcendental appearance or illusion; that they do not cease to be wrong about art or science and their relation to the real, that neither art nor science ever imitates *the* or *a* real, neither relatively nor absolutely, that they do not consist in attempting to approach a model or already-constituted real supposed to be accessible, in rebelling against it and emphasizing the supposed liberty of their operation. This hypothesis assumes an "ontology" of art or science that would no longer have anything to do with philosophical ontology which serves as a basis for aesthetics and epistemology. Positively, in order to save itself from anticipated idealist interpretations, it is necessary to postulate that art or science are autonomous practices without a dependent relation with philosophy, or else one that is superficial since in these practices, as we will see very shortly, a language (ML) is associated that is not specifically philosophical, a meta-practical language certainly impregnated with philosophy and through which art or science become philosophizable. For example, it is in this manner that we generalize the equation *mathematics = ontology*, including both the axioms of mathematical practice and the postulation of the real within the duality of practicity. What is then the meaning of this hypothesis, which unravels aesthetics and epistemology and limits them to philosophical idealism in its voluntarism and spirit of conquest?

From Practices to Non-Philosophy

The philosophically implausible equation *practice = ontology* here forms part of the meta-practical or constituent language. It begs the question, what is philosophizability (rather than a determined philosophy) without the contribution of art or science, what decisive impact can these autonomous postures and practices bring to the philosophical operation? The posture of artistic or scientific practice can be repeated under certain conditions by constituted philosophy, becoming aesthetics or epistemology, but there it is a vicious circle. On the other hand, the thesis concerning the reality of transformation is in fact a real or anaxiomatic axiom, a radical presupposed. Because of the preceding reasons already discussed which touch on the structure of the future, we are forced to posit the empty or non-sufficient necessity of the Real that *if there is anything of the real in philosophy it is given by practice* and only by it, by this structure which we have sketched. Or else practice gives a real that is not that of philosophy and that is not specularly projected as a reflection of reflection. It is already a "thesis" oriented by non-philosophy concerning practice but which is not yet that of the Real as One-in-One, which would mean on its behalf that non-philosophy is no more definable as theory than as practice. A thesis which already goes against philosophy's pretensions as the only giver of the real, confusing it in an idealist manner with an act of position. Here, on the contrary, the axiom of the Real's position is not confused with the former, an axiom which would at once reconstitute a philosophical thesis and position. In the first, RO and ML merge, doubling back the one over the other within a unique "real" or a "same" that is Logos. But they form within

118

practicity a duality proper to the presupposed and remain within that state, so that in philosophy they are considered as a dyad, unitarily unified by the third term: Real = Logos. In other words the presupposed as a uni-lateral intention is no longer a synthesis of the identified real and signification within the intentionality of consciousness and aimed at an objected object and potentially the World. Within the philosophical pronouncement, the intended object and the World merge. This is presupposition as unity or unitary, whereas the real and ideality of axioms are distinguished but within some presupposed that is a duality.

So science is first a dephilosophized quasi-ontology which acts as a guiding theme in order to break towards the most theoretical non-philosophy, while as deaestheticized artistic practice it would serve as a guiding theme for moving towards art as future, or towards religion as future. In the previous works of Philosophy II the affinity of non-philosophy with science also rested upon a certain autonomy of scientific practice outside of epistemology. But we never quite knew how to choose whether we should start from materials as separated postures (philosophy, science or art: whether brute practices or even reduced to the state of base materials for philosophy) or whether we should start from materials like epistemology, an idealist appropriation of science or art. In any case we cannot remain with practices in themselves, for they apparently do not have any philosophical sense, and all must pass through philosophy only when the latter is reduced to its basis and a meta-practical language (the scientific or artistic "real"). In reality they have an already philosophical but dissimulated sense that would bring about a return of the repressed. The solution consists in providing the specific autonomy of practices, but their relative autonomy as well, and each time on account of meta-practical language that isolates them from philosophizability and at the same time allows for their subjection.

Practices are not made out of philosophy as such, there is [il y a] as much a specific practice of art as there is of science, even a "regional" practice, but the "there is" [il y a] no longer simply recaptures [*reprise*] them in and by philosophy, namely their interiorization in the Concept. More specifically, practices are not opposed to the philosophy of such muted practices as we briefly thought before, they have a meta-practical language and ontology. Hence the equation art or science = ontology as thought/Real. But we do not maintain that certain works or understandings are the fundamental or unique text of ontology. The works of art or science are not the text itself, because they are a practical structure and it is this structure that is a quasi-ontology. This is not a determined theory, like the classical philosophical move, as if we said that Kandinsky is the essence of painting or that mathematics in the form of set theory is ontology. Philosophy lives off that alternative, or from that work, that fulfilled [*achevée*] knowledge, or philosophy. On the contrary, the structure of science or art resides between two branches of the alternative and reserves the autonomy of practices as practicity.

All practices are thus utilizable within non-philosophy and all of them, in a sense, are equivalents since all are equal as pentadic structure. Nevertheless science is first because within science the distinction of the two uses of language is more radical, and this is why philosophy represses it and utilizes it more than the others, more than art, religion and technology. This would have to be the criterion for choosing the first practice, science being the most decisive. We will rediscover the distinction by moving between a *general (i.e. more critical)* non-philosophy (but from the point of view of practice, and not from specific structures of non-philosophy itself) and from *special non-philosophies* completely equal from the properly non-philosophical point of view, but not from those of the critique however. This is non-philosophy; it is not immediately non-science or non-religion, and it only becomes such by philosophy's mediation either as epistemology and theology, or by using science or religion as a base and meta-practical language. This does not free us from not having to expel philosophical sufficiency, but on the contrary any practice is possible through its relation to philosophy, with and within non-philosophy.

120

From this point of view alone there is a principle of optimality of choice with an eye towards the best efficacy given philosophizability, and it is science that represents the best first decision. Of course non-philosophy does not allow for a choice between this or that material, it under-determines the choice of practical material and only imposes it in a forcible way within its full concept of philosophizability, but philosophizability perhaps imposes as a priority the choice of science as first practice.

Practical Unilaterality and Ontological Difference

Philosophy in its most self-conscious contemporary form reveals itself to be structured by "difference" in various modes: signifier, ontological, textual, desiring, etc. Its most celebrated form, Ontological Difference, is exemplary of a philosophical style as such combining a certain unilaterality with a reversibility, assuring the primacy sometimes from the one and sometimes from the other. The being is being of Being; Being is the to-be of the being but it is more so, or if we can put it this way, at once more and less, than the inverse. The mechanism is that of a global reversal which only functions with a dominated unilaterality of the "otherness" type rather than "presupposed" type. Even when it seems relatively determining as it is within deconstruction, it is the convertibility that remains absolutely dominant and that signals its philosophical subjection and its globally or finally specular destiny. Difference always has two heads, for it reads itself in a privileged sense but finally also within the other that it serves as horizon or hinterhorizon, so that convertibility, which undoubtedly is no longer the first plane, conserves itself or re-appears as its theater or its backstage corridors.

Let us return to the comparative structure of practice and philosophizability. All these practices are constituted under the same model of a *compound or ternary (the constitutive procedures of OK) + ML/RO (the presupposeds)*. The structure of the practices is finally a quaternary or even a pentad. For example, for Science RO, ML and the ternary of OK which contain the forms of reality and knowledge relative to one another in the totality of knowledge [*connaissance*]. It is here that the status of the in-itself of practices is *specifically autonomous and constitutive of the substance of the reality-world*, the remainder being a philosophical appearance that later takes up the practices through their associated language. As for philosophy, it is a limited or abridged practice, a ternary or quaternary, the dyad of base + the double One, as an absolute or transcendent and as transcendental or relative to the dyad or experience. This is precisely not a true practice, the constitutive ML or RO fuse within an appearance. Science is close to philosophy in both its destination and intelligible aspect, and art by its incarnated and sensible aspect. But if philosophy finishes by exchanging the two sides, then art and science do not exchange them, or do so poorly and maintain their duality, assuring the irreducibility of the presupposed.

So there are only specific practices, not beings or things (*contra* empiricism and dogmatism, the first forms of realism), in order to form the substance of reality or of the World, except that one of them is a false practice, philosophy, which simulates the others without then being one itself and presents itself as claiming to be the form of the World. Philosophical "practice," if we can hold on to this term, is not an associated meta-language, it is already a practice of language and it is for itself its own meta-practical language. It is already philosophy that speaks when it speaks, so that there is no meta-language for it, just local effects of meta-language. Or still philosophy and meta-philosophy tend to merge, philosophy is a transcendental appearance, already its own language associated with it and is indistinguishable from itself. Hence an identity of the object-language and meta-language.

So here it is a problematic less precipitated than those of the philosophies, which have as a practice their own quasi-cogitative experience (the enlarged *cogito* of philosophizability) and concentrated in a premature way in a transcendental appearance of terms or sides that the practices distinguish, lacking for that reason their principle. Though it would in principle be necessary to isolate a practice of language as philosophy's core, but under what form? That of a necessary, but particular, ternary of the kind where concepts are transformed by themselves. Ternaries are assembled in various ways, which would explain why practices properly speaking *resemble philosophy, which re-appropriates them so easily due to an excess, whereas it is instead philosophy that must resemble them by default.* The philosophical ternary, and not only its theoreticist pretension wholly from appearance, would then be what must be "unraveled" by determination-in-the-last-instance or Uni-laterality. Philosophy is a ternary/quarternary, a limited or concentrated practice which has the means *claiming* to realize the telos or presupposed of the other practices and to reduce these to a simple presupposition. Philosophical practice puts itself in a state of exception in relation to other practices. In relation to them this is not a "bad" ternary, but its simple ternary structure allows for its hallucinatory belief in the Real.

All authentic practices (and not merely the scientific ones) suppose this disjunction in regard to their procedures between a real practical object and meta-language. This is a fundamental disjunction irreducible to philosophy's diverse differences, nevertheless without being a contradiction. It falls outside the philosophy that it delimits, and of which it allows a genesis, by showing that it does not respect this disjunction or makes a simple difference of it. A genesis of philosophy is impossible as long as the starting point is still philosophical or idealist and as long as philosophy has the pretension to effectively encompass [*englober*] all other practices without remainder.

"Thought-with-the-presupposed" is a very general formula and can make us believe in a new unitary structure that reabsorbs unilaterality. It is necessary to attend to the *practical* form of unilaterality as irreducible presupposed in every presupposition in order to find the first serious rebellion against this specular-all, before being radicalized in its non-philosophical form. From this angle, but not only it, non-philosophy is the radicalization of practices as thought-with-the-presupposed and cannot itself be the *object*, of language, of a practical, worldly intentionality. Uni-laterality has for an object this All of the thought-world, which by virtue of its nature, it necessarily bears, being uni-lateral or utopian, it is turned without consultation to the All. And even though it is concerned with language (ML) or the real (RO) that belongs, in principle, to the All or stems from it, they function then as material of the presupposed or of unilateral intention.

Thus philosophy only appears to be a practice exceeding or transgressing its status as practice, finding in its conditions for practice the necessity to overcome it. What philosophy overcomes, from the side of practices, is the distinction of the operative and thematic-object, and what is overcome sufficiently shows that practices, above all science, have an affinity with non-philosophy. To distinguish object and meta is undoubtedly to distinguish object of knowledge and real object, or Thought and Real, but non-philosophy does not posit the Real as *intended* [visée] in an opaque way as science does, and there is undoubtedly a unilateral duality within meta-language and within the immanent usage that non-philosophy makes of language. What in general are the prospects of meta-language and of its distinction from the object-language within non-philosophy? This indicative distinction is radicalized in the sense that it pushes the Real to a dimension that escapes the *epekeina* dimension of philosophy which ordinarily claims to give the Real.

But is the problem in regards to the non-philosophical becoming of practices themselves? Non-philosophy merely changes their function rather than their structure in relation to philosophy. If there is no longer anything but quaternaries that claim to exceed one another, non-philosophy is the reduction of philosophy's pretensions with an eye to ensuring the practices' safeguarding against those pretensions. Is it then a negative theory of simple practices as outside-world? Or strictly speaking as practices with a "world," with pre-worldly or associated pre-philosophical language? Or must it break down all the structures and try to constitute subjects *for* them? This alternative is largely misleading because non-philosophy has higher ends, it is undoubtedly an aid to the destruction of transcendental appearance, but also to non-philosophical exposition and modelization of philosophy and the thought-world's mechanisms.

Indifference and Combination
of Philosophizability and Practicity

In order to open the angle of "philosophy" to the greatest extent as an inevitable passage towards the thought-world, we will admit that it is "divided" a second time in a duality that is no longer that of *Idealism/Materialism* but its "radicalization," *Philosophizability or Auto-specularity or Auto-encompassing/Knowing or Practice.* Non-philosophy's object is no longer the experience or being that are the correlates of intra-philosophical entities as Idea or Being, whereas the *de jure* correlate of philosophizability (except in the reduction to effective philosophy) is a practice of autonomous knowing. Philosophizability has its proper structure in a dyad/triad, the form of Philosophical Decision, and ultimately a duality of every philosophy is that of Decision and a specific practice. This duality is probably no longer intra-philosophical or even formal and structural, but it appears constitutive of philosophy as a thought-world when these are already understood by non-philosophical practice.

Can we still define this duality of thought-world as a contradiction? Not exactly; the contradiction is a syntactical phenomenon and would assume in an idealist manner that specific practice in its irreducible duality is dissolved within a unitary syntax or understood as simple division. In its third axiom, non-philosophy, already non-philosophically interpreted, recognizes this duality but assumes that this duality is not liable to be reversed. At least not in theory: for in philosophy's historical or restricted effective practice it is possible *to believe* that one privileges a practice over the philosophy-form, even if this has no effect, since this practice is always in the last resort beholden to the philosophy-form. Thus it is impossible to reverse that duality except through an idealist interpretation of it or a reduction of all content to philosophical syntax. It is therefore necessary to distinguish philosophizability's core (which induces theoreticism) and the material base that it appropriates and whose "content" it forms. The thought-world is not necessarily idealist, it is only such when the practices' material reference is absorbed by philosophizability. In this way we avoid an indifferent juxtaposition or a brutal and thoughtless struggle of the disciplines. From the side of these practices assumed to have an absolute autonomy, this is a precaution that also avoids rejecting philosophy either as a simple error in language or representation, or as an ideology within which science rains down fury and condemnations. *On the contrary, this duality of the thought-world is what would require us to find (non-philosophical) unified theories of philosophizability and a practice = x.*

From the side of philosophy assumed to be absolute and independent from practices, a first correction takes place in the form of philosophy's blending with practices, blendings to which we now give a more intelligible rather than empirical sense. Indifferent duality becomes antithetical in effect when it is admitted either because it resolves itself in a blend organized by philosophy that names and characterizes its practices which are the basis of these blendings or because science and philosophy, for example, form an unequal contradiction where science holds the determining role and philosophy the dominant one. These derived knowledges have practices for an object, be it epistemology or aesthetics or theology. Whether science, art, or religion, the logic is the same. By passing from the indifferent and thoughtless opposition (but which in reality philosophical presuppositions immediately penetrate) or passing from indifference (for non-philosophical reasons) to an antithesis and then moving on to a contradiction in the post-Hegelian dialectical spirit, the implicit or hidden role of philosophy may seem to have diminished to the point of no longer being nothing more than a part or an "idealist position" in front of the other. It is nothing of the sort, all these solutions or attempts to think their relations remain philosophical to various

126

degrees or in any case philosophizable (even materialist contradiction, cannot escape it). Even if the saturation of the philosophical sphere has as a goal to show that any step beyond this limit is impossible, that it is absolute, this operation of delimitation remains philosophical or inscribed within its mobile and constantly moving borders.

This antithesis and its idealist solution have the drawback of fostering belief in a dissolution of science within epistemology, of art within aesthetics, of religion within philosophy, and so motivating or justifying a reversal (above all in the case of their contradiction) from the *pro* to the *contra* of domination, to a rebellion of dominated entities. These revolutions are idealist and philosophical acts that then limit the critique of philosophy to a deconstruction, although still an extreme form of auto-critique. Philosophical idealism continues to reign over this type of critique of "philosophies of ..." science, art, religion. To grant everything to philosophy from its pretensions (as non-philosophy does) should not mean giving it everything in the mode of idealism (which is still a narcissism) but to agree with it subject to an objective demarcation which does not let itself be carried away by habitual forcefulness and haste. This objective demarcation of the philosophical within materials calls for an evaluation of the autonomy of practices in light of philosophy such that it is no longer reserved as the only authority of philosophy but would be an understanding of the possibility of an attempted philosophical takeover of these practices. An idealist reading of philosophical mastery is a permanent danger to be submitted to non-philosophical vigilance. A certain *starting point* — an occasional starting point — for non-philosophy within these blendings is very limited and in any case is intra-philosophical, as is every preparatory work of materials, but inevitable. It conveys the thesis of the supposedly ultimate philosophical sense of these practices. Therefore it is suitable to put forth both the potency of philosophizability over practices and to reserve the specific or proper autonomy of these practices, such that philosophy is fundamentally discernible from their relative autonomy in the sphere of philosophy. This is what we will now examine.

Meta-Practical Language and the Philosophical Appropriation of Practices

None of the anti-thetical or dialectical (which is a rational or philosophical instrument) forms perfectly allow for the formalizing of the relations of science, art, and religion with philosophizability. They leave intact philosophy's *first critical narcissism*. The philosophy/science hierarchy is itself a philosophical or self-interested representation even when it takes the form of an unequal and dialectical contradiction, not greatly idealist like epistemology. These practices are heterogeneous in a way that is original to the philosophical gesture and forms at best its material base. Yet the latter, in spite of the language that is associated with it, is neither *integrally* philosophizable nor simply irreducible to philosophy. But in order to avoid simple philosophical domination in the guise of epistemology etc., it must first free heterogeneous postures and irreducible practices in philosophy as the fundamental and imparting "practice" of language and sense. Undoubtedly these practices are accompanied by a meta-language, here a meta-practical language, which carries philosophy *de facto* and *de jure*. It is thus necessary to accept the existence of a meta-practical language in the same way that we can accept a meta-ontological language for mathematics (moreover without always seeing its continuity with philosophy) to such an extent that philosophy can explicitly graft itself onto this meta-practical language. Philosophy is the most devious thought capable of returning beyond its repression. It is the most encompassing, more than the other meta-practical languages of various "regions." Supposing that the two principal postures both claim the Real, (even science by its meta-practical language also wants the Real) this scientific "Real," albeit autonomous, is still ordered by philosophy and is in any case philosophizable and threatened by idealism of the sort that does not let us overcome this risk. This is *the precaution principle against philosophical risks.*

128

The solution consists then in posing without contradiction the specific maximal autonomy of science as a distinct, consistent posture of philosophy with which a meta-practical language is associated, as carried out by certain modernists. But also to posit science not as an in-itself, as we have thus fashioned it, but as inseparably *de facto* and *de jure* (philosophically) betrayed by its meta-practical language, able to be re-appropriated on this basis by philosophy. We will similarly pose the relative autonomy of religion as practice (of faith) associated with a concrete meta-language that is *de jure* and *de facto* philosophizable, which is to say a theological meta-language.

Is this thesis of the consistency and autonomy of practices outside of philosophy interior to the philosophical decision, albeit as a dogmatic thesis in a materialist spirit or at last discovered and legitimated by non-philosophy? Is it absolute like the modernist and mathematical cut [coupure] or like the cut of religion or gnosis which, in the Platonic sense, use the same kind of absolute cut in relation to philosophy? This would not take into account their associated language through which philosophizability infiltrates, and covers up the cut or effaces its "cutting edge." The difference between these two Platonic solutions is that in one case this first break is determined by nothing, it is a mathematical dogmatism, whereas in the other, non-religious gnosis seems to presuppose non-philosophy, thus the Real, in order to affirm that the practices or instances are relatively autonomous.

But in this last case, the confusion bears on the notion of "relative autonomy." Certainly it comes in-the-last-instance from the radical Real, but there is another form that decides itself in relation to an assumed sufficient philosophy. However, it is necessary not to confuse the two, since science is not relatively autonomous from itself in the same way: vis-a-vis philosophy to which its associated meta-practical language is finally connected; as well as 2. through the operation of non-philosophy. If we invoke non-philosophy while reducing philosophy to religion and Platonic gnosis, it is because we are given religion as separated from philosophy without having examined thoroughly the materials from the point of view of philosophizability and what it is able to do — it will return under other forms.

Under the threat of not having sufficiently located and identified philosophizability, there is a meticulous examination to be made of the materials. Otherwise this is a dogmatism of mathematical science within philosophy, which represses or denies philosophy, or a dogmatism of religion within non-philosophy. Non-philosophy is not therefore the work that philosophy could and should do, on the contrary it effectively begins with the work of philosophical auto-analysis (though already under the condition of the Real or certain of its philosophical symptoms, such as immanence in general) completed at least at the level of principle, when it is no longer possible to fashion "from" philosophy surreptitiously. Once this work is completed, it is possible to posit that the whole sphere of materials is given-in-One and that the Principle of Sufficient Philosophy is raised (which reigns in philosophy and in science) *but only through its associated meta-practical language.* Non-philosophy only has an effect on the sciences and the arts in so far as philosophizability has infiltrated their meta-language, and it does not have any effects on the practices themselves. If we do not first posit a certain autonomy of practices in relation to philosophy as auto-encompassing, and thus by relation also to non-philosophy, we proceed from idealist presuppositions which we have given up. Finally, having been too spontaneous a philosopher from the start, one in the end becomes a philosopher again within non-philosophy despite oneself. So the specific, rather than relative, autonomy of science frees it from philosophy without cutting off all effect of philosophy over science.

Finally science and philosophy as postures assumed to be separated are given together in a complex apparatus, in the form of an auto-encompassing that indirectly envelops the specific structure of science, the idealism of philosophizability and scientific realism. Philosophizability is the apparatus that has the spontaneous will to integrate the two schemas. Science thus represents here the base or the dyad, while philosophy takes it back again not in order to constitute itself but in order to give itself a solid base within the reality of experience. It transforms it into the sense of science, its concept of the object, of the transcendental and knowledge (in reality this is not the same object, it is an opaque and black transcendental, knowledge is not the *a priori* but only the support of the *a priori*). So it is philosophy that needs science, appropriating science as its base and so changes the meanings of its elements. Science is autonomous but constantly threatened by a philosophical repossession that transforms it into the base, which it is not spontaneously.

This complex blend of relations of domination and determination is the material to be dualyzed. How is the equality of the-last-instance introduced between science and philosophy, between the old "regional-specific" of practices and the "fundamental?" This "utopian" equality resides in the constitution of a subject or *force-(of)-thought*. Non-philosophy will invert the order of the base and the appropriation, since it is in a way the radical autonomy of the real base that will itself appropriate philosophy against the transcendental appearance or philosophizability.

Non-Philosophical Practice and Practices

The first condition for the possibility of philosophy's decomposition is its being-given in-One, which allows for the distinction of philosophizability and its sufficiency, followed by the liberation of practices in relation to the philosophical structure. But does this not assume that the practices are themselves in-One and given in this way? Or that the immanent Real limits its effect to associated language alone, confusing epistemology with knowledge, the appearances always being a question of folding one plane upon another? How in turn is the duality practiced affected by its being-given-in-One? *This poses again the problem of the affinity of not only science, but of all practices, with non-philosophy.* The One-in-One has no constitutive relation with the practices but simply *exists* as

131

a radical practice or as the unification of the practical duality and philosophical difference as transcendental.

No doubt the concept of Unified Theory seems to make sense only if the non-philosophical Real has an effect on practice, but it only has an effect on the associated language by which philosophy interferes with the practice and gives way, for example, to epistemology. Thus it is this epistemological or aesthetic appearance, attacking the duality of the language-object and meta-language, which we must undo. The core of theoretico-material procedures is only modified when it is extrapolated towards philosophy. The Unified Theory, unification of the forces of practice-science and philosophy, is only valid for the materials of epistemological or aesthetic appearance. A non-philosophical combination of means of quaternary practices only capable of fashioning itself *under the condition of an epistemo-logical language common* to science and philosophy, thus within language and the appearance from which the subject is woven, and additionally under the condition of the Real. The Real, no doubt, displaces the practices' pretensions but they rightly only have this pretension through the mediation of their associated language, as if the necessary meta-practical language for every science and for the description of science were derived in a philosophy and an epistemology and assumed *practical duality*.

The difference with epistemological idealism's starting point is that by idealism and through epistemological appearance we have not exactly understood each time the same thing. In one case the confusion of epistemology is immediate and thus self-confirming, in the second case it is recomposed or given this time as an effect and no longer as a nature which would justify itself. Indeed, how do we know that epistemology is an appearance and not a nature? An artifact and not an essence? There would be little reason to critique it through the usage of philosophical materials alone, which could only give us a comprehension of this appearance (like nature or like appearance undifferentiated between philosophy and practice) that is itself idealist.

Hence the interest in a critique of philosophy, of a delimitation of philosophizability through the practices before passing to effective non-philosophy. However, as we have said, we do not have the right to discern the practices and dualyze philosophy, appearance included; which under the non-philosophical conditions have already been posited. By what right is practical duality opposed to philosophy if philosophy still presents itself as it normally does, in a massively authoritarian manner, as one or unitary? It is perhaps only through the removal of the Principle of Sufficient Philosophizability, which runs through every philosophy regardless of its vastness, which can allow or justify (at the least authorize) a first decomposition of philosophical appearance or make philosophical authority appear as an appearance. It is necessary *to pay attention to the order of the forms of the symptom,* the first being the effect of the Real itself, the second being possible in the interior of the first and under its condition.

The Real Field of Struggle

The idea of non-philosophy has required understanding precisely the thesis of a reality and relative autonomy of those instances which compose a philosophy. The consistency of a particular philosophical decision resides in the tension that runs through the blendings between *its two sides, that of the absolute idealism of philosophizability and that of the reality of practices, of their non specular realism.* The Idealism/Materialism duality is internal to the precedent that generalizes it outside of every doctrinal position already empirically effectuated or already blended. The idealism that no longer does anything but make a reference or allusion to practices is a pure product of this blend or of this effacing of duality. The third axiom must exhibit as much as possible *the most secret and the most universal* form of philosophy. For example, Platonism remains a doctrinal position and at most leads to the general thesis of a sufficient specularity, of which the philosophizable nature is not interrogated as such and which above all is deprived of its correlate of non specular practices. Even Hegelianism and

Nietzscheanism are positions such that the Platonic reference or allusion to the empirical is mentioned only in passing. It is necessary to generalize this schema for all the relations of philosophy and regions of specific practices, art or ethics. The complete but abstract schema of Philosophical Decision can be filled out with art as a base taken within this structure by appropriation. A philosophy of art, for example, is in general already constituted with its implicit scientific base and subsequently appropriates art. The same goes for religion in so far as philosophy re-appropriates it, not in so far as it would be the unique material of non-philosophy standing before the Real. In this last case, showing further that religion is perhaps not the best symptom of non-philosophy, philosophical resistance is not dualyzed. Non-philosophy has as a primary objective dispelling the domination of dominations, philosophizability.

Three remarks:

1. If non-philosophy in the narrow sense is the strict respect of this third axiom and product of unified theory, we will call it *first*, universal or general, concrete as it must be in the form of a unified theory. And every non-philosophy must ground itself on a third axiom which gives itself either a doctrinal position or a practical knowledge as determinate or co-determinate of philosophizability and duality of the thought-world; we will call this *second or restricted.*

2. As practice of the human utopia of the possible, non-philosophy extends the list of its principles, Principle of Sufficient Philosophy, Principle of Philosophizability or Precaution, Principle of the Consistency of Practices, Principle of Double Relative Autonomy (of philosophy in relation to non-philosophy, of practices in relation to philosophy), Principle of the Exhaustion of the Thought-World's Ingredients.

3. Does non-philosophy have an effect on practices? Only on philosophizability, not on the practices of knowing. But it is also why an artistic or scientific modeling of philosophizability will be possible, by recourse to the operative practice of art or science, as a unified theory of philosophy and art.

This extension not only exhausts all philosophical possibilities, it furnishes the most adequate materials for cloning the transcendental subject-organon, which in this way should come to be operative on the entire field of the thought-world. It should make possible multiple activities of modeling between philosophy and science, philosophy and art, leading all the way to risking a *modelist explosion* [*explosion modélisante*]. In a concrete way we would proceed to an extension of modeling beyond its epistemological, scientifico-philosophical concept.

LET US MAKE A TABULA RASA OUT OF THE FUTURE OR OF UTOPIA AS METHOD

Imaginary Utopia, Real Utopia

Having accomplished this route into the past of philosophy, let us return to the future which manifests or gives it. A consequence of this conception of the determinant primacy of practices is to correct the initially apparent arbitrariness of non-philosophy as a theory always threatened by a return to theoreticism and of making it in turn suddenly appear as something other than a simple practice, at least in its practical aspect or from the perspective of practice but still transcendental, within the extension of practices. Thought exists but is not by its nature philosophical, and it is the "practical" style, integrated with the transcendental, that non-philosophy resumes.

The change in terrain, as we say, thus presents itself. The place of thought is no longer unique, it is itself as in theoreticism and idealism. It is double but in-One, speculation that claims to be auto-determinate *and* a practical place foreign to speculation. This is to pass from idealist utopia where fundamental thought only returns to itself by an effect of the almost real, to a true but strange or unattributable place by which thought is determined. In fact, the problem of thought's "locality" is more complex, between the idealist utopia that is a place but an imaginary one (the philosophical all-place) and the real utopia, that of the unattributable Real. The presupposed practice is in effect utopian as unplaceable or unlocalizable, and more precisely as determining the philosophical relations of place and non-place. It is at least in this way taken back up or assumed this time by the human Real as radical utopia, which is not extra-worldly but that which allows the radical inversion of the logic of the World. Non-philosophy only demands the status of utopia in so far as it is that of the Real of the in-Man rather than the completely imaginary utopia of philosophizability.

Philosophies have been quick to fill in utopia with social and political images, drawing from past and present times which condition these images as "futures." At best some have abandoned this confusion or this transcendental appearance and have settled on a utopian modeling of reality, they have in fact a model object of construction and modification charged with rendering life in the city intelligible and amenable. But this conception of the model remains positive and philosophical, it comes from the imagination. We understand that utopia has "taken a wrong turn," as if philosophy had transferred it from the World and diverted it from its vocation (to unilaterally come to the World). Instead of making use of *the tabula rasa in a negative, not positive way,* of the one-sided blade of the razor, they have continued, under the name of utopia, to project images drawn from the World and to make of themselves aides and servants of the worst persecutions, giving the World the noble and idealizing version that is theirs. The problem will instead be that of rendering the radically human (non-)acting, vacant or free from all images or models, of making utopia('s)-force applicable to everything that transcendentally assumes it as affecting History, the whole of time.

No doubt utopia as the Contemporary's alterity represents a novelty and some progress over the positive or metaphysical utopia, but it also remains for a "last" time still within the traps of conformism and shackled to the force of its weakness (its "weak force," if we can say that) to the mirages of domination and historical power. It still submits positive determination to the indetermination of alterity in place of positing the Real as that which determines (in the form of a subject) the relations of positivity and alterity. It continues to introduce, but more mildly, the worldly positivity into the little of utopia that it tolerates, a utopia which philosophy uses to get over its philistinism.

The All-Place and the Non-Place: Philosophy's False Utopia
Meta-language and Real Object, the couple that constitutes the presupposed of practices and so the practices as presupposed, has as its place a radical exteriority or without status, Uni-laterality, except that it is these conditions, undefinable by a context, and which are such only by *their position and their theoretical function* or determination or ternary of concrete procedures and also the equivalent ternary (2/3 or 3/2) that forms Philosophical Decision. Thus we must distinguish within philosophy two statuses of transcendence as its deep structure: the *thematic, that of which philosophy speaks* (*meta* and *epekeina*) and the *operative* that we presuppose here in philosophy. And yet the operative has neither definition nor place, it is its presupposed, only it does not recognize it as such and from this arises the misunderstanding that carries it to transcendental appearance. The thematic-object and its ternary also inscribe themselves and are determined by and within *a presupposed but invisible exteriority and repressed with a furious energy by the "official" and yet already overwhelming thematic content*. Although this exteriority (operative transcendence) is not properly speaking a transcendence but that which determines it, it divides itself into a meta-language that posits it (because there is a language or at least an effect of meta-language for philosophy itself) and a real object (because there is a real for philosophical practice itself). But this presupposed operative side is regularly denied. It is a necessary and determinate non-place that allows for philosophical transcendence to be thematized, and from there the other ternaries as well. So it is that philosophy as well presupposes a non-place but strives to deny or forget it in order to present itself as all-place. Then in the loudest voice it feigns recognizing a presupposed understood as Place, Other, Other Scene, so that it only thinks of reducing any of them to the state of a presupposition, gnawing away at them: this is the ruse of the imaginary All-place.

But why does the practice of these two transcendences produce this effect of reciprocal reshuffling and not a distinction of ML and RO within a Logos, whereas on the contrary, the distinction is maximal within science? It is that philosophy conceives the Real as Unity of experience or empirical materials, thus of the OK and the Real. This problem depends on transcendence and its relation to beings, which cannot be the same within science and philosophy. Philosophy is the transcendental gesture that applies itself to the concept as *a priori* valid within the limits of experience as unity of reality and rational concept. This unity of the concept and reality (cf. Parmenides) is broken by science which refuses the intuition of the Real and breaks the Unity of ML and RO. Within science it is the concept and the neighboring apparatuses or formalisms that determine the material of reality in the form of knowledge, of the distinction of RO and ML. There is no scientific equivalent of *epekeina* nor perhaps even of the *meta*. Science is determining, art is postulating or searching, philosophy is the unity of the two, of determination and reflection. Science is a non-place of ML, art is an unlocalizable place, philosophy is the unity of place and the unlocalizable, it is driven by precipitation and achievement, the need for globalizing or world-making [*de globaliser ou de mondialiser*].

The non-transcendence demanded by certain philosophies only indicates at best an immanence in an undefinable manner but *in relation to* the thematic transcendence of the ternary, still relative to transcendence. It will take non-philosophy to posit this transcendence as such and to invert the sense and origin of the "non," since it thinks in-Real, *in a non-place* or in a utopian way without desiring it but by thinking it as a future lived affecting the life of the World and the subject. The operative plane that assumes non-philosophy is thus not in reality a plane but a *non-place that is not definable except by its effect of determination.* This non-place is devoid of transcendence or understanding. It is only in starting from the non-place that we can think it, even if philosophy has folded it over transcendence and its ternary. This non-place has a vague affinity with the thing-in-itself as Real, so it is only Kant who posited it secondarily in opposition to science and its ternary, as an exterior limit and then recovered it in the traditional way as a principle of auto-limitation, whereas non-philosophy will never make a principle of an "auto-" nor even a veiled ultimatum in the way of Heidegger, but the immanent real object as given within a transcendental axiomatic. This is a return to Kant and the thing-in-itself in an apparently dogmatic way but modifying the theoretical position of philosophical discourse, thus inverting it.

Naturally we will not make of the presupposed, either a ML or RO, or even philosophy's operative non-transcendence, which generates or engenders through a procession the ternary of conceptual practice. We must in a sense self-give it, for it is a form of unquestionable intelligibility, other than by way of philosophical appearance. The presupposed, even that of non-philosophy, engenders nothing, it determines the structure of practices that are the given of the World or of reality and which it is impossible to constitute piece by piece.

The principle of non-sufficient utopia or uchronia cannot plunge the future into time or into a nothingness of time. Within non-philosophy, the Other-than … or Uni-laterality as Future conveys the metalinguistic non-place and ends in uprooting it (or unlocalizable operative transcendence) from philosophical and ontological localization. With his problem of the place of Being (of its locality) Heidegger is close to a negative utopia but he is still chained to an empirico-metaphysical sufficiency. Non-philosophy develops the real as a *necessity but a necessity of possibility* that makes practical duality necessary. Man-in-person as subject cannot localize the unlocalizable, this would be to return to philosophy, but he posits axiomatically the non-place of ML or RO as identical in the in-Man. There is nothing here like a double negation, radical immanence cannot be a new negation, even if it is the Other-than … or being-separated. This is an immanent real, not the identity attached to negation which would form a system with it.

Man-in-person and the Practical Subject

The structure of practice and its "critical" determination of theoretical appearance allows us to understand the necessary unilateral distinction of Man-in-person as Real or determinant future and the subject as determinant and determined in-the-last-instance. Distinction of the *Who?* and the *How?* The subject is the operator or agent that in his person identifies, but only in-the-last-instance, the presupposed·(or the Real of practice) and the properly practical operations. The confusion of the Who? and the How? that is simply differentiated internally in a unique instance is the symptom of philosophy or theoreticism: the symptom of man as theoretical subject. For example, a titular radical Ego of auto-affectivity is also said to be "real" only by its being known as a *how* and thus as a transcendental operator (certainly real as a consequence), but it is *primarily of a transcendental nature*. This philosophy of radical immanence dissociates the transcendental nature of the World's first relation, which it retains, and the ecstatic nature of the representation of this relation, which it rejects. Non-philosophy simultaneously rejects both as it refuses to separate them and as a result must distinguish two "relations" with the World, the real or noetic and the transcendental or nometic, that of Man and that of the subject, the latter derived from the former rather than the inverse. Theoreticism continues to determine the egological philosophy of immanence as soon as the *how* seems to have exhausted the *who*. The paradox is obvious: the excess of theoreticism is an excess of philosophical "practice" and in the end practice overcomes the Real. Hence the primacy of practice over the Real, its non determination by it, leading to the primacy of theoreticism over practices. We will oppose the following unilateral order to this system of primacies (which are in reality dominations): 1. primacy of the Real over practices; 2. primacy of practices over philosophy; 3. primacy, within philosophy, and so philosophically of its theoreticist appearance over its practical aspect, and non-philosophically of its practical essence over its appearance.

Future as Organon: The New Tabula Rasa

The destination of the subject is now precise. Utopia fashions a rigorous and practical method within the subject. Allowing itself to-be-determined according to the Future is the same thing as working to insert the Future into the World and History. The subject as cloned is a place, the only possible place susceptible to still being named as such, between the imaginary All-place of the World and the non-place of the without-place of Man-in-person. It still concerns the identity of place, but the identity-(of)-place is itself unlocalizable. The subject is what we would call an "*instance of unilateralization.*" The subject neither creates nor receives the Future in the manner of phenomenological consciousness, the Future is already given as in-Man itself, but how can a utopia without imagination (real-without-effectivity and so non-acting) affect the form-world? It is that the form-world is already given in-One and so in the mode of the Future even before there has been something like a subject, and is not brought from the exterior by an agent. The subject then is the recovery of the Future, but this time in a transcendental manner and by definition affects the World. Each subject is one such organon and the Future becomes an organon or takes responsibility for a transcendental force in relation to the World. Each subject is one such unilateralizing factor of the determination of the undetermined World (qua appearance), but also, what amounts to the same thing, a factor of indetermination and unlocalization of the All-place. If the subject determined according-to-the-Future is himself future, and if he assumes the World, it is at best to dis-alienate himself from faith in the World. But utopia only belongs to the Real, Man-in-Man alone is the proprietor, and it is in the subject that his "negative" weakness or his "being forced" becomes a force (of utopia).

The Being-Forced from the Future and Utopian Forcing: The Necessity of Nowhere

The Future (Uni-laterality, the (non-)One, the Other-than ...) bears witness in its way to the radical Immanent, to which it belongs and which gives it its "essence," as a dimension of No-Where [*Nulle-Part*] and by unattributable necessity and so void of determinations. Man-in-Man is not synthesis but the immanent

143

identity (not to itself but in-Man) of the being-given of Man and the Future. It is he and he alone who by right introduces "into" the World a future or rather who introduces the World and History to a radical future. *The non-imagined or real Future has primacy over the World and the imagined future through History.* Or, in order to undo Parmenides, *the Future and thought are identical in-the-last-Humaneity.* Or in yet another manner, *the future determines History in-the-last-Humaneity.* Being-thrown into the World is a transcendental appearance that reduces the immanent Future.

The human future is thus not a vague or fuzzy possibility, a modality of consciousness, but that which "precedes" or rather that which has primacy over the ek-stase [*extase*] of consciousness and which determines or removes its sufficiency with the aim of transforming it. This is instead a necessary contra-intentional arrival as the Real, not a forcing but *being-forced, which is the same thing as the being-given of the Real.* We had reduced it too much to the inert state of a being-given, certainly without-givenness but too easily reducible to a passive given of the phenomenological type and opposable to the action-position of Idealism. The spirit of non-philosophy is neither that of passivity or phenomenological givenness, nor that of idealist activity (Fichtean, for example). It is the spirit of radical immanence that (incapable by definition of being of an order, nor of a point, nor a tendency, of an effort or an impulse) is the being-separated-without-separation. In other words, the future is even a being-given in the mode of the in-One but being-given-in-One is itself open or rather counter-openness, counter-ecstatic. Naturally, "counter" cannot signify here, as we have said, a point of departure for going against the World, a counter-current of History, as an infinity of separation brought against the World. But a force, rather a being-forced that is not the result of forcing, namely the necessity of the Nowhere [*Nulle Part*] which inverts every possible sense. The Future is inexstensive in space and time, pure uni-ference which gives the World rather than coming to it. We understand then the Born-Again subject as a subject determined by the Future, as its envoy.

Man is this being from Nowhere that haunts the World rather than the World haunting him, this Distant without distance, this utopia finally without topology. This is only possible from now on if the World is given in Man by Man rather than Man "thrown" first in the World. The Contemporaries' being-thrown must be dualyzed. The Future comes to the World because it gives the World in this same gesture of coming that is not a return, or a being-thrown. It would be necessary to wait for the subject and force-(of)-utopia in order to see Man turned in his way towards the World that reclaims him. He is thrown there only in so far as he is alienated there, and thrown as if into a Whole rather than into a phenomenological horizon within which he would remain definitively a prisoner. Is he a living utopia? A utopian lived experience? On the condition that the subject and the attribute are not separated or divided and posit Man as this X determining in a non-sufficient way the relationship of the subject and attribute. Lastly we distinguish being-forced or being-future, given or manifested without forcing a futuring, and their transcendental revival in the form of a subject that is a force-(of)-future or (of)-utopia directly affecting the history-world. Unitary being thrown is then destroyed by the Future which is the negative condition that determines it and suspends the alienated forms.

A Rigorous Utopia for the World

The problem of a rigorous utopia at play for the whole of the World is evidently paradoxical and at the edge of contradiction. How can we "imagine" one such that it is not a repetition of the history-world if it must provide us with the totality of necessary means in order to conceive it? How can every means required for utopia not be affected by the spirit of the World that it would nevertheless transform or abandon? Hence either the dualistic rupture between the two worlds or the splitting and shameless reviving of the past (the imagination of a future in the blink of an eye) with these half-solutions that consist in modifying utopia's space and time, its horizon, its depth, and its structure of double transcendence, the whole symbolized by the island-machine or by the machine as island. In each of these cases, utopia is a scission or dissidence and so an imitation rather than a heresy that proceeds by one division or by another, even a hyper-frontier. It is a dismemberment of the World, an arbitrary choice which loses its identity.

Man-in-person is in-Man and not an island. The dimension of unilateral utopia is foreclosed to the history-world from which it is separated and in this way falls to the exterior of it, while given according to this dimension. To such an extent that negative utopia is never an intention or transcendent noesis, in the end filled up by a noema of the World. It is an empty intention to the extent that, separated without an intention of being, it draws its last force from Man-in-person and not from the history-world. On the other hand, the means that it utilizes as a utopia of transformation and not imitation are necessarily drawn from society and from history but it is precisely they who are transformed when transcendentally taken hold of again as subject or force-(of)-utopia and become the *a priori* content of this force. Utopia must first be the means before being the ends in order to continue speaking this language. Thus the lone concept of a utopia that is real or in-Man, necessary and negative with regards to its non-sufficiency or its powerlessness to act but not determining whether history presents itself, resolves the contradiction of a utopian transformation of the history-world. We may call it a non-Platonic utopia, Platonism as a philosophy-model which has given the model of utopia as an imitation, namely authoritarian, local and localized upon a part of this history of society but incapable of affecting it as World and of transforming it.

Last Definition, Utopian, of Non-Philosophy

Originally, non-philosophy theoretically signified 1. the refusal of hermeneutic and comprehensive practice; 2. the co-intervention of science within philosophy; 3. the concern of a *theoretical domination* of philosophy; 4. the initial belief that the Real implicated a theoretical activity because of its indifference. All these initial elements came to be taken up again and nuanced after internal difficulties became apparent.

These problems are the following: 1. the demand for practice since non-philosophy does not exclude any opposite; hence 2. internal difficulties concerning the combination of philosophy and science; therefore 3. various combinatory definitions of aspects but always to the benefit of one of them, theoretical practice, practice of theory, practice theory, practical theory, transcendental practice; 4. the emerging risk of a "theorist" normalization and the opposite accusation of "theoreticism," thus of "practice" against non-philosophy; 5. the excess of formalism or abstraction from the isolated perspective of some "discipline" and carried to the absolute as non-philosophy's assumed true meaning, more generally the separation of discipline and oeuvre, of the discovery of the Real and non-religious graft, or the non-philosophical method and poetry, art, etc.

The solution put forth is born 1. from the impossibility of defining the Real and thus non-philosophy, the Real = X determining in-the-last-instance the relation of theory and practice; 2. from a new understanding of the third axiom and from its bipolar composition of philosophizability and content within the practices or forms of knowing. This new definition and opposition of philosophizability and practicity takes place around the question of meta-language and the real object. United or fused within philosophy, they are irreconcilable within practice, and therefore science; 3. altogether non-philosophy mobilizes philosophizability (the transcendental or oracular, thus a theoretical element in the philosophical sense), and a practice in a new sense, first and foremost science but not only science (art, religion, etc.). Thus the initial definitions of non-philosophy as theoretical have been undermined and solicited from all sides. This was not to head in the direction of even more theoreticism. On the contrary, the practical aspect, but in a new sense of the term, has gained in importance and sticks to the definition of non-philosophy in so far as it is possible through its constituents. It is indeed a practice but a transcendental one (this is the theoretical aspect coming from philosophy). Practice here includes the theoretico-scientific aspect and does not correspond to the theoreticist concept of it (or if it does so only to a small degree). Thus the double aspect is indeed conserved but only for the instruments of non-philosophy. As for the Real = X, it limits the definitional possibility and demands a "non-definition."

This research allows and obliges us to give a new, more precise definition of non-philosophy, no longer as theory but, as it would seem in the first case, as *transcendental practice*. If it only treats practices in a wider sense, how would non-philosophy not be a practice? We have defined the practices, as a material substance of the thought-world, through *a ternary of procedures* + *a presupposed of ML/RO* distinct by various degrees from the ternary terms. Yet non-philosophy also defines itself globally by a ternary: 1. the material in two forms, in-itself or absolute and in-One; 2. the Real as transcendental identity of the clone; 3. the transformed *a priori* contents of the materials and a presupposed, the radical Real. Non-philosophy is then a practice, but a transcendental one, with the duality of a radical Real and a ternary formed from a material, from a transcendental essence with a production of a finished product which is the *a priori* or "mixture."

How is it then still a theory? If it combines philosophy and other practices, it should principally be a practice and secondly a theory. Having defined philosophizability as a practice that completes itself in theory in the form of a theoreticist appearance, it is by definition opposed to practice in the larger sense like theoreticism itself. Is non-philosophy then the unified practice of theory and practice? Or a theory determined in-the-last-practice? Or a theory determined in the mode of a practice of-the-last-instance?

A great misunderstanding in fact threatens non-philosophy, that of its spontaneous definition as a theory or even as a practice. It is neither one nor the other, of course, neither practical theory nor theoretical practice or "of" theory, but *a future thought or in-the-last-instance, determining a subject for the (non-) relation of theory and practice*. Two important points are found here: determination-in-the-last-lived-experience of some combination that we intend to test, and the composition of this combination. What combinations? Theory and practice are from this perspective a couple amongst others. Philosophically, sometimes one term is privileged and dominant, and sometimes another. This couple as well as its branches of theoreticism/practicism, such that they are in general thrown onto non-philosophy, are maladjusted, though not absolutely, but through their philosophical pretensions which are materials and are not determining of the "last" Future. Everything depends on their disposition within philosophical materials where they always come together and are only able to be isolated as artifacts serving to name a doctrine. But theory philosophically dominates practice, and so non-philosophy can be characterized according to materials as a theory but determined-in-the-last-Future and in any case includes practice. But it is also possible to call "practice" the cause of non-philosophy by privileging in this way unilateral duality. This is why we will define non-philosophy rather as *an immanent thought whose arrival determines-in-the-last-Humaneity or according-to-the-Future the (non-) relation of practice and theory*. Non-philosophy is thought made into an ultimatum.

OUTLINE FOR A NON-INSTITUTIONAL UTOPIA
L'ORGANISATION NON-PHILOSOPHIQUE INTERNATIONALE (ONPHI)

The A Priori Defense of Non-Philosophy

ONPHI can inscribe itself within a more general objective: the *a priori* defense of non-philosophy which comprises its theoretical framework, a formula that must not be understood in its common meaning as a fortress forbidding every approach and critiquing "on sight" every attempt to modify or to even interpret it. It is a defense by means of an *a priori* understanding which concerns it rather than an obsidianal reaction. *A priori* must be taken here in its philosophical sense rather than the banal sense of a "mechanism of defense," and in its non-philosophical rather than philosophical sense. A philosophy defends itself precisely by combining two styles, one of them being the anticipation of *a priori* arguments which are also added to the attacks, the other being the reaction or delayed action to arguments that have opposed philosophy. Non-philosophical defense brings these two styles together in a different way and for other ends. It is against the World globally and the Principle of Sufficient Philosophy rather than against this or that particular system or objection. And it brings them together within a unique style, that of the transcendental statement itself referring to an empirical material, but ultimately to an *a priori* content such that it is extracted from these empirical occasions.

Therefore, it is not clear that non-philosophy needs to attack certain doctrinal positions better and that its means of combat are here re-enforced towards that end; this is not its problem, which is more vast than its apparent conflicts with Plato, Hegel, or Nietzsche. Non-philosophical defense holds back the attack which it would become in a prolonged way simultaneously *a priori* and

151

a posteriori. The concept that dualyzes every strategy of the philosophical type is the *a priori* defense that forms itself according to occasions. Non-philosophy in one sense "takes the initiative," but not in the sense where it confiscates the space in front of the adversary in order for it to deploy its weapons. Non-philosophy brings its own "initiative;" it is an ultimatum in that it does not belong to the adversary. This is then no longer a preventative war designed to demonstrate its force, to intimidate its adversaries, nor to completely destroy its weapons of destruction before using them. Non-philosophy leaves them as the space of their deployment. This coming-to-the-front without being in front of …, without belonging to the opposite space, this is the key for *a priori* defense because it transforms the adversary. For non-philosophy, defending itself is not the only possible attack (the attack, if there is one, deduces itself from defense rather than the defense taking the attack as its cause), but more simply it is its mode of acting or its practice. This is still not about whatever defense is habitually grounded on the same type of weaponry and the same type of effect as those of the adversary.

Is it necessary for non-philosophy to be defended since by definition it is intended to leave only very weak traces within the philosophical sphere, perhaps like those that leave victims rather than heroes? Or Heretics rather than Masters? Or the indisputable, as much as inadmissible, traces of a Stranger who decidedly would not face the World except in so far as he would never be caught there in a face to face? And yet he does not complain of the tense indifference of the philosophical-professional public, an indifference which is necessary and in each case inevitable. Non-philosophy does not trace itself but lets itself be determined as trace in so far as this public resists it. It is engendered as its own intermediary without tempting the constituted philosophical schools, which non-philosophy cannot form, but by going to seek out that which lets itself be interpellated by it as subject-existent-Heretic. Moreover, does it make an oeuvre or simply a trace, or, neither making oeuvre nor trace, does it unveil a Utopian City of heretics, built with world-materials, which would fall from the Sky or come from the Earth?

Undoubtedly a defense against the silent misinterpretations and falsifications, against the return of philosophy, but why *a priori*? Is it a refusal to hear and to understand them? The formula of an *a priori* defense is susceptible to an immediate harmony which is easy but introduces certain misunderstandings that are those of self-defense. More profoundly, it is possible to outline the framework of possible misunderstandings, the *a priori* form of denials which is applicable for every possible objection of a philosophico-worldly origin. Consequently partially legitimating them since this *a priori* form is what introduces us to philosophical materials and deduces them from within its final conditions, materials at once transformed in an *a priori* of the non-philosophical style. Do we then refuse every critique as simply "exterior?" But there is no such exterior critique, even the "exterior" of non-philosophy (i.e. philosophical sufficiency) is posited and justified in so far as we have the means of showing its double character that is moreover consistent with transcendental hallucination and illusion. The defense against the critique here stands in for the first critique, its criticism and its contemporary forms. But if this is still a critique of the critique, the concept of critique must be unilaterally transformed in light of its identity within its status, its possibility and the extension of its domain.

A defense must be grounded on an instance that is more real than a simple *a priori*, which is insufficient within philosophy and still more so within non-philosophy. Only the transcendental is higher and more real than the *a priori* but on the condition that it no longer admits its idealism and posits it as a function assumed by the Real or Man-in-person himself who is not yet exhausted there. What we call the subject-existent-Stranger is the bearer of this rigorous defense, it is the transcendental subject engaged in the World but capable of bringing it out by extracting, in-the-last-Humaneity, from objections and resistances, their *a priori* form. A form that thus begins with resistance but above all does not reduce itself or complete itself in-the-Real-of-the-last-instance. It is impossible to name every process of extraction of this *a priori*, it is non-philosophy itself in action, but it is possible to condense it within this simple formula of "*a priori* defense." In other words, the non-philosophical subject is a defense or dis-alienation of itself under the conditions of its determination in-the-last-Humaneity.

In this way, through the force of its unilaterality, or its inexistence as assumed face to face, the subject defends himself with-and-against objections, certainly using them "against" themselves, but without contradiction or differentiation and instead as effects determined in-the-last-instance. It is not in a state of self-defense but takes its defense from the more real than the "self" assumed from a subject. The *a priori* defense of a subject is thus not really "of itself," it is an activity that possesses a reality and an autonomy, but only a relative one, and which does not then dissolve itself any longer within the all-philosophy (criticism, Nietzscheanism and still partly deconstruction).

The One('s)-Blow or Single-Edged-Blade

Provisionally resumed under a form analogous to that of psychoanalysis, though wider, the goal of non-philosophy is to evade the most devious traps of philosophical mastery and domination characteristic of other domains, while respecting the absolute necessity of "going through" it. In this task two qualities that only indirectly arise from syntax or technique are required of the non-philosophical apparatus: rigor and a cutting edge. But appreciation for their role can diverge according to the interpretations that appropriate this apparatus. ONPHI may be designed to give them the non-philosophy they would ordinarily lack, on the condition that it would avoid the risk of dispersing its identity within a multiplicity of interpretations that claims a supplement of authority.

Rigor is made up of insistence of respect for fundamental oraxioms, refining the technique and its distinctions, the sophistication of procedures. None of this is exceptional when it concerns grounding a theoretical discipline and determining a practice.

154

As these demands are here a little different from philosophical ones, they seem particularly difficult but stand in for the difficulty of comprehending the classical systems. On the other hand, as one odd half of non-philosophy, its real phase (One-in-One, Other-than …, Occasion) or Uni-laterality, is unapparent though determinate, it appears obscure and communicates its opacity and its strangeness in the set, which in effect has no equivalent but only resembles a wave within philosophy, as if non-philosophy were a huge joke[2] designed to amuse and deceive the philosophers. There is nothing formal about the rigor put into the analysis of "Philosophy" or with respect to the procedures of dualysis, it is transcendental and must render non-philosophy fertile, meaning it must eradicate the traps of philosophical appearance without claiming to eliminate philosophical appearance in the mode of philosophical absoluteness.

The strong or scrubbed minds of psychoanalysis retort that the refusal to be tricked is the surest sign of erring, without always seeing that it is necessary to recognize that there is no trap and leave philosophy in this state at the extreme end of its trickery. This is not knowing; if there is a philosophical hallucination that we worry about then it is this faith which accompanies it, and this naturally two-fold belief is the hallucination that does not know itself within the subject. It is not brute alienation that we are continuing, but the faith in this alienation, which comes to double it and re-enforce it.

Non-philosophy knows a rigor rather than an orthodoxy since it is no longer a doxa but the identically scientific-and-transcendental treatment of philosophical doxa. From the perspective of the first axiom, rigor is the demand of having to respect philosophy's being "devoid" of the Real as Other-than … philosophy, and which in this sense is a simple negative condition. But this rigor within the negative condition demands as a counter-result a rigor proper to the materials that must be reduced to its ultimate,

---

2. English in original.

minimal, and radical elements. The analysis of the third axiom, that of its materials, is fundamental in order to define the rigor of non-philosophy, but this rigor depends first on respecting the Real's uni-laterality.

What about the "cutting edge," a dangerous notion like "purism" and difficult to treat, but fundamental for debates over the signification of non-philosophy since, apparently, it is one of the objections that is made against it, that it lacks a "cutting edge" owing to its "liberalism." There may be several kinds of cutting edge that may come from diverse origins and which concern the kind of decision or cut proper to a discipline, to its dualities, to their acuity and irreducibility. In non-philosophy it is uni-laterality and unilateral duality that provide the cutting edge [*tranchant*] as a simple single-edged blade [*uni-tranchant*], under a form irreducible to every "discontinuity" and "heterogeneity," or even any "cut" and "alterity" known by philosophy. It is no longer concerned with "slicing into …" as required involuntarily by non-religious gnosis, but to land a blow of the One, the strike of the uni-lateral cutting edge. The non-philosophical kind of rigor excludes the unitary "cutting edge."

Since for rigor, the cutting edge is not a primary concern of the sole materials upon which we fixed its choice; rather it is that this choice overdetermines the unilateral Real and dulls its edge through presuppositions of the philosophical kind. Effectively, philosophy knows a certain unilaterality or asymmetry but as inclusive within a reversibility and not at all as first or determined in-Real. But this debate can be overdetermined by a certain religious and Platonizing thematic, through a gnostic need to be "decisive" [*trancher*] and following the dis-alienating struggle of the subject against the World, through a "hatred of the World" or a condemnation without an appeal that must be reconciled with a salvation of the World. Hatred, purity, a cutting edge [*tranchant*], this constellation shines in a bizarre way, as the ray of death in the occidental sky. It will give even more ground to an analysis that would raise the effect of a precipitated usage of non-philosophy according to the Platonic transcendence or chorismos. A furtive bilateral cutting edge, called upon to cut off [couper] intelligence or heads, can only have another definition than the transcendence of the blade. The "cut" of the Modernists, mathematics, Cartesian and above all Platonic, are of the same metal. For a long time it has been the case that the blade is double-sided, one materialist, the other idealist. The philosophy that is most aware of its own means was careful to blunt the razor's edge (of Ockham) by limiting the naked power of transcendence. But its recourse to immanence is in general too weak to do anything other than stipple the point. Unilateralize the duality; this is not to load transcendence to the point of excess, in the way of Plato, Neoplatonism or Levinas, nor is it to aggravate it, or even tone it down and make it tasteless, pulling the hood over it, but rather to order it according to radical immanence, or the Other-than ... by which Man-in-person holds himself separated from transcendence, only approaching it as a subject.

On ONPHI as Non-Institutional

What is it that distinguishes ONPHI such as it exists from any ordinary institution, association or organization, as in psychoanalysis, for example, to teach, authorize and sometimes finance an activity? An association regulating an intellectual activity is an institutional *a priori* device designed to organize and define its activities, its norms and instances of legitimization, and is inscribed within an international, political and geographical context. It is about "welcoming" to better "control," of "subsidizing" to better "manage," of "electing" or "co-opting" to better "select," altogether to interpolate homeless thoughts in order to constitute them in subjects of authoritarian instances and finally in the World.

Can we imagine a different kind of organization, one that would be composed of "heresies," heresies lived in-the-last-Humaneity? Of a constitution and coordination of subject-existing-Heretics? An organization that would no longer be an organization serving to control the possible deviance or no longer a disciplining force

157

for rendering them socially reproductive? Nor, inversely, to intensify these forms of deviance as if it were concerned with "illegalisms" capable of giving rise to new forms of knowing? Globally and seen from afar, non-philosophy is a lived but sober utopia and uchronia that tries to bring together the last forces of struggle still theoreticallly pertinent to the name-of-Man against the thought-world, with philosophy in the lead. It possesses a side which reflects the World and institutes itself on its model, for example, through a self-proclaimed decision of its existence and its direction; and also a "side" of radical utopia or defense that would immediately have to transform the worldly side, at least if the radical future is not merely contemplated but implemented.

Why in the Name separate from Man-in-person? Contrary to what passes for philosophy, the principle of determination of laws and rules must be disassociated from their application, this is their presupposed, for those who want to create a new kind of heresy, non-worldly heresies, those which, by explaining the World through what is specifically unintelligible, can only transform the World. The discourse on the disciplines and the Nietzschean cynicism that forms its base does not lead to a overall critique of the philosophy-world's authority but only leads to a better re-enforcing of it in a spirit of complicity. If transformative and liberatory heresies are possible (as much as they are necessary) they will eternally sin if they do not become actual. If they come into being, it will certainly not be in order to fill up a void deserted by philosophy folded back onto itself, freeing a space in order to better conserve and conform itself to its own tradition. Since philosophy has despaired of life by transforming it within a World, a World whose destiny we are constrained to follow, we proceed to exploit it and make "full use" of it in order to set up our heresies in their proper non-place(s), not in its place or within its functions.

So does it, then, concern a positive utopia, with determined but idealist contents, futurist and coercive dogmas and institutions? On the contrary, it is a "negative utopia," which is to say a utopia necessary to transform the World and its form-philosophy but without contents determined by an order as the Name-of-Man, or the "Unmanned" [*Inhomme*] on which it "grounds" itself in a sense like every other utopia, for it neither is nor has worldly, political or anthropological content. In its own way the Principle of Human Non-Sufficiency is what limits the exorbitant and dangerous pretensions of utopias that repeat the past and lead to authoritarian philosophical ends and worldly goals. Ours, which is as much uchronia as utopia, does not project any imaginary world of forced happiness ("we will force them to be happy"), but forces-without-forcing the World into its basic human salvation. Thus, from a future already dead we will make a tabula rasa. However, the problem is more complex if we approach the possibility of an ONPHI.

The Limits of a Non-Philosophical Organization

ONPHI has not claimed to modify the essence of non-philosophy, even though it is generally understood as a possibility *de jure*, without speaking of a permanent temptation, for a modification or even a subversion of that essence. It of course corresponds, but in a way more assured than in theory, to its material conditions of existence (in a similar way, moreover, to philosophy, which has some of the same such conditions), but it is of the same essence. Moreover, philosophy can also be treated as a practice which possesses a presupposed as well as material and institutional conditions, to such an extent, indeed, that they are also one of the objects of non-philosophy that must raise their philosophizable form and appearance. ONPHI is one part of the "aggregate" of these material conditions of pragmatics, in the manner of the seminary or the school, the publication and diffusion of which has non-philosophy as an object and which must be torn from their philosophizable form.

The fate of ONPHI then plays itself out not only in the clear position of its axioms, but practically speaking between philosophical subject and subject-"Strangers" which themselves close out these axioms. From this perspective, the auto-dualysis of the subject-inventor does not distinguish itself from those of the other subjects implied in the ONPHI-operation, even if these psychological conditions and worldly oddities have had to be re-assembled. In the work of its inventor and in his heritage, we cannot separate the discipline and the oeuvre. One such motive for separation is found in the modification of the theoretical status of the three "oraxioms" and the creation of a "new" non-philosophy rather than a new effectuation of it. The desire, moreover, to extract and isolate a common discipline must eventually realize itself but only on the condition of recognizing both its limits and its sense. Heresy is not at all a universal key, for there are normalizing heresies or ones that return to the sect. It is the philosophical confusion of the essence of non-philosophy as invention and of the invention of non-philosophy, which leads to the consequence of it supposedly being open in all directions. The uchronia of the Name-of-Man is then destined to be lost in the measure of its manifestation.

On the theoretical plane, meanwhile, ONPHI is not the re-foundation of non-philosophy, or even "other non-philosophies," but rather the power of inventing disciplines as "non." On the material plane, it develops its conditions of existence, since there are some, thus saving them from inevitable institutionalization, or at least makes sufficient use of them. The extension of its means of production, distribution and diffusion cannot serve to create new spaces but to gain new theoretical and practical subjects in its cause as it tries to be negatively universal. Concerning the varieties of non-philosophy, rather there must be variants or currents. These varieties must come from philosophizable materials, and naturally these materials are sometimes very far from philosophy, but nonetheless non-philosophy's variants come from philosophy that is not reduced to the state of materials. The initial reduction of the World and the exact comprehension of its power are decisive, as in phenomenology, and engage with divergent forms and "currents."

Of ONPHI as a Negative Utopia

The third axiom, that of philosophizability, apparently supports a multiplicity of interpretations that exhibit or dissimulate the extension and constitution of philosophy as materials, and also place it next to other disciplines. From our point of view, it confers maximal force and extension under the name of the thought-world as materials for a unified theory of the first rank. The thought-world, furthermore, sets in place two poles, that of philosophy or philosophizability itself and a practice = X, an exemplar of practicity which unifies and transforms them according to determination-in-the-last-instance.

The first of the transcendental axioms is that of the Real unilaterally determining language and thought. Both this axiom and the others are necessary so that an intellectual activity is recognized as "non-philosophy" without excessive pretension, even by the World or from the point of view of History. But everything that is necessary and determining on the basis of the first are never sufficient to give its reality and consistency to this activity. They are only assured the minimum of validity concerning its transcendental conditions for truth.

The first axiom, let us recall, only posits the presupposed of non-philosophy but is still not effectively non-philosophy. The Idea of a presupposed of thought is philosophically frequent, but it is then, as we know, a confusion of the presupposed with the famous "presuppositions" that are always susceptible to a reappropriation by the philosophy that posited them. It is necessary to distribute the real, reality and thought, syntax and semantics, altogether differently in order to recognize in the presupposed its irreducibility. If it eludes every enterprise of thought and must remain what it is, it is necessarily "negative" in this way, and it only determines thought within its being-real, syntax included, thus putting into play the second or mentioning it (without making further reference) but without being determined by it. The presupposed is not a dogmatic beginning (a semantics from which we will later deduce the syntax), but an identity of semantics and syntax.

161

Dogmatism and skepticism, and thus their most critical synthesis, are effects of the presupposition in the philosophical sense, the blend, that is, of the presupposition and the presupposed. Of course the non-sufficiency of the Real forms a system along with the duality-without-dualism of unilaterality, which assumes the explicit provision of a second term (already given-in-One anyway), that, namely, of the materials of so called instance-worlds, with their own consistency and objectivity, on which the presupposed exercises itself. ONPHI cannot then be in any ultimate way a construction upon unshakable foundations, built with the intention of lasting for eternity. The materials are quite considerably solid within this order, together with the Name-of-Man, which is of another order altogether.

Consequences: Limitation of the Non-Philosophical Struggle in all the World

ONPHI is thus not the armed or secular wing of non-philosophy. It is necessary that this organization not be made exterior or even interior to a doctrinal body that is itself closed; to exteriorize it as purely worldly means, tool or instrument, under threat of delivering theory to the rediscovered sufficiency of philosophy. Or to interiorize it in an assumed non-philosophical essence as its simple institutional aspect. Whether empirical or rational, experience of this kind is both exterior and interior to philosophy, but what there is of the empirical, or more exactly of the practical in ONPHI, cannot maintain this ambiguous double relation to theory. ONPHI is in its concept undoubtedly an organon or a subject in the sense intended by non-philosophy, meaning an organization-existent-Stranger. Stranger to the World of philosophy, but without maintaining with the thought-world a simple face to face relation susceptible to forming an opposition or contradiction, under the threat of stagnating in the worst, most "dialectical" way. Moreover, it is in its essence a practice, as is theory itself.

ONPHI thus aligns with the *a priori* defense of "theory." It is an added arm if we think that non-philosophy can borrow the channels of philosophy's communication and merely satisfy itself with deforming them, for it is not then directly necessary to its internal functioning or its structure. It is a necessary wing if it assumes its own channels of diffusion and a specific diffusion. Or we can assume, because of its material conditions, a certain stepping outside the theoretical sphere and entering into the World, which is not heavy artillery at all, always authoritarian, charged with intimidating the combatants and making them march together, "with synergy," or even of pushing them to the margins proper to non-philosophy, which is to say into nostalgia for philosophy. It is true that we are all nostalgic for old world thought and ready for commerce, but non-philosophy takes as its task to finally bring this re-appropriating to an end. In any case the statutes of ONPHI are no more "formal" or "institutional" than the axioms, but real-transcendentals although non-sufficient or not fixed on themselves, either analytically or synthetically or by some other combination, like the reality of the instances from which the arrangement is foreseen. In other words, we must distinguish amongst instances of ONPHI, those of the Real, which is only the last but necessary resort, and the other or properly called instances that are the subject's materials. ONPHI is not a positive instance of control or surveillance assumed to assure the sufficient reality of activities that are taken up, not a simple formal framework, but it is, however, just as positive and restrictive.

The Idea of ONPHI seems then to operate by jumping outside of "pure" theory into the World. This is not the case. This would be just a philosophical way of defining it and justifying/annulling its existence. ONPHI's problem, rather, is that of finding the minimum form and institutional realities compatible with this *a priori* defense, with a subject, that is, of the heretical and utopian kind, not within the World but with institutional elements in the world-form. It is the aspect of non-philosophy which takes account of its "reception" via the middle, in particular of its "inscription" in the same material and institutional givens of conjuncture, simply because these givens co-belong to the structure and life of philosophy. The Council of-the-last-instance, assumed "to enforce" the proper rigor of non-philosophy, is nothing more than the material and institutional aspect of the subject-Stranger which guards the fundamental axioms of non-philosophical utopia against the backwash of history and the enterprises of the World.

ONPHI is not an instrument of conquest in a rivalry with philosophies and sciences (on the contrary, non-philosophy hopes for their continued "development") so the only conquest that it can hope for is that of expressing itself through the usual channels but also by transforming them through this act, of expressing itself once each time, without repeating forms of knowledge already known or words already spoken, but because of the silent force of its axioms which still use the most known forms of knowledge and words already recorded on the disc of tradition. The phrases of non-philosophy remain strange and mute, voiceless and stupid before the intelligence of the World as long as some other dumb or deaf mute does not come along to transmit their secret unintelligibility to the others.

On ONPHI as Positive Utopia:
Extension of the Struggle in the World

Now can ONPHI also be a positive utopia in the space offered by the World? A forced insertion of a certain kind of heresy into the structure of auto-encompassing transcendence? A dangerous way, full of perils, for making heretics return to the proximity of the World? ONPHI does bring a supplementary dimension and some new means to this task. The set of these means and their effect exceeds the non-oeuvre or the oeuvre-existent-Stranger of which it has been a question, and now places itself "within" the World and must be evaluated from the perspectives at once of absolute autonomy and the relative autonomy of the World. To work in non-philosophy signifies also its inscription in the hallucinatory sufficiency of the common World and precisely as common or co-mmunity, and it is that work of insertion that can and must serve a similar organization.

It is thus necessary to distinguish between the World for Man-in-person and the World for the subject. It is only for the subject that one such extension or ex-sistence of struggle according to the World imposes itself.

This extension of non-philosophical struggle implies a qualitative change in that it attacks the worldly repression of heresy at the level of consciousness reflected in the World and must complicate its functioning. This extension is utilized by non-philosophy rather than by Man who only thinks ONPHI negatively, but it always risks reconstituting a new Earth or new Heaven within the World and giving rise to a philosophical interpretation of this repression and the struggle against it. It is inevitable and useful to go down, not to "go down again," but to go down for the first time into the Cave willingly or by the force of non-philosophy in order to trouble the good conscience of the World with heresy. This return to the Cave is no longer constitutive of Man, whom we would assume to be philosopher par excellence, as in Platonism and thus destined to inscribe himself within the World, not merely being separated from it and struggling against it via the subject. Platonizing philosophy returns, forced by vocation, we might say, within the World which Plato however only made an allusion to without taking it seriously — this is the entirety of philosophy. Man-in-person is radically independent from the World which only becomes a cause of the subject in an occasional way, a subject which takes it seriously, which forms there as a subject-Stranger more than as an allusion and can penetrate there in order to imprint his trace there, forming a kind of pedagogy of heresy.

The Two Aspects of Struggle: Stranger in the Cave

An "organization" is particularly paradoxical if it is concerned with non-philosophical heresies as lived utopias. This could be a way of making heresies return to the World, or in any case of obliging them to be in the perilous company of "Mastery." While the worldly and non-worldly senses of this ONPHI are not elucidated and this enterprise is simply brought back to utopian imagination in general (that which is tangled up with the history-world), ONPHI is an overly anticipated contradiction and a nest of aporias. It is necessary to begin to distinguish the two readings of the non-philosophical effect, of specifying them according to a statute attached to the resistance to the World, which is also a double statute according to what we consider the real subject or the subject-in-the-world [*sujet-en-monde*].

The first reading accepts that PSP is raised first by the human Real, that it forms itself strictly in-immanence; this is the first phase of utopia, its being-forced-without-forcing, utopia as negative tabula rasa. The altogether "negative" causality of Man-in-person does not put itself to work or trace itself but in-the-last-instance determines the subject constituting itself as Stranger-to-the-World. If philosophy disposes of these two concepts, work and trace, in order to speak of the effect, then non-philosophy neither determines effect as work nor as trace as the sufficient product, for example, through the insistent blacking out of this oeuvre, where it would still concern an adequate entity in the World, a relay of resistance which would not at all be a stranger to it. Non-oeuvre, which in its essence is the subject-Stranger, is not strange in all of its resistance because it uses the World in order to de-present itself radically through its unifacial structure (a structure also known as a "clone" or unilateral duality) but not through a "sufficient trace." The practice of the subject-Heretic can only leave a trace (albeit negative or non-sufficient by its cause) if resistance makes a return as Humaneity produced by this dis-alienation. The second reading forms itself under the hypothesis of the PSP, which is always acting initially for the subject (but not for Man) and which sustains this utopia through an attempt to reflect it in a consciousness, or better still, in a thought-world where the subject locks itself up as in-World. Let us then distinguish the City of Nowhere, which is only determining in a radical manner, and the effect of the trace or work which it frees in the person of the subject within the complex of the thought-world, meaning "in the eyes of the World." This is the same utopia, for these two phases are identical in-the-last-Humaneity. So it completes itself within the constitution of the subject as autonomous activity, within a Utopia of Strangers or a City of Heretics which for its part is then neither of Heaven nor of Earth but simply non-philosophical practice itself. Even outside the character of this organization (as conforming with the style of non-philosophy), all it can do is protect the insistence of this kind of trace in the interior of the World and for it, rousing philosophical resistance in order to make it somehow "conscious" of itself and to make it work on itself.

So it is that the Stranger makes a return to the Cave without engaging in his destiny as Man, as is the case in Plato. The process is inverted in relation to the return of Platonic philosophy. It stays at first in the Cave, by leaving and returning there through operations of forcing ex machina, completing a perfect circle with the nearest Good. But the non-philosopher did not start off in the Cave of the World, even if he has unceasingly been thrown there, just sufficiently long enough in order to draw from the Cave the materials needed to constitute his existence. He has been "in-Man" for all the eternity of the Future and exercises himself as "force-(of)-void" even to the World so as to finally produce himself as a subject. Immanence is a radical "law" that we must follow and it implies the initial raising of resistance, so utopia is not for us a promise but immediately accorded. Thus if there must be a resistance, it is utopia that will return, or will arrive for the first time, it is the Cave as resistance which would make a "return" and not the non-philosopher. Utopia is not primary, but it has primacy over the World. As a matter of course, just as Man-in-Man is (that) who comes once each time to the subject-Stranger, the Cave also comes to the subject in the same way. The phenomenal content of the Platonic return to the Cave is that there has never been a return but an arrival, one time every time.

Resistance is not first in the constitutive or determinate sense, it is not even second in relation to being-in-Man, but cannot come, if it must be considered for the first time, except under the primacy of the Real, a primacy which has been suspended, separated from itself without destroying it. On the other hand the subject integrates this phase with the transcendental phase that he constitutes, and it is the subject that renders this resistance effective and makes it happen for the first time, as resistance not with regard to the Real but only with regard to the subject and in some sense adapted to him who is capable of fighting against it. It is in this way and for the subject alone that resistance makes a return, but a return once each time, a return as happening, so the Cave "returns" rather than the non-philosopher returning to it.

Thus this concludes the positive sense of the provocation of the kind of subject that is ONPHI designed to maintain resistance to the World and sowing the spirit of heresy amidst contempt and scandal. This is the way that non-philosophy and ONPHI may become positive utopias, but contingent to the extent that even the arrival of the Cave must be re-included into the unilateral immanence of the Real.

ONPHI as the Modeling of Non-Philosophy through Philosophical Resistance

It is necessary to combine several dimensions in order for the resistance of ONPHI with itself to start working. We can envisage that, from the perspective of its positive side, it is an organizational modeling possible for non-philosophy within the conditions of the World. But the concept is extraordinarily complex and, unable to follow the analysis here, we limit ourselves to a few indications.

Without being formal, the non-philosophical oraxiomatic allows for particular interpretations of "models" that make it concrete under the general conditions of philosophical system-Worlds. Strictly speaking, non-philosophy is rationally incomprehensible within its presupposed but can be rendered philosophically intelligible through its modeling, certainly here an objective appearance. For its own constitution non-philosophy uses an effect of meta-language: philosophy, which, since it is not reduced (with the preceding reservations and complications) to an occasion or materials, can, as appearance, serve as non-philosophy's mirror.

"Positive" ONPHI would not create a modeling of philosophy with a view towards non-philosophy but of the former by the latter. The meaning of ONPHI may itself be understood in this way as an effect of axiomatization and may only be a semblance of the return to the World.

The modeling must form itself within the conditions of resistance. These models can only make resistance appear if the conditions of departure (under which they make non-philosophy appear for the subject, still not the World reduced or given in-One as occasion) are assumed as an absolute autonomy or in-itself but yet still under the ultimate primacy of the Real. ONPHI in this way highlights the concrete place of resistance.

Non-philosophy not only puts into play the practice of external communication but also the practices of internal communication and writing. These are practices in the sense that non-philosophy has defined them, as non-specular presupposed, without any face to face with philosophizability. Thus now it is according to a primacy of practice over the theoreticism of philosophizability that we must elaborate the concept of ONPHI. The complexity of the problem is contained within what we must transform, namely the materials-practice of communication and its usage, and transforming them through the mode of a unified theory, except that here it is precisely to pit against non-philosophy once again a brute new practice. In every way the material of non-philosophy is always the duality of two sides but in the form which posits the primacy of practice over theoreticism (Ideology/Production, Specular/Operative, Philosophizability/Science, all these correlations and contradictions direct the same invariant of the thought-world without saying the same thing).

In other words, ONPHI must be a way of modeling on the basis of the operative practice of philosophizability's communication and appearance. It is not about the modeling of non-philosophy or about giving a practical and communicational interpretation but of modeling philosophizability on the identity of community and philosophy, of the operative and philosophizability, through a radical transcendental communication, which is to say by giving non-philosophy a communicational and working version rather than giving it a simple cloak of this kind. Does it concern a unified theory of philosophy and communication? That would assume the materials of a philosophy of communication. Or even a brute or worldly practice of non-philosophy? No, rather at best a communicational modeling of philosophy (including communication), under a regime that is itself non-philosophical, but assumed as directly applicable to the thought-world or directly able to be thrown into the World. This communicational modeling may serve as an intermediary between the non-philosophical bound to the regime of philosophical primacy of theory and the communicational order of the World. This theory-modeling is the subject which exists-Stranger to All-communication.

However this doctrinal mundanity must still inscribe itself within the legitimacy of last-Humaneity. If the World is still presupposed here and may only be in this manner explicating one such project, it is a World which records the non-philosophical effect and which no longer precedes it, in some way gathering, like a mirror, the signs of this effect. ONPHI is the universal model (it has particular modalities according to philosophical systems) which interprets (in a more axiomatic than philosophical sense) non-philosophical axiomatization.

What can we expect from the operation of this "Organization?" Certainly not a useless and dangerous institutionalization of non-philosophy. Moreover ONPHI must exclude every so-called "democratic" vote, predicting on the contrary its auto-dissolution and fixing itself within the limits of time, here still with a precaution and always in the same spirit of vigilance. There is a double benefit, first, the evident coherence of non-philosophical axioms, demonstrated by the possibility of constructing a model or an example of this axiomatic; second, the benefit of proving a certain fecundity. However, this would be to confuse the real-transcendental axiomatic with a realization of philosophy that considers this double effect sufficient in order to demonstrate the validity of non-philosophy. Its true validity is determined in-the-last-Humaneity rather than by its criteria of formal coherence and verification through the construction of interpretative models. It is also through this contingency of empirical interpretation that ONPHI must not be considered as the armed wing of non-philosophy and cannot be taken as its form or its pre-destined institutional nature. Naturally, there will perhaps be a combinatory explosion of the types of non-philosophical theories and enterprises, each unified theory, for example that of philosophy and art, may give rise to an "interpretation" that would come to engender a universal model of that unified theory and sub-models according to this art or that practice. One such explosion of possibilities is not able to be assumed by a single (Heretical-) subject, but can be assumed by their multitude of principles. An organization must understand itself through the subject and limit itself to the organon of which it is the occasional condition or its institutional existence.

From the Encyclopedia to the
International Organization of Heresies

Every philosophical system realizes itself as an explicitly unitary (Hegel) or multiple (Nietzsche) encyclopedia, under an empirical form (Aristotle) or a formal one, for example as an Idea of a system of faculties (Kant). This finality, inevitable as soon as it concerns the encompassing circle of philosophizability, is within non-philosophy without an object, a non-philosophy that by definition reconsiders [*remet en cause*] the constitutive character and even simple regulator of the philosophical system, and displaces it as materials susceptible through itself to hallucination and transcendental illusion. The theme of transcendental appearance is transformed and extended in every possible encyclopedia.

That which we propose to substitute for the encyclopedia but which is quite a different thing, is thus this idea of ONPHI (under certain minimal conditions, within the effectuation rather than the interpretation of the elementary axioms of non-philosophy). Non-philosophy cannot form an encompassing sphere of self and its sub-disciplines, since it necessarily exists in a unilateral way "to the exterior" of itself, in the form of a relative autonomy of its objects and instances, articulated under the regions-materials which form the World's content and which are the actual "philosophical" practices rather than its objects. It is grounded on a maximum of immanence without empirical contents but this is radical since it is (if we can put it this way) the sole contents of itself, and founded on a maximum of transcendence of its philosophical or worldly contents. But these two "maxima" are articulated within a unilateral duality. The principle of the encyclopedia is that the relative autonomy of its object is finally measured by the absolute of philosophy's essence which dissolves this provisional autonomy. The principle of ONPHI is the radical relative autonomy of its objects, in the sense that the relative-absolute autonomy that gives them the philosophy in which they are dissolved, is in its way radically relative, the radical opposing itself to the absolute as much as to the relativity that the absolute tolerates. This opposition of the radical relative to the absolute relative opens the theoretical possibility of a non-hierarchical organization of non-philosophical activities, a field of possibilities that the spontaneous practice of philosophy has concealed.

The general form of these disciplines is what we call the unified theory of philosophy and practices or forms of knowledge, for example philosophy and science, or art or ethics. It assumes, as discussed in a preceding chapter, an autonomous theory of practices and that which distinguishes them from philosophy.

THE RIGHT AND LEFT OF NON-PHILOSOPHY

Topology and Utopia

We will try to make a quick comparison of topology and utopia, not as they are in-themselves but in the interior of non-philosophy.

An attempt at a first classification of "non-philosophers" is required by ONPHI, in order to compose a picture they form. One such clarification is also a response to certain recurring objections about the meaning of non-philosophy coming from the only explicit and fertile objections made openly about non-philosophy and which have sparked some theoretical revisions by those who have tried to share this problematic. The series of discussions that have accompanied the constitution of its theoretical corpus take the form here of a topology of positions which can voluntarily represent this discipline or sometimes fight for this discipline with their bodies, or rather what some of them have a tendency of projecting as a new discipline. Those who make use of non-philosophy find themselves arranged on a map of its possible blendings with philosophy, according to their radicality within the exclusion of the doctrinal forms of philosophy and within its usage as material.

The theoretical status of this classification and topological organization is itself problematic, for it demands the elucidation of its possibility and its limits. It nonetheless remains that the Idea of non-philosophy (often poorly understood partly due to the tentativeness of its elaboration and to each new exploitation clinging onto one of its stages or moments) is a nebula which exists and always propagates itself from individual researcher to thinker, never conquering pre-formed groups on the basis of a philosophy.

To the extent that philosophy is made hierarchical by its in-equalities, but is also auto-encompassing and unified, it knows of mirror phenomena or symmetries. It is likely that it allows for a topology of its positions in relation to one axis, which is the line of demarcation that it always begins by tracing. Undoubt-edly a line finally enveloped in itself or an auto-enveloped cut, it functions as an axis which distributes the positions and doctrines symmetrically, in an unstable and labile way, but there it is rightly a transcendental topology and not a structural one. On the other hand, non-philosophy functions according to a grand principle or "logic," that of uni-laterality and not bilaterality. It does not know the symmetrical positions through itself because in any case it rightly excludes every specularity and reversibility and in gen-eral every topology. Why speak then of a right and a left of non-philosophy, yet never of the center or the middle, for does it not trace this line of demarcation in order to subsequently reabsorb it? All the apparently neighboring positions, which have a fam-ily resemblance with non-philosophy and which demand certain principles or even simply a "free use," have been arranged also on the vector that joins the One-in-One to philosophy. But this vec-tor is cloned in-One and thus is uni-rectional rather than di- or bi-rectional. All these uses of non-philosophy are necessarily laid out on this uni-vector, because they are all considered primarily as a material reducible to philosophy. None can claim to get beyond, exceed or leave this vector, if non-philosophy is at least rigorous and adequate in its concept. But if this vector prohibits for itself every topology assumed to be constitutive of the Real, then it tol-erates the objective appearance of a topology since it is in any case conveyed by philosophical materials and material itself. Without non-philosophy really being in the center or the middle and not being an orthodoxy in relation to some heterodox position, which would precisely be a philosophical situation, non-philosophy ar-ranges schematically symmetrical positions from within this ap-pearance.

But then why is it mixed up in this affair? Because through an aspect of itself it necessarily falls into the objective appearance that creates the philosophy that contemplates it. The topology of non-philosophy owes its necessity to a reaction like resistance to immanent practice and only has meaning for the philosophers that we all are and who fall into the Cave. This topological appearance is not false, it is even "true" but its truth is complex, assuming the perspective of philosophical resistance despite or because of the exercise of non-philosophy. As philosophy remains for itself that which it is, its representation of non-philosophy also survives it. This appearance, philosophical in origin, is in every way objectively hallucinatory, or else the philosophical hallucination projects an appearance well-grounded in topology. To such an extent that unilaterality excludes every topology as constitutive by reconstituting itself as a topology around non-philosophy under philosophical pressure.

Radicality excludes centrism in every sense of the term, the happy and Greek middle between symmetrical positions. But also linearity, for example, such as we understand it in Descartes as an order of reasons. It combines the primacy that determines priority itself, and the priority or beginning, being radical also, of thought. Everything happens in-Real but is exchanged in non-philosophy or according to the Real. In relation to Platonic disparity as uni-laterality through transcendence, the radicality of uni-laterality through immanence gives the impression of both rightness and justice [de la justesse et de la justice]. These two postures, which surround non-philosophy, and these two divisions together compose a renormalization, a justice which returns non-philosophy to philosophy.

We will display a little more concretely a sample of this topological appearance using the case of neighboring doctrines of non-philosophy, for either they have preceded non-philosophy historically, as with Saint Michel's philosophy of auto-affectivity and Life, or they are contemporary with it, as with the philosophy of the pure mathematical multiple of Saint Alain, or they have even accompanied and followed non-philosophy as with the non-religious gnosis of Saint Gilles. This topology of contemporary philosophy, at least the most inventive, is a weak equivalent of the Transcendental Dialectic exposed by Kant in the Critique of Pure Reason, a dialectic which is hardly any longer adapted to the style of contemporary philosophy, more topological than straight-forwardly [*linéairement*] dialectical or antithetical. Or it is still an equivalent to the Holy Family of Marx and Engels. We will show that these philosophers, unlike Lacan, ignore every structural topology (even in reduced form as we have proposed it), because as "philosophers" they have wrapped topology up into itself within its own appearance. They do not at all have the same reasons that non-philosophy does for refusing topology. They have denied it altogether in presupposing it, while non-philosophy has the means to allow it but suspends it as secondary, as a relative autonomy of appearance. For example, Saint Gilles thinks an "absolute" in the name of religion (or non-religion) and identifies the doctrines thereof within "mastery" in the name of an overly exclusive transcendent Platonism, simply balanced by a symmetrical immanence which has not been elucidated within its structure and its primacy over transcendence. From there all the doctrinal positions, and even non-philosophy itself, are rejected by an Absolute Rebel on the single rule of non-religious gnosis. Non-philosophy may even be a deviation from gnosis.... It is true that we ourselves have posited that Saint Michel is a deviation of non-philosophy, though one that has preceded it. Gnosis possesses a unique non-topological hand and, because of this ... packs somewhat of a wallop, for this is the way that "theoreticism" exists as a practice. There are no theories to the left of this gnosis; it does not have a left hand precisely because it refuses the practice which divides theory sometimes to the right, sometimes to the left. Does a unique hand make man? Is it not the phantom hand of the Absolute rather than the pair of hands that still belongs to who is in-Man? Regarding the auto-affection of Life by Saint Michel, being found only to its left where other neighboring thoughts have

176

tossed it, it too has one hand but it is not the same. It is impossible to reconstitute a man-in-One with these two halves. Philosophy has never been a body, a human body, that is.

The game of deviations and normalizations is infinite and specular. Non-philosophy has never found the principle of some decidability regarding the relations of the Real and philosophy, but has instead discovered the determinate identity in-the-last-instance of the decidability and undecidability of these relations. This is why it is neither the normalization of an anterior "deviation" nor a deviation in relation to a norm or general thought which non-religious gnosis would be, for non-philosophy downgrades these two antithetical positions and throws them back to a non-controlled philosophical cause, an objective appearance.

Insufficiency of the Preliminary Analyses of Philosophy

It is curious, though undoubtedly significant, that the positions of right and left in relation to non-philosophy form a truncated analysis of philosophy, either as simple specularity, or as unity-of-contraries, each time deprived of the principal piece, the unity which closes the two into a system. The position of Saint Michel is here a decision, and this is clear from the beginning. The philosophy of Life as immanent auto-affection draws an overly simple picture from philosophy, that of the dyad of the real and ideal but deprived of its unity which is both immanent and transcendent. The unity of contraries is an empty phrase, for it is reduced to the duality of terms without which their unity receives some value or significance, whereas it is the philosophically dominant piece. Here we find already an abstract and truncated image of philosophy, deprived of its concrete and amphibological dimension. It is perhaps possible, but only once it has been given-in-One, and certainly not posited from the start as the most sprawling concept of philosophy. The thought of Saint Michel is a philosophy of immanence as presupposition, not as presupposed. A presupposed may not take place immediately within philosophical materiality in order to amputate it under the pretext of reducing it. As far as the sufficient specularity that strives under the name of "mastery" is concerned, that of the non-religious gnosis of Saint Gilles, it oscillates from one extreme to the other: on the one hand, it lacks a superior unity of system, and confides in the dual and imaginary specularity, whereas philosophy itself is Trinitarian, although not merely in the manner of the symbolic. On the other hand, it off-sets this intra-philosophical duality through the effective appeal to its only dimension of real or epekeinaphysical transcendence as one of the terms of this duality. It abandons the form-system of philosophy in favor of "oriental philosophy." The philosophy achieved is tantamount instead to ambivalent identity and not separation, or indeed the flat identification of these functions of unity. It is easy to prefer religion to philosophy if we have already begun with a religious reduction of philosophy.

In the second case the All of philosophy is not given imme-diately as an object of theory but arrives in pieces or by aspects according to still intra-philosophical needs. The philosophy of Life combats only the "Greek presuppositions" of philosophy and above all in philosophy, being the only base dyad or the only meta-physical dimension. Within philosophy the gnostic only combats and transforms the epekeina-physical dimension alone. Both divide the All-(of)-philosophy, limiting from the start the range of its enterprise and so their entire range as well. In each case philosophy returns, in the one with the primacy of the tran-scendental off-set by divine auto-generation, and in the other with the Platonic transcendental stowed on the exterior of the non-philosophical Real.

The two foundational terms which are lacking a third in the philosophy of Life, the two terms of specularity or the dyad of mastery and rebellion within gnosis, represent two deficient analy-ses or limits of philosophy. The reduction of philosophy to two imaginary terms (to which Lacan would add the third of the sym-bolic then the fourth of the Real, progressively knotting them and doing so certainly within immanence but always as chorismos or exteriority) render the struggle against it impossible, for this struggle

178

has not been recognized in the structure of its most enveloping thought-world. Emasculating philosophy as imaginary makes the task easier but must be confronted with its return in the form of the sufficiency of a theological or philosophical "absolute." They are vestiges [*survivances*] of intra-philosophical decoupages. If there is a problem of survival [*survivances*] it is that of the philosophy or mastery which survives itself in every attack. The "radical immanence" invoked is then a wasted effort, like a sword stabbing water, and this is no way to break the mirror of philosophy.

The Four Discourses of the One: Utopian Topology of Unilaterality

Schematically, the unilateral trinity of the Rebel (Saint Gilles) is a return of insufficiently analyzed philosophy or religion and it is not sufficient to add the hat of the Real without profoundly transforming the syntax of onto-theo-logy, without elucidating the relations of the Real and the transcendental within a Neoplatonic frame. Opposing the philosophy of Life we find an overwriting of transcendence deprived of autonomy over the One assumed immediately immanent, a refusal of the Logos to the benefit of the words of the Gospel. Non-philosophy takes into account philosophy as a forced hand, rather than as a religion, and of the One-in-One as the necessary-negative condition of the recourse to whatever card is played. It holds the middle ground between the extremes of the religious which, from its perspective, think in an abstract way. Life itself gives the One rather than the thought-according-to-the-One, the Rebel himself gives religion-according-to-the-One rather than philosophy, the Stranger himself gives philosophy-according-to-the-One.

Uni-laterality will thus be declined under four principal modes, according to the degree of radicality of its immanent cause or of its exclusion from every relation of convertibility.

At one of the extremes, the trinity or better still the quaternity of philosophy can contain unilaterality but as co-extensive with reciprocity, out of which reversibility is omni-encompassing.

179

This is the standard contemporary model completed by philosophy, specifically by Nietzsche and Deleuze, though with some gaps continuing to spread, namely with Heidegger and Derrida, all the way to the most distant pole of this model, (though it is always more akin to transcendence) with Levinas.

At the other extreme, we have non-philosophy, (the one most opposed to the preceding example) in which the One can be called uni-lateral (duality also follows in the transcendental mode), since the duality of the One and the reciprocity of the World is real or given in-One only by the immanence of the One. And so the duality of the World with the One is in-the-last-identity or transcendental, and the being-given of the World is the unique face or unique Stranger to reciprocity or to the World assumed as sufficient. This is the discourse of non-philosophy. In actuality, these two positions are located less at the extremes than they are articulated within a unilateral duality. This is why the topological disposition begins here.

To the right of non-philosophy, the One can be unilateral in the transcendental sense where it is posited in relation to the exclusion of reciprocity, and so it is unwillingly impregnated by a reciprocity that it makes interior or by a World that it refuses. This explains its definition as having a final transcendental relation to the World. This is the philosophy of the auto-affection of Life or the Transcendental Ego, an acosmic Christianity.

To the left of non-philosophy, the Trinity as structure of thought can be unilateralized in this way, the three terms form two unilateral dualities, "oriental" cousins or neighbors of the Christian Trinity. This is non-religious gnosis, dualities of the One and the Transcendental Rebel, of the One and the Angel or of the Rebel and the Angel.

From there four figures of discourse define themselves in relation to philosophy as a sphere of reversibility. 1. The philosopher or the Master is complacent in the World and is himself a World, as One he can only withdraw from the World or supersede it in order to better re-institute it, he loves the World from the World;

2. The Stranger in-struggle with the World identifies in-the-last-instance struggle and the World, he is that clone of being-in-struggle-with-the-World; 3. Life is the refusal and contempt for the World, for as a One life is immediate negation of the World which remains as a gaping wound in its side, and in this way Life distinguishes itself from the World that it does not want to know; 4. The Rebel is in-hatred of the World, for as One he is superposed with the transcendence of the World, with the Trinity or Quaternity, and he thus hates the World with the means of the World.

These four figures are in reality dependent on the One which lets itself be penetrated to various degrees by the World and is not happy with giving the World a future or a utopian way. Philosophy, Life, the Rebel, they have in common not so much bearing a relation to the World in general as they do in not having preliminarily defined or reduced its sufficiency, which is to say the World's own belief in its being in-itself, being assumed real or independent from the One-in-One. The World can only be determined in-the-last-instance if it is already given in-One or in the "future" mode of the One, being in a non-relation which is not simply "of struggle" but which is "in-struggle" or "in-an-identity-(of)-struggle." The World's sufficiency must already be suspended in a real way (this is real indifference that does not exclude the World, which on the contrary, assumes it, but which is only an indifference to its sufficiency, or Other-than it) in order that it be or can be taken into account, in any case despite the One within which we think. Struggle then becomes a transcendental function that is the essence of the Stranger-subject. Thus the One is so immanent that the World or auto-position of transcendence (their identity) is as well, or is immediately deprived of its sufficiency. Thus the World can intervene on its behalf without contradiction with the One thus calling it to a transcendental function. The causality of the One does not overcome nor render useless that of the World which protects its relative autonomy without nonetheless being still determinate but merely occasional. Immanence must be protected along the chain of deduction, under threat of being definitively lost and put in the service of transcendence. From the start its blending with transcendence is interrupted for its benefit, the one and the other cease to be dominant on a rotating basis according to the philosophies. And immanence is nothing more than determining without ever having been dominant. The One-in-person is only granted to the other figures through bits of immanence and thus through the primacy of immanence over transcendence.

What does it then mean to say this maxim: treat immanence in an immanent way? It is not a question of an immediate auto-application of immanence, which would exclude every discourse and even the cry of the mystics. Transcendence remains a necessary means. On the other hand it no longer concerns surreptitiously utilizing transcendence either as auto-positional or as operative presupposition of it, but only a non-thetic transcendence (of) itself within its essence. There will always be transcendence and at best it can be used as non-thetic in-the-last-instance in order to deal with immanence. Rightly, the last-instance signifies that in spite of the necessary introduction of transcendence by and within thought, it keeps an immanent essence and the One continues in being determinate. In a more banal way, non-philosophy's discourse, by definition so as to use the means of philosophy, is put to use under the conditions of radical immanence. It is the One-in-One that uses the Logos, it is not the Logos that uses the One as within philosophy. It is thus no longer possible to juxtapose (though maybe without wanting it, but philosophy wants it anyhow) a discourse of subject and object with a doctrinal position. Taking such a position inside of immanence becomes a simple contemplated theoretical object, which resides at the basis of the blendings of non-philosophy and religion, either Christianity (Life), or gnosis (the Rebel), or even Judaism (Deconstruction).

Parricide: Or How Saint Gilles Rectifies
Non-Philosophy with the Sword

Saint Gilles is an excellent example of a leftist normalization. He supports certain positions (theoreticism) assumed to be non-philosophical but which we contest because of their Platonist orientation in the way gnosis is used from the perspective of a rigorous non-religion. It is problematic and opposed to the spirit of non-philosophy within its argumentation, its intentions, and its effects. The non-religion that he developed is just a new orientation (we will soon understand the orientalizing reasons for this). How does non-religious gnosis orient itself within ONPHI? Recall that what will inevitably be suggested is that non-philosophy will be an occidentalization, so the matter becomes how to occident it, rather than orient it, within thought? It is not clear that the problem of ONPHI, or more widely that of non-philosophy, is that of its orientation. We can divide the space of non-philosophy's materials but not the undivided cause of its usage, several "non-philosophies" may not exist (in the literal sense of the uni-lateral — uni-literal?). In the case of Saint Gilles we will therefore critique the major confusion between the effectuations and interpretations of non-philosophy's axioms. We will look closely to see if this caution is a new orthodox-esque closure, or if on the contrary the strict respect for non-philosophy's style is not the very means that it uses to liberate itself as much as possible from the chains of philosophy as a superior doxa in order to better detach itself from the religious chains.

The context of Saint Gilles' interventions, barely metaphorical in his mind, is that of the war with and in favor of the World, and so too with the University. Included there is a war on the same model, but this time with and in favor of non-philosophy. Under what form? In the philosophical and psychoanalytic traditions there is no other name except "parricide" for the kind of gesture that he has made. The term suits a Platonist. For there to have been a parricide, there must still have been a father. But in reality it is parricide that, in this tradition, constitutes the father or else enjoys giving itself a father. We assume this function, being designated as such haphazardly and leaving us to ask ourselves in what way the proper name of an inventor can still be attached to non-philosophy. A symbolic operation in every sense of the term, the parricide of profit, it allows a reduced doctrinal heritage to subsist (non-philosophy is only worth the "discovery" of the Real) but utilizable and above all better utilized by him than by the Father who did not know how to make his money grow, and at least a doctrinal authority is left vacant and so it becomes possible to re-assume it. Who will be the new leader of the non-philosophical phratry, he who has devoted himself to the tasks of the theoretical order, understood well, and who is even a "theoreticist?" In this order, does he unify the horde of non-philosopher brothers (and sisters?) by the war of all against all or everyone against everyone? Therefore railing against a certain pacifism, and still more detestable for him, an assumed soft liberalism of non-philosophy. From now on the old dictatorship of the proletariat will be carried out by Christ with the Sword in the name of the people.… But separately from the unconditional refusal (anti-Hegelian) of war as situated within the Real of the Last Instance, for we see nothing like liberal pacifism in non-philosophy, meaning specifically within the subject defined as "in-struggle." Who would serve in the struggle if it was one of liberalism rather than one of liberation, if not of dis-alienation from the World as such? Non-philosophy also makes use of gnosis but this use does not have a double in the Nouveaux Philosophes or in what remains "proletarian" in our author. Gnosis par excellence belongs not to a doctrine (hence the problematic character of the usage of unique materials) and the heresy allowed by it cannot serve to identify (in the ordinary sense of the word) a thought or an individual, a new holy family. Gnosis is rather a factor or an exponent of philosophical material, the "yeast" [*levain*] or the "salt," closing down what must "raise" [lever] struggle and does so by fomenting a rebellion. Regarding the conclusion of this discussion, it may be that only non-philosophy can practice the parricide that gnosis esteems (in a certain impossible

184

or hallucinatory way) within its concept, knowing for a Father only Man rather than God, and of crime only that of the subject-in-the-world against another. With Saint Gilles we are here on an already known terrain which we will continue to call "Platonic." There is also much of Platonism within non-philosophy, although no more, perhaps, than in any other philosophy, if only because Plato is the herald of a divine philosophy or the principal adversary of "human philosophy," the first in a long theoretical march of which Hegel and Nietzsche brought up the rear.

Saint Gilles' argument takes place in three moments, which will surprise no one.

a. The apparent general goal is the breaking up of ONPHI (as cause and destination of texts) because like the risk of every official doctrine, non-philosophy risks being an "orthodoxy." For he reduces non-philosophy to an interest in a simple discovery, that of the Real, an innocent discovery moreover, as if one beautiful morning the non-philosopher laid his hand on an unexpected treasure and so must have been confused and a little undeserving. Even the proper name of its "inventor" is only hinted at so as to be placed between parentheses. In this way, deprived of an author and more profoundly of philosophical contingency, non-philosophy is reduced to three relatively formal and neutralized axioms, as a management tool or catch-all. Against the all too famous risk of "orthodoxy" — a true head of Medusa, which the non-philosopher jokes about being scared of — Saint Gilles poses the equivalency of interpretations on the basis of a Real that has become abstract, an empty shell and skeleton key, and moreover for which language has become indifferent. If it is the Real, it is not in its naming within non-philosophy, and if the Real is fore-closed to the name of "Laruelle," then its naming is not. Even the discoveries of mathematicians and physicists, as well as psycho-analysts ("be a Lacanian if you want, I am a Freudian" — Lacan), have proper names. Not to mention the names of philosophers since the System of Absolute Knowledge carries the name of Hegel as well. It is pointless to say that we believe very little in the Idea

185

of an isolated non-philosophy as a neutral theoretical discipline opposed to personal work — all of that is imaginary — and we do not wish to say that it does not have a theoretical-disciplinary aspect to develop. It is on the basis of this formalism that we authorize ourselves to posit the equivalence of various possible and rival "non-philosophies."

b. But this ultimately formal peace was only a scrap of paper, because everything reverses itself and this reduction of the assumed non-philosophical sufficiency was only the preparatory operation that would allow another interpretation of the Real to slip under this name, that of non-religion. We have sufficiently denounced the peek-a-boo politics [*la politique du coucou*] that is philosophy in relation to science, so we are not surprised by this last "peek-a-boo!" that non-religion presents to us. Be careful! A baby could be made behind your back [*Enfant "dans le dos"*] or substituted for a child in your crib, as you like! If a language like the religious is chosen in the work of Saint Gilles as a function of the criteria of the cutting edge and the power of division ("say anything as long as it cuts," formula of the idealism of language and which, in addition, is Platonically echoed), how can this language not become determinant of what we mean by the Real itself or of the concept that we give it? It cannot be a question of "saving" the lone Real and abandoning the lone thought to the risks of religious language. This would be to assume a pure language of the Real or in-itself and one uncontaminated, as language, by the chosen materials. This would still be treating the Real and language as two bilaterally distinct entities, while language is not separated from the Real which gives it in-One, language which serves us and only serves us in naming it. The rule here is to indeed take language into account, but only as a symptom, no more (language in-itself or determinate) and no less (any language whatsoever). There is in this conception some linguistic fetishism and a secret of the idealism of all-language or of language as absolute. In these conditions it is the Real which is furtively engaged, implicated and not "neutral" like it was supposed to be, it is the Real as "immanent division" — what we would like to speak about, as we already know, is the Platonic chorismos, the overview of being-separated as division. Finally there is even a hierarchy of vocabularies, and non-religion is frontally opposed (without passing through the work of a unified theory) to non-philosophy and as more effective in the struggle against the World. The equivalence of interpretations was a ruse in order to get rid of non-philosophy and posit the superiority of non-religion. This is the great theme of its "rectification of non-philosophy." Evidently this is not a rectification but is instead a new interpretation of a set of axioms which allows for this substitution, a worrying rectification by the sword....

c. What then can come after this dyad of contradictory positions, one flattened out or made equivalent and the other valorizing religion? The third term, of course, is the third term of the system. And it is, we will include it, the same term that assumes this function for "non-philosophy," but a term completely overdetermined and incoherent which must keep the advantages of its "classical" form and those of non-religion, and thus coalesce. Here we are once again in the bosom of the philosophical system. In this ambiguity, two refusals compete for their share: the refusal of saying "God" in place of the "Real" but above all the concept of "oriental philosophy" or religion which either excludes occidental philosophy or includes it as an incomplete moment. "Religion is more thought-world than philosophy" (Saint Gilles?). It is more menacing and criminal (so gnosis also goes wild?), but it does not provide either the adequate vocabulary nor the critical technique that philosophy provides and which are necessary in order to be able to speak of non-religion in the name of the Real. It was thus a philosophical operation. Its other names, "reaping the benefits...," or "divide in order to rule...." The "multiplicity of non-philosophies," the "current," the "version" or "Laruelle variant" (formulations known by chance through exchanges with various non-philosophers on the Internet), these formulas only have an already approximate meaning for the effectuations and cannot rightly constitute descriptions of non-philosophy and its practice. It would be necessary to shed light in particular on the vocabulary of non-religion and not to push past the dazzling oriental lights into the blind night of unlearned knowing or non-knowing. Non-philosophy is not "philosophy with eyes closed" or philosophy "blinded" by the Platonic sun. That being said, a unified non-philosophical theory of philosophy and religion is indeed urgent. Regarding the critique of the present non-religion, it continues in what follows.

A REBEL IN THE SOUL:
A THEORY OF FUTURE STRUGGLE

The Unified Theory of Philosophy and Revolution

It is necessary to welcome a certain return of gnosis against philosophical, institutional and academic [*universitaire*] conformism (amongst other things), but we have to ask ourselves, how do we finally make room for it when it has been condemned to an eternal rebellion. Is it possible to introduce gnosis into the very foundations of thought, even if it means shaking those foundations? It is true that gnosis is also condemned to periodic returns, like philosophy. If there is any future for rebellion (having a gnostic motif rather than a classically philosophical one) then it is a rediscovery of contemporary post-Marxist gnosis. It is with this rebellion that non-philosophy has some squabbles. The latest of these returns can be an occasion to test non-philosophy, which from its very beginning invoked gnosis as a possible source, as a kind of *a posteriori* source. The force of this gnosis is the power to combine, for example, the Great Proletarian Revolution's regime of discourse, its slogans, its watchwords, its dazibao, with the form of a "theorem," by grafting its discourse onto a renewed notion of the Real which held a neighboring place for non-philosophical theory, as a Platonist Idea posited on a new material base. The revolutionary effects attached to the Proletarian Revolution are conserved despite everything and their reach takes on a new direction. But this is a crucial test for non-philosophy: is it capable of carrying the Idea of Revolution to a higher power than Marxism, be it by contesting the philosophies of history and their criminal implementation, or does it remain a theoreticist activity without a tomorrow? Does it at least establish a new relation between the future that it promotes as an ultimatum and the absence of "tomorrow?"

189

The gesture of a "reduction" of the Great Revolution to philosophy does not aim to dissolve Revolution within philosophy, nor even within philosophizability, but attempts a radical unification of the critique of philosophy which subsists in Revolution and the revolutionary proletarian critique. It is impossible here to rise up "against" this kind of discourse, even with its assumed excess of formulation or its own hyperbolic nature. In its non-religious usage, gnosis is perhaps too hasty and short-circuits a necessary phase, that of interpreting it through philosophizability in order to immediately "graft" it onto the Real in place of non-philosophy. This is not a refusal of Revolution (on the contrary), but rather the demand requiring it to pass through this intensifying filter of philosophizability as the condition for its heightening. Non-philosophy, exposed as such under its apparently theoretical form, is certainly an organon which remains open to numerous unified theories including the unified theory of philosophy and revolution, but in reality it is already a unified theory of philosophy and science, the only problem being that of knowing if that theory is fundamental for the others or one amongst others. In other words, the attempts to reclaim itself under the title of "non-philosophy" or under another label, must be put into a certain order. In particular, all the critiques of non-religious gnosis that non-philosophy bears here only touch on the hasty intervention into non-philosophy by non-religious gnosis (its aspect of leftist deviation), but in no way whatsoever bears upon a possible usage of this thematic.

A good understanding of the objectives of Unified Theory may allow us to dissolve certain ambiguities introduced into these conflicts. It discovers the fundamental illusion, meaning the transcendental hallucination hidden in philosophy's depths. In place of merely denouncing the illusion carried by religion, it takes notice also of its enveloped and dissimulated complexity within philosophy.

Religion is such that it allows itself to be developed according to its regions in several kinds of unified theories and "tolerates" them. But also several types of much "shorter" theories that are short-circuits of the unified theories, either leftist or rightist, and which undoubtedly put into question one of the principles of non-philosophy, by knowing the correlation-reduction prior to the "regions" or particular regimes of discourse and practice prior to philosophizability, evidently before isolating them as practices in the most precise sense. This is why "non-religious gnosis," itself so fascinating, so invigorating, but also so authoritarian, cannot be anything for us but the occasion for re-initiating non-philosophy.

Rebellion as a Problem

Rebellion is taken here as an example of an object that can be treated by non-philosophy, but also as one putting non-philosophy to the test. It posits the real primacy and practical priority of theory over its objects, philosophical, religious or otherwise, which may concern the revolt or the era according to which revolt spreads itself. This is not the announced enemy of the same revolution nor the future, a new wager on history. With history there has to be a wager on Good and Evil. With the future, there is nothing to wager, just an ultimatum. Non-philosophy hopes to release these objects from their philosophical imprisonment and possibly from religious historical conformism, without once again making slogans and banners out of them. But non-philosophy will ask itself if it makes an oeuvre out of rebellion, if it makes or is an oeuvre, or if it destroys all oeuvres, or if it is like madness, without oeuvre. Our principle intention is not to refute gnosis in-itself but its contradictory usage, at once non-philosophical and in-itself, gnosis as a doctrinal position introduced into non-philosophy as a critique of it. We will then defend along the way non-philosophical rigor against these objections, objections that are naturally the object on the left flank of non-philosophy. We will show the possibility of presenting it as a unified theory of philosophy and gnosis, but as materials and opposing the usage of gnosis as doctrinal position. Here this is not a question of being opposed to certain philosophers (like Plato, or gnosis itself, and above all not to its force of rebellion and its persecuted), but on the contrary being opposed to its religious and Platonic recuperation. Its a question of saving gnosis, as is insisted upon in *Future Christ*.

We previously called for rebellion in an older book, *Nietzsche contra Heidegger*, directed against the Nouveaux Philosophes amongst others. There we tried to propose a Nietzschean usage, so plainly philosophical. Then this problem was repeated in the more recent *Future Christ*: 1. calling back into question the axiom that it is right to revolt, refusing that there is some sufficient reason in rebellion, that would be to deny rebellion; 2. distinguishing rebellion from every reflex of auto- or self-defense, of vengeance or hatred; 3. positing an *a priori* defense of man which would be a self-defense or auto-rebellion. The problem of rebellion is one of risking the introduction of resentment and reaction into the struggle against "mastery" and so returning to the war, to the project of waging war against war. What is within rebellion that is not of the self-defensive order or a reaction? A reflex action? The non-philosophical solution asserted, as a condition of rebellion, is that (non)action of Man-in-person, the identity that we call real or negative, is non-sufficient for practice. How can one not think action as positive and victorious like Nietzsche, at least as the first action of radical identity ruling out that it would be a reaction? Every philosophy of force and action is contaminated by division and reciprocity of action and reaction, which makes action turn into a reaction. We must think a mastery that is not merely a re-action but an occasion, and a human (non-)action that is a pure force of action-without-reaction.

Overmastery or the Place of Philosophy in Non-Philosophy

In order to practice non-philosophy, which is a practice of theory, the method that is most pedagogical and oftentimes the most misleading is found in preparing the conceptual materials and doing so within the limits of philosophy; to reveal the maximum of its parameters, to leave the minimum of hidden determinations, to lay out the notion on the most comprehensive structure of philosophy. Three questions rightly stop us here. By what right do we speak of Philosophy? By what right do we philosophically interpret rebellion? Finally, by what right do we consider philosophy as the principal adversary, as if it were the mastery-form par excellence?

Regarding the first question, philosophy itself tells us what it is, for it exists in the best of cases as a system that posits itself and auto-thinks itself; Plato, Aristotle, Leibniz, Kant, and above all Hegel and Nietzsche have designed, projected, defined, sometimes effectuated this Idea as a system of a universal *cogito*. The "capital P" of "Philosophy" [*le "la" de "la philosophie"*] is understandable first as a self-auto-affecting Whole, and this is the affair of philosophy itself, philosophy understood a second time as the Whole('s)-identity, and this will be the affair of non-philosophy.

Regarding the second question, rebellion is perhaps still not philosophized but let us ask anyhow if it is philosophizable, in order to satisfy philosophy's pretensions without prematurely denying them. We only philosophize rebellion on the condition of recognizing its maximal or absolute pretensions, which is to recognize it in its blending with mastery. Non-philosophy assumes an extreme generosity with the philosophy that is our true adversary. An adversary must always be recognized under the threat of it returning after its apparent defeat, a brief return of the repressed. The most serious error is that of believing that this reference to philosophy as mastery is contingent and arises from an obsolete empiricism. Here we find a first objection against non-philosophy. Some have reproached it for oscillating between the love of structures and the empiricism of materials that it would take up randomly according to the tastes of the author, thus of waffling between a theoretical discipline and a more or less arbitrary personal oeuvre. But the structures of Philosophical Decision (philosophizability) themselves form a concrete vocabulary or an empirical object, for they are the most embodied and invested in empirical objects. Non-philosophy is not an empiricism; it is experimental in so far as it is theoretical, and it bears a relation to an experiment [*expérience*] which is the form-philosophy or form-world itself. Already the distinction of theory and oeuvre is hardly possible even from the material point of view. As for the knowledge of whether it goes to market or makes its own market, as has been objected, by going from the theory of understanding to that of ethics, then mysticism, aesthetics, and then probably the erotic, the problem is simple. In reality it goes into the form-market, not to or on the market to exchange this merchandise. It goes into the form-encyclopedia as much as into the various materials of it. The market-form is as before invested here in some determined merchandise, and its objects are in effect merchandized but inseparable from it. It is this merchandise that is the principal object even when we are dealing with a variety of objects. Additionally and above all, non-philosophy itself does not exchange itself in this market, not even against the market in general, but transforms it or appropriates it, appropriating mastery by way of a rebellion that by definition does not perform any exchange, having no cash-equivalent for this operation. Non-philosophy is what we call the market('s)-transcendental-identity or encyclopedia('s)-transcendental-identity and what distinguishes non-philosophy from All-market and All-encyclopedia.

Regarding the third question, why designate not just an adversary but the Adversary par excellence within the systematic and historic universality of the philosophical system self-thinking itself, philosophizability as a form of the world, the Master of masters or the master-form as such, while there are other masters and more apparent ones at that? This primacy and priority of philosophy over religion and politics within the constitution of materials is a methodological and theoretical principle, its refusal bears witness to the religious ideology and political ideology as determinates. Only philosophy can be the consistent object of a somewhat rigorous theory. Let us unpack some of these arguments: 1. It is consistent and objective, almost performative, because philosophy is inseparable from its exercise, from its structure and language, from its own thought, which is not the case for religion which determines the relations of its object, faith, and the thought of faith, theology, in an ambiguous, unstable or contrasted way; 2. It is identifiable as a structure that can be articulated or formalized but always concrete or incarnating such fundamental-regions of reality. There is no formalism here to couple with an empiricism, sometimes objectifying one or the other to non-philosophy; 3. It claims to reach or want the absolute and to satisfy the highest desire of man; 4. It has the spontaneous and natural pretension, it matters little if it is a symptom, for philosophizing religion and every other domain or region, politics and science, while the inverse reduction (for example of the philosophical to the religious) is difficult or ideological and in any case collides with philosophy's formidable powers of resistance and struggle; 5. This is a device of the World's appropriation through meaning, truth and value, a device of resistance to the critiques and rebellions, of auto-enveloping but also of the World's enveloping. Those philosophers for whom the pretension to sufficiency is the most affirmed, Hegel and Nietzsche, have thought religion either as a figure or as a deficient mode of the reality that is philosophy; 6. The adversary is designated par excellence by its nobility and its height. We will say that philosophy, unlike religions, forms a "world," that it is the form, always concrete, of the World, the field of struggles. And all these characteristics are relatively capable of being mastered all the way to including their auto-variation and auto-affection. So will the problem instead be that of completing this challenge, becoming capable of thinking this universality, this thought-world that claims itself capable of thinking everything? In short, how is a theory of the Whole and the Auto-encompassing possible without giving rise to a simple redoubling in the form of a meta-philosophy?

Here we find a second objection against non-philosophy, namely, that it lacks a cutting edge and a radicality.... But it would be a more serious objection if it did not lack a true object. It is with non-philosophy, with this extreme and inconvertible mastery that is non-philosophy in so far as it exercises it, that one must first settle the problem of mastery and rebellion, since this problem is too crafty for non-philosophy to ignore. As a matter of course non-philosophy must provide the problem with its most complete concept, the largest possible, auto-encompassing philosophizability rather than this system of philosophy. For example, defining it by "sufficient specularity" (with the Real) is possible on the condition of knowing that it is sufficient because it is auto-specularity, which will allow for a definition of an auto- or an over-mastery of a philosophical essence.

So there is no reason to make a non-religion without delay or, as Deleuze insisted with his objections, a non-science. As far as mediating a non-religion, this is possible but on the condition of ordering religion to philosophy, not letting religion determine the essence of philosophy, or non-religion determining the essence of non-philosophy. The practice of faith (of science, or art, etc.), in one sense only knows that it is, it only has its intelligence in its pre-supposed, or even in its theological interpretations, that concern spontaneous religious representations or elaborated dogmas that engage with philosophy. The Orient tends to identify religion and philosophy, faith and thought, but in this case effectively, since the practice of faith has lost its own presupposed, and non-philosophy does not have any great meaning. Moreover we can assume that religious mastery is mortified, but on the condition as well of admitting that it is philosophy which gives the plenitude of its meaning to death [*mort*], for example ending in the nothingness of every determination as Hegel fashioned it. Why introduce religion here rather than philosophy (at the risk of metaphor), which suffices to define the scale of the means of oppression? If philosophy has for its task the elucidation of concepts and understanding of the World, which is not the goal of religion as it pursues other ends, it is more interesting to unmask within this philosophical objective the most subtle means of mastery. Religion overdetermines philosophy, or else it is too immediate and limited a phenomenon in the manner of those 20th-century philosophers who had centered their entire critical enterprise on representation, which was only a decoupage undertaken on the Whole of philosophy, either as a complement or a supplement to the Whole. The overdetermination of philosophy by religion is obvious, but as a simple material, not as a point of view. We will challenge any of those who have religion, and then have non-religion, to provide us with something other than ideology that has not passed through the philosophical filter and then the non-philosophical one. So we are speaking here of semblance and mastery only on the condition of giving them some content ... controllable as transcendental illusion and hallucination. And able to be mastered here meaning according to philosophy ... but in order to better undo it. Without this reservation the "religious" appears as a hardly solid fantasy, which allows for a para-non-philosophical construction, being a metaphor for all the oppression and servitude that follows it. Non-philosophy only has meaning if its object, that which it attempts to explain and destroy in its sufficiency, has begun to be posited within its own limits or its auto-encompassing, precisely, not within a continuum of fuzzy representations. We can flout this prudence and these precautions which would be those, it seems, of a master, who savagely runs through the field of philosophy, knocking down concepts bluntly in the name of love and hate. Non-philosophy must speak to him in the context of gnosis, trying hard to take into account the work of contemporary philosophy, Lacan, Derrida, Deleuze, in their scope and their means (which are at the least, critical). They refine and fill philosophy out by diversifying the Platonic outline of philosophy and moreover in this way do not stop verifying its validity. In short, it is a principle of theoretical precaution but one which conditions a principle of interference in other disciplines, of any granting whatsoever of its pretensions in philosophy, a means of driving us to weakness in order to better overcome the cunning resistance of the Master. The force of philosophy will paradoxically be our force of rebelling.

All of this is still para-, quasi-, ultra-, faux-Hegelian or Nietzschean, authors who should not be overlooked under a non-philosophical pretext. But once non-philosophy has effectively begun, all the preceding notions afterward or rather "beforeward" take on another sense, universal in another manner than that of philosophy. They do not deny philosophy, they will widen and modulate it more — this will be philosophy('s)-Identity. In short, we now know that neither rebellion nor mastery are solitary entities, that they are rightly and necessarily, regardless of the empiricity chosen as an object-guide for non-philosophy, a dyad of mastery and rebellion, but reversible to various degrees that they self-determine reciprocally but unequally. Not to the benefit of mastery but of overmastery or auto-mastery, which contains within it the rebellion it has disarmed or domesticated. A somewhat advanced philosophical analysis extracts the concept, not of mastery, but of *overmastery*. Above all this is what we are concerned with and so we will avoid these overly religious notions of "mastery" and "rebellion" that emerged from the Nouveaux Philosophes and which Deleuze denounced in his day, but on whose terrain he nonetheless remained, which is to say within philosophy. There is a *final inequality*, because there is not overrebellion if not as an effect of overmastery, which is the absolutely absolute Master and not only a relative-absolute one. Yet it will be necessary to analyze the absolute of overmastery from the non-philosophical perspective of the defeated. Overmastery may be effectively suspended but this also signifies that rebellion will never be pure or absolute, but that it will be radical, which is to say, if we can put it this way, a rebellion that is non-rebelling (of) itself.

Struggle and Utopia
or the Place of the Non- in Non-Philosophy

So then what is to be done? To enter now into non-philosophy, which is to say where we enter or go only because we are already there, we Humans, and it is given to us to do this against the Master. Between oracle and axiom, this mysterious phrase that must eventually end the mystery in appearing and manifesting itself in its place, which is the first and which is said in a whisper, "we-Humans." We, Humans, are capable of "receiving" rebellion, thing and word, by the Logos of philosophy which can alone give it to us. Being capable of receiving not just any object nor even the perceived World as in phenomenology, but the philosophy-world in person and that through a concrete concept like that of rebellion, this is to be capable paradoxically of … giving it or manifesting it, just as Humans manifest themselves, in-person. Thus manifesting it under another form and for another destination than those under which it spontaneously gives itself from itself, that is to say "philosophically." Thus knowing in the form that we are, we-Humans who are not defined by mastery nor by rebellion, but who are capable of seizing mastery as a weapon that we transform and already make our own in the same moment that we seem to receive it from the exterior as we are being wounded by it. Who, us, identically singular and plural? What is this us that can take weapons from a Master and above all from an Overmaster? What is the time of this us that defines itself by this already! By which we welcome the present, and we liberate it, this future which always comes after the present but which it has already transformed? This is the future proper to rebellion. The kind of future that, while seemingly produced in connection with the present, has in fact vested the present, making it an occasion, that has befallen it, without ever having been belated.[3] We call future this radical coming ahead of the present, this priority of ultimatum, of last things that precede the present without delay. Rebellion is the radical inversion of the Master, his In-Verso rather than his reversal.

By definition no one is able to simply snatch his weapons from an overmaster. In any case, no subject of philosophy can do so since philosophy is already the overmaster. It is precisely because philosophy is the overmaster that it wants to tear in general, and in order to tear itself away from domination and thus from itself, it divides itself or forms a two (a master and his rebel) with an

---

3. C'est le futur propre à la rébellion. Ce qui, produit apparemment à propos du présent, l' a déjà versé et en a fait l'occasion et chute sans avoir jamais été en retard sur lui. The French words *occasion* and chute have the same root: casus, cas, cause, what befalls. T.N.

overmaster, thus forming a new overmaster with this two. Because there is a universal exception, which is no longer an exception, no one unless there is a subject capable of positing and of thinking (in this manner) an axiom of the future of rebellion rather than a thesis or an injunction. This axiom says that the struggle with the overmaster is necessary but possible or "empty" from the point of view of its effectivity or its outcome, by principle uncertain. It signifies that the overmaster is already defeated (at least the belief that animates him) even if the battle has not yet begun. Effectively before entering into combat and in order to be able to enter there, it is necessary to posit and to know in a non-positional way this position: we have never been defeated immediately or *a priori* as the Master tries to persuade us or make us believe, and that our defense is in a certain way already prepared, as soon as we refuse the belief of the Master in the desired victory, assumed to be effective and certain. This refusal of positive belief proper to the overmaster is the struggle, or rather the in-struggle, the spirit of struggle, in as much as it is the negative condition, sine qua non, the condition of a future or non-temporal rebellion. The Rebel knows in an indirect way that the struggle, not to say the immediate victory, is within his grasp or is necessary in its possibility. What is it that binds this "us" and this possibilization of battle by struggle?

No one goes into an effective struggle if they already only postulate themselves in the position of the winner, already being in the position of power implying that as well of their defeat. The postulation of possibility is thus susceptible to several interpretations. Either we already postulate victory, its possibility immediately reducing itself to its reality or reabsorbing itself in its effectivity: this is overmastery. Or we necessarily posit the possibility of victory as a simple necessary possibility, as a struggle that no longer depends on the certitude of victory, struggle in the manner of an empty axiom which no longer has the intuitive character of effective or engaged war, but as a simple presupposed, and this is the Rebel. What the Rebel knows, he knows "from struggle."

He is fundamentally a militant, not triumphant, a militant "in the soul" before even actually going out on a campaign. By principle, this allows for a contingency of victory, and this extreme weakness of the Rebel becomes victory made clear by his force of struggle. If capital-philosophy, and the other, examine and regulate the whole problem in superficial terms of gain and loss where humans are the losers at every turn, then on the contrary, it is up to us to examine our force ourselves, the constitution of our force as real being-forced or force-(of)-utopia.

Third objection against non-philosophy. When it speaks of a force-(of)-thought, does it not justify force? There is a state of force as possibility and it is through struggle that the Rebel is defined, and it is effectively though a force exercising itself that the overmaster is defined, but this is hallucinatory because it forgets the incontrovertible necessity of presupposing struggle as victory's non-sufficient possibility. Because nothing yet, not even this axiom, effectively offers us weapons that we could have had or that we need anyway. Between necessary struggle (though uncertain regarding its necessity) and the victory that takes itself from mastery and rebellion, there is no analytic appearance and yet here we find true victory, the non-rebel rebellion of itself, nor is there synthetic judgment and yet nonetheless here we find a contingency of the conditions of the final outcome.

Speaking Germanically for a moment, the Rebel ignores the Blitzkrieg, the lightning-war, in general he ignores the lightning, the flash, that is Heraclitean love of the One at first sight by which philosophy has lit up the Greek sky, or the nuclear flash that has definitively darkened it. The Rebel waits for victory as a future, a radical waiting which has already suspended the Overmaster, reduced to showing for all to see that he was only reeling in the wind of history.

This axiom of struggle is our presupposed; it is this axiom that defines this "us" and gives it its content, but this is rightly not the presupposed of the overmaster, which wants to know nothing about it. If the Master flies in ahead of the victory, the Rebel comes, ahead of the battle's future but this is not the same "ahead of." Let us oppose the radically future rebellion to the anticipation of victory. The overmaster engages himself in the victory by "believing it," the Rebel is engaged in struggle unwillingly. The overmaster believes immediately in the reality of victory, he considers it as necessary or effective as soon as he wants it and since he wants it anyway. Belief for him is sufficient. The other, the Rebel, knows a necessary knowledge from struggle. He has something more than the overmaster, who is something less, he distinguishes the necessity of struggle and that of assumed victory that justifies itself. Mastery only self-authorizes itself, meaning as Overmaster, while the Rebel does not self-authorize himself as a subject except through the nearest struggle to him, he must accept struggle as a presupposed, or else he adds to the belief of the Master. From there victory will then be given increasingly as a form of grace as soon as the Master has engaged in hostilities; he is only overmaster from having always already engaged or anticipated them. But the haste of the overmaster will be fatal for him, he does not believe the time of real possibility to be necessary, while the Rebel takes into account the relative autonomy of struggle that is real but not effective as victory. This is why the Rebel exists as subject-in-struggle who is never reabsorbed into the fact of victory. Victory as a way of thinking (because the Rebel can win but this is not how he thinks) is the fact of facts, semblance even, an auto-encompassing justification that can even be hallucinatory.

Negative Necessity and Sufficient Necessity

There is thus an amphibology of necessity proper to philosophy but we have made it appear at least as an illusory appearance, that of negative or non-sufficient necessity and sufficient necessity. What is terrifying about the overmaster or "semblance" is no more nor less than the ontological argument it resorts to. Sufficient necessity is the resort of the *cogito*, of the ontological argument, finally of the set of philosophy. It is enough to think but if we think then we are necessarily real, it is enough to think victory; which

202

is to say, to provide the means in order to be victorious. Possibilizing necessity is more modest, it declares that it does not suffice, or more exactly that necessity only announces itself in the form of a real possibility. It is like a minimal and "negative" struggle (this is the presupposed of the spirit of struggle) that will not become positive, but which will remain a real possibility when it will be effectuated. The conditions for the real possibility of rebellion are not a way of differentiating or slowing it down, but of making a future-in-person happen.

This disjunction is fundamental for several reasons, especially in that it is not transcendent. It leads to several other distinctions:

1. Between Man and the All of creation. I alone can posit this axiom with which I am bound to Man, Man-without-an-operation-of-rebellion, all the rest is overmastery (meaning mastery and rebellion in a blended state).

2. Between Man, by essence without-rebellion or even non-revolted Man but compelled to be capable of struggle, and the subject-existent-Rebel or non-rebelling (of) itself (we will return to this formula).

3. By way of consequence, between the philosophical subject, which is engaged and disengaged according to various proportions, and the Rebel-subject which as Man is "non-engaged" rather than dis-engaged. Non-engaged is not opposed to the spirit of struggle, on the contrary, it also signifies that the Future Rebel is not engaged in a philosophical way (for example an existentialist one) and struggles against this kind of engagement.

4. Between rebellion blended with mastery and the rebellion non-rebelling (of) itself or in itself. The rebel is often a factor for unrest and war and always risks simply turning war against itself again. Thus there is some meaning in speaking of a rebellion non-rebelling (of) itself or in itself, which is no longer to enter into a war against war or of which the Rebel has not won through the spirit of vengeance and resentment. Generally speaking, this is the same essential problem of rebellion and only non-philosophy can tear it away from self-hatred and prevent it from extending into mastery or from reconstituting it. Non-revolted Man has the primacy of the Real and determines rebellion by struggle but rebellion is the radical and transcendental beginning of combat. To such an extent that rebellion is an effectuation of struggle in the sense defined here and is inseparable from it under threat of returning to the anticipation of victory. Struggle has primacy over rebellion but rebellion is the way in which struggle exists. It all begins with or in rebellion but all of it is determined by the spirit of struggle.

In reality all of these relations are a little more complicated and do not happen between distinct and bilaterally opposed entities. These are indeed dualities, but one side of which is precisely that of primacy, Man or Real, which is separated-without-separation as if it were absent or had not fallen into representation and so into mastery. This is the "Man" aspect, an aspect of real possibility, as a struggle to prevent rebellion in its way being reabsorbed within the effectivity of mastery.

Finally, we distinguish three instances: Man who is without-rebellion but not without a struggle, the cycle of overmastery (mastery and rebellion blended), and finally the subject-existent-Rebel (itself complex) which rises up at the intersection of these two. He is real in-the-last-Humaneity, his transcendental essence is the spirit of immanent struggle, and his *a priori* content is mastery and rebellion both transformed by this essence. In order to end this chapter, we will examine certain objections that have been put to non-philosophy in what concerns the type of articulation called unilateral of these three instances, and from here we will even continue to distinguish the usage that for its part non-religious gnosis makes of it.

The Rebel or the Place of Non-Philosophy within Non-Philosophy

A. The Man-ultimatum as presupposed of the Rebel and that which thinks it as the Rebel. Non-revolted Man, who has the primacy of the Real, prevents (this is the spirit of struggle) the blending of these instances. We do not blend them any more than we distinguish them by opposition. They do not count, above all non-revolted Man, despite the "three." These "three" instances are not separated or bilaterally distinct, arranged in a space which would furtively be that of transcendence or philosophy, of overseeing or overhanging. It is Man that possesses this property which flows from its radical immanence, it is separated-without-separation or Other-than, or still a negative or necessary possibility, or spirit of struggle, and is as such through its own immanence even if these traits are destined to take on a transcendental meaning and are then assumed to have taken into account the already given mastery.

Three consequences:

a. Man is and institutes a radical or intrinsic finitude, that of the future which will go along with itself up to mastery. No overseeing or domination, nothing more of its (non-) action is representable, even if its objects are. The Rebel works with transcendence or even mastery without being within transcendence, as if manipulating it at a distance or from the "absent" Real with the help of a robot displacing dangerous masteries or of a screen visualizing a flux of otherwise invisible particles. Except for here there is precisely no distance whatsoever; utopia thus opposes itself with the distance necessary for the manipulation of the essential weapon of the master, transcendence. The Rebel is a quasi-robot or an automaton but without having the materiality of a robot. Because he is Man-in-person or the future, without distance he effects [*agit*] distance, and so also the weapon of the master. This is the rebellion non-rebelling (of) itself.

b. Their unilateral duality with the Real implies that mastery and rebellion are accessible and given in the mode of Humaneity (in-Man or in-One). In-Man does not signify that they are parts of Man, for they have nothing of the Real, above all for the instant where only mastery is involved, and what mastery will pass on to the subject-Rebel uniquely. There is no question of connecting Man and Master from the exterior, the pretensions of the overmaster will never be invalidated, but merely undermined, and this will be its deconstruction. Overmastery must at least already be invalidated in or for Man, even if the pretensions of overmastery remain effective in their order. Real (-transcendental) invalidation is struggle. Why then also transcendental? Because it goes through the Rebel-subject which necessarily carries the foreclosing of Humaneity to overmastery.

c. There is no intervention at the heart (in-itself of overmastery) of mastery in general. There is a non-philosophical identity of mastery, but not for it or for itself, which does not mean that there has not been a rebel action and that non-philosophy ignores transcendences. But mastery remains what it is in the sense that its functioning and its illusions remain constant for it, but no longer for the Rebel. To transform the World, as Marx demanded, but not for the World (that would still be to interpret it) but instead for the rebel-subject that does not reconstitute a second World (or a second Capital). This objection of indifference made to non-philosophy may be cynical, as already discussed, because it lacks the sense of the transcendental that it reifies as a pure thing, inert and not directed by experience. In reality, what matters here is that the Rebel concretely constitutes his proper domain of non-mastery, by transforming the blend of mastery and rebellion. There is also a Kingdom of Rebels, or at least a City of Heretics and Irreconcilables, but this does not take the place of mastery or install itself in the World (that would require proceeding to an "Organisation Non-philosophique Internationale," ONPHI as we have said). Rebellion in this sense does not make an oeuvre, or it is the Rebel in person that is precisely this oeuvre. Rebellion is then a (real-) transcendental acting. Why also the real or in-Man? Because the transcendental is the Real itself but as a function that it assumes in the form of a Rebel (the spirit of struggle thus become an essence of struggle and rebellion) which would directly confront the structure of overmastery (and not only as preceding the belief that animates it). If these three instances were assumed in the philosophical and theological way as separate and distinct in transcendence, then we must in effect imagine a direct intervention into mastery or within the World, or even to say a creation of the World, but it is an external intervention which goes back into this sphere. This is why all transcendences (according to the usage made here) are in general not the same, they are only the same from their point of view or in so far as they remain auto-transcendences.

B. The Rebel and his transcendental constitution. If Man is without-rebellion, then Man cannot directly intervene and must determine a Rebel that would take his weapons from Man (in the form of struggle or real possibility) and from the mastery which is the owner of all the necessary means for struggle. Non-philosophy has some chance of annihilating philosophical sufficiency if it, without making the transcendental absolutely autonomous, can generate it starting from this double causality, and thus that of mastery. The Rebel in his complete concept is real, transcendental and even *a priori* (forming the link with the experience of mastery yet also extracted from it).

The subject-existent-Rebel is the clone, in which the Real-Man fills the role of transcendental identity, which is the essence of the subject in which the materials of transcendence are transformed in-and-by that identity serving as *a priori* content. One can certainly say that "a Rebel" is only a transcendental moment isolated by abstraction but it is precisely nothing more than a moment or only the essence of the subject. But the subject is more than the simple transcendental that would have no meaning without an *a priori* experiential content which is the transformed result of materials. If we, in our way, resume the thread of the vocabulary of (non-) religious gnosis and say the Angel, if we are fond of this term, then it is as just that aspect of the blend of mastery and rebellion but yet such that it appears transformed in its transcendence within the Rebel-subject. The Angel, then, will be the *a priori* content of the Rebel-subject.

This theory of the non-Platonic Rebel can of course also be read as a non-philosophical critique of the dialectic of Master and Slave [*Valet*].

The Transcendental, the Rebel and Struggle

Non-religious gnosis (Saint Gilles) tends to oppose a pure transcendental Rebel, without direct efficacy of mastery, to non-philosophy's Rebel, a being who is always transcendental but directly "connected to" or acting *a priori*, as we have said, on mastery. This, of course, assumes an abstract Rebel which needlessly comes to double Man himself. But there are profound reasons for this conception. That which distinguishes the two versions of Rebellion is certainly clear enough and engages with the concept of struggle. This non-religious gnosis, furthermore, also accepts the immanent human Real but speaks about it and treats it (without giving an account) in a transcendent or Platonic way. Non-philosophy, though, affirms that it is necessary to speak of the immanent Real in a way that is itself immanent, to speak and to think the One according to the One. The sense here of the according to is that it is necessary that radical immanence be practiced and not only discoursed upon or contemplated — for we will see, by this new persona, the being of the Angel, which comes to the aid of gnosis. The discourse of non-philosophy, on the contrary, is that of the Rebel-subject himself who articulates it and who confronts his existence with just this theoretical discourse that is at once also practical. On the one hand there is a fear that the Angel of theoreticism is haunted by a fourth figure in addition to the three instances already counted. And in effect there are four, which is plenty: Man or Soul, Rebel, Angel and Master. In reality the Angel is the Philosopher but in a religious mode by means of which religion redoubles itself. While philosophy claims to include the philosopher who must not be ex machina (save for another finer analysis), religion assumes a heteronomy of itself, a celestial persona ex machina and not merely a "conceptual persona" (Deleuze). The partition of Heaven and Earth, their division, finds its echo in the theoretical apparatus [*dispositif*]. Non-religious gnosis is in reality the exterior perspective of the Angel or the People who come to theory or support a theoreticist position.

Except for an unexpected return of Platonism, the Real does not tolerate a transcendental double alongside it. We see gnostic mythology emerging here as a result of Platonism in the form of a unitary double that is no longer empirico-transcendental, as Foucault would say, but rather real-transcendental. This is why for our part we have always written these terms with deferring parentheses arranged to break this characteristic of the doublet and to indicate the being-separated of the Real and the occasional contingency of rebellion, both necessary in order to effectively have a Rebel. We cannot place their indifference to non-philosophy beyond reproach, itself advancing one such transcendent concept of the transcendental that returns to no struggle, neither a possible nor an effective one, but only to the theoreticist concept of mastery itself. If this contemplation is what gives thought its cutting edge, then we will gladly leave this division of Heaven and Earth to the care of this more traditional Platonic cutting edge.

Moreover, in the gnostic solution there is no effective genesis of the transcendental. Yet, for all that the transcendental effectuated there, another is still always necessary, a second cause, of course. This is only a weak and ad hoc cause, the kind in which Plato undoubtedly makes an allusion to the sensible, but a cause, nevertheless, whose function does not supersede this role as an immediately effaced signal like every idealism insists upon. The pure transcendental Rebel is of the order of a transcendental metaphysics, in the tradition that Kant called the "transcendental philosophy of the Ancients" having formed those famous "transcendentals." It is a pure transcendental, absolutely and logically separated. Hence the result is a hatred of the World that conditions the general structure of the apparatus utilized, and brings with it a certain refusal of cloning, the love of pure theory or theoreticism, the refusal of practice up until the point of theory, and the excess of logic as Aristotle and Plato called it. The objection made here against non-philosophy rests then on the conservation of an undeclared transcendence within the Real or Man from which immanence is contemplated, and which is incapable of any access to mastery. In being only mastery, the cause and the sign are not immediately thought in-One, but thought by the Angel offering this thought to the Rebel. Yet from the outset the Angel must give itself the conditions for accessing mastery of Humaneity, though it is a mastery which it does not participate in, an access which passes through a struggle. Non-philosophy's element is separated immanence, without a doubt, but not separated by transcendence or through a surreptitious operation of separation, but only separated by immanence itself. This is the unilateral identity of Man and mastery together and thus also of the Rebel (the clone) such that it renders useless the intervention of the persona of the Angel, except for cloning it in its turn. Mastery is independent, but it can precisely only be thought as independent according to the Rebel. In sum, then, non-philosophy is not merely Platonic, but also Aristotelian, not merely Hegelian but also Kantian.

The pure transcendental of gnosis is without a relation to mastery, which is only a simple reference. Yet in philosophy the Rebel and the Master are bound together, and the thesis of a simple "Platonic" allusion to mastery is an artifact produced by philosophy. It is the Real and the Real alone which is without relation to mastery, not the transcendental. It happens to be the essence of the subject but it is an essence which comes forth as a simple function assumed by the Real at the request of overmastery. A simple mention or allusion to mastery cannot make the transcendental emerge without active intervention.

Consequences: current gnosis, as non-philosophy speaks of it, can provide the identity of Religion, but immediately gives itself the latter, short-circuiting its cloning process and its being-given-in-Real at its inception. It acts as if Man is enough for the identity of mastery, assuming a reversibility of the "of." But if Man gives this identity along with its "empty" trait, a second gesture becomes necessary, that of cloning, in order to complete the process and take mastery into account, which is something that gnosis does not do since it immediately posits a transcendental Rebel; but rebelling for what? We do not really know, perhaps for an invoked mastery, but absolutely inactive, like the sensible in Plato which serves as a neutral springboard, but nothing else. It comprehends occasionality as a simple signal or suggestion, not as a secondary causality, and this is why it needs a second, more serious occasionality, in order to pass from Rebel to Angel. The process is typical of Platonism, which disposes of abstract entities offset by intermediary entities; such is the Platonic root of religious and gnostic mythology when non-philosophy has not appropriated it in the form of a unified theory of philosophy and gnosis.

How can a Rebel which doubles the Real as its image act otherwise through another intermediary? As always within every philosophy, even more so in Platonism, the problem of the suture of instances is regulated in an abstract way, by the presupposition of a transcendent unity that forms a horizon and gives a final consistency to philosophy or to Mastery, precisely the Overmaster … which is everywhere, in transcendence and in immanence, but the nature of which is never elucidated because it is hidden in the suture as an operation. This is the argument of the third man or here the third persona, the Angel but also the Rebel, both making a double use of Man-in-person and the one with the others. This is the black box of mastery and of every battle; here it also takes on this conception of the pure Rebel, and also functions as an act of knotting rather than one of cloning.

If overmastery is to be found everywhere, then it is up to the Man-in-person and partially also to the Rebel to be nowhere, and from here we get the Idea of a Utopian Rebellion in-the-last-instance or just in-the-last-utopia, via a uchronia. The Rebel has ceased to be this fugitive hiding in the forest; he no longer has a geo-philosophical place, such as Norway or Iceland. Cloning can be as enigmatic or obscure as contemporary gnosis suggests, but it is less so than this pure transcendental Rebel who has no cause, because the Real without mastery is not even a cause. To continue, the suture is bilaterally-overwritten, and thus opaque, while cloning is a unilateral identity.

Is cloning precisely the initial situation, the first phase of rebellion, that of real possibility, the struggle posited as necessary without there still being an effective rebellion, meaning an effectuated one? How do we pass from this possibility of struggle to its effectivity? The Rebel arises out of necessary possibility and the spirit of struggle, a first weapon the Master has not yet used. Still it is necessary that the Master engage in combat, or else the Rebel has no reason to exist. However, combat is always engaged or exists as philosophy itself, and this is the rashness of the Master. We would be wrong to not take mastery seriously, regarding it merely as passive and massive. It is an occasion of Rebellion, its second phase which takes mastery into account and assumes its perspective. This is the problem of the origin of the transcendental which, as Kant and the Modernists wanted, is no more a supercategory, a transcendent term, as the pure Rebel still is, but a relation of conditioning of experience (here of mastery). Evidently this is no longer a substantial term but a functional term. Platonism, and even more so Gnosticism, introduce a spirit of verbal fetishism, its "theorems" being a few common but "trenchant" affirmations, allowing for the use of religion and capable of transforming the cutting edge into an effect of religious style. What is then important is "dividing itself," which is to say affirming division as a style without fearing doublets and redoublings....

And yet they must come to agreement. The Rebel is the unilateral duality which forms the clone, but its essence is identity because Man adopted or assumes the mastery that solicits him. The Real digs a hole, an absence, more exactly it places the void of negative possibility into the heart of mastery and its apparatus of transcendence. Yet that necessary possibility as the One is the non- of the (non-) One, which makes out of transcendence in general a non-thetic transcendence, or out of Rebellion a non-rebel rebelling (of) itself. Man is not a rebel, he can only exist as-Rebel.

In the end, cloning explains the genesis of the transcendental through the Real but also through an account of experience, and not through a Platonic allusion to the sensible. It destroys the bilateral double of the Real and pure transcendental in and by a unilateral clone (the Rebel). Lastly, it does not uselessly multiply entities, and thus, is truly rigorous.

Against Platonizing Gnosis

The gnostic interpretation of non-philosophy does not merely reside within the limits of its axioms, and in particular, of a few added in between them that we refuse to notice. As always in philosophy as well as in non-philosophy, the critique has to reach only so far as the axiom is deployed, not beyond. Its critiques of non-philosophy's alleged liberalism and lack of a cutting edge are an effect of a Platonic perspective, tied to the principles that they start with and which reverberate down the long chain of deductions. Thus what gnosis calls its axioms also have a doctrinal intuitive content or an intra-philosophical determinant content. It all rests on a resulting differend: indifference or hatred, cloning or not cloning, the force or weakness of thought, the relation to the World, liberalism or a cutting edge, etc. This differend is a symptom; it concerns the relation to immanence, both the usage and the non usage of it. The question bears in fact on the coherence of the problematic of immanence and the language used by gnosis.

"Say anything as long as it cuts." This maxim of Saint Gilles, which in its way rings like a new injunction, is the declaration of criteria for discourse. How does this enunciation ground or legitimate itself? "Anything," the arbitrary choice of terms or declarations is nevertheless limited by the transcendence proper to the Angel, and this is the criterion posited. In its way this criterion or the Angel is "oriented" by the Rebel or the subject, pure theory or the pure transcendental. Yet to bring it back by conditionally does not allow one to reach the Real in its specific effectivity. Thus gnosis is condemned either to arbitrarily giving itself philosophy and thinks starting from it, empirically grounding its criteria without being able to reach the Real or in reaching it only in order to determine it in its empirical way, or it's condemned to giving itself the separated Real, but then mastery or philosophy is absolutely contingent and without a relation to the Real as another world or another strangeness. Gnosis has a choice between two solutions: either to not effectively be in-Man if the criteria is given and if thought grounds itself on this criterion, or being in-Man and in this case Mastery is absolutely contingent and no one knows why it would be necessary to revolt, since there is no reason, even non-sufficient, to revolt.

No name, however big it is, not even Plato or Hegel, sums up Philosophy or can substitute itself for it. No proper human name of history can substitute itself for the name of "Philosophy," a quasi-performative name, *cogito* of philosophizability, more exactly an abbreviation for a formula that will run something like: Philosophy is the identity of philosophy and philosophizing, in each case an auto-encompassing All. This formula contains, besides other things, the Platonic demarcation of this discipline of thought and makes it the interior of thought as much as it is able to. The names of Plato, Hegel, or Nietzsche designate exemplary philosophers but despite any singularity of their character they are reduced to the state of examples of Philosophy. On the other hand, it is impossible to make Platonism the alpha and omega of philosophy because it ultimately privileges transcendence (epekeina), the logical chorismos, mathematics and finally even religion, without balancing them against inverse tendencies, like physics and biology. If, as Kant said, Plato is the father of every digression in philosophy, then non-philosophy (which betrays a necessary digression in philosophy) can also recognize in Plato this father, which his children have "completed." These somewhat ridiculous attempts to classify philosophers according to a scale of proximity to the auto-encompassing All are nevertheless still fundamental for the formulation and delimitation of a philosophical order which also includes possibilities for disorder. It is certainly necessary to posit the possibility of a hallucination proper to philosophizability but first we must posit the sphere or the type of reality which is proper to it and which will be the seat of transcendental appearance. Thus the two senses of "Philosophy/a philosophy" [*"la (-) philosophie"*]: one belongs to transcendental appearance or is auto-signifying, sufficiently able to define it in an internal manner; the other is its non-philosophical identity.

Undoubtedly, Plato has once and for all posited every possible transcendence, including the religious kind. But he did not posit transcendence in-Real or in-Man in-the-last-instance. Yet in order to treat it and so transform it in this way, it is necessary first to give it in the in-the-last-instance of Man, in-Humaneity, meaning that we must assume that with his doctrine Plato claimed to rival the Real, to think it at least, to measure itself in him. Or else we connect outside of it two incommensurable things, Platonism and the last instance, which does not mean that the Real will be at all commensurable with Platonism. This exterior connection is, in effect, materialism. Non-philosophy, though, is like psychoanalysis, which must begin by accepting that there is something like a philosophical symptom (and consequently a transcendental function of the Real). For gnosis, however, there are no such symptoms, as the religious, Platonism or mastery are not symptoms but brute givens which we must or should resist without knowing why in so far as we are in-Man. Like the religious itself, non-religious gnosis is a permanent power grab [*coup de force*], meaning a philosophical or absolute type.

This problem yields two forms: one concerns the Idea of non-philosophical practice said to be "immanent," the other the transcendental form of materials dealt with. It is necessary to "knot together" these two problems, for gnosis forms this knot as well but without being aware of the requirements for the idea of an immanental treatment of the discourse of immanence. As Saint Michel and several other minds attempted with the theme of radical immanence, the gnostic interprets it in an ultimately philosophical and transcendent way, i.e. religious. In Saint Michel the symptom is found in the formula "(love) with your eyes shut," which implies a last operation ex machina, so that non-philosophy does not shut (its) eyes, never having opened them in the first place, being born blind, born-without-birth, as it were. In gnosis

215

the symptom is found in the privilege accorded to Platonism. The gnostic has not left the Platonic cave for if he does, he is seized and fixed, paralyzed, by the blinding sun. Non-philosophy risks passing for an excessive wager on intelligence, and on philosophy, while gnosis wagers on popular stupidity, on the poor in spirit. Why does it not give up on intelligence as soon as it is concerned with philosophy and let it account for itself, for example the divine Plato himself? Because from the perspective of the Real, unintelligence, stupidity, or idiocy is radical, not absolute or total, which would be contradictory. It must nevertheless ... be intelligent in some way, for inversely would we not ask if gnosis is not still too little concerned with the One and the Real, if it is truly delivered from the gaze and the view or if it is happy to shut its eyes, being a dazzling intelligence like all the Platonizers? Why would it not wish, in its own way, to give up on Platonism?

Non-philosophy's question concerns the radicality of immanence. What to do with language itself or thought when the Real is strictly immanent and determines language in this way? Here we have the central question of non-philosophy and it is not Platonism's question, either, which on the contrary provides itself with language and reflects it through ontology, nor even that of Neoplatonism which remains dominated by the doctrinal taking up of a position in favor of Platonism. Yet one of non-philosophy's axioms is that it excludes (without at all excluding philosophizability) any particular doctrinal position taken, even that of Platonism (which subsequently introduces gnostic and religious heterodoxy). It can make use of Platonism but as already reduced materials, not as a doctrinal position. So that we can schematize it, let us posit as a principle that it is the immanence of the Real that determines some material = X and that determines it as symptom for non-philosophy. Inversely gnosis leads not to an exemplified non-philosophy through Platonic materials, but to a non-Platonism, to a non-materialism, to a non-religion. Here this is a universal restriction: the difference between a unified theory of philosophy and gnosis and a gnostic or non-religious posture.

216

Moreover it is also the misunderstanding present in Deleuze's objection to non-philosophy: why not a non-science?

What does it mean to say that philosophy is a symptom of non-philosophy? The Real is radically, not absolutely, indifferent to all language, of which contingency is also not absolute. There is of course some recognition of a certain causality in the naming of the Real which the radical nature of it tolerates but also determines. The Real is indifferent to language, Other-than … it, only if language presents itself or is already given in-One. To speak is not only to use language as an inert tool; we are already engaged in it and cannot consider it as absolutely contingent. Thus language does not determine the Real, although it does determine part of the way that we go on to speak of the Real. Yet only philosophy, and not religion, is capable par excellence of being this symptom of the Real and its language, of simulating this immanence through its auto-encompassing character.

This gnosis says that there is nothing but transcendence which Plato unveiled, certainly, but philosophy does not reduce itself to transcendence so objectified, but in its blending with immanence over which it is dominant by virtue of their blending. It is thus a system of auto-transcendence, it is philosophy in person. Its reduction to transcendence alone is already an abstract religious thesis concerning it.

Non-philosophy thus supports three theses: 1. it is the philosophical and not the religious which is dominant in the blending of these two languages; 2. philosophy is what most closely simulates the Real and yet it is precisely that which is the farthest from the Real; 3. finally philosophy is the most intelligible and at the same time the most devious and greatest sham. There is a language, the philosophical one, which wants to pass itself off as the Real and this is what defines its intelligence in everyday life. Of course, it must give philosophy all its dimensions and not only epekeinaphysics.

If the Real is indifferent to language, can we not then use any language whatsoever? But when one invokes the Real, at least to be dogmatic, the game is already over, and in any case we use philosophy while partially using another language and it is with them and in them that we must fight. In gnosis, religious language has not been philosophically reworked but juxtaposed with the Real in an authoritarian way. So must we hear by the Real a religious notion, God evidently, but yet we are not told how to philosophically reduce it?

If philosophical language is what is the most devious and deceptive, the most enveloping, then there is also, correspondingly, some necessity in having a psychoanalysis that is either adapted or at least equal in power. Non-philosophy is neither indifferent to nor holds in contempt deconstruction or psychoanalysis, yet non-philosophy is the transformed form of psychoanalysis (amongst other disciplines), rendered adequate to the complexity and originality of its object. In the wake of contemporary philosophy, can we object to its novelty and specificity by saying that the system of philosophy is already predesigned in Plato? This is the symptom of the Greek refusal of Judaism in thought (Levinas, Derrida). Plato is the model or paradigmatic philosopher, but by no means all of philosophy, not even counting the fundamental and innovative cultural affects like Judaism and Christianity.

Non-philosophy thus recognizes Philosophy itself as the only dominant master or mistress (and in addition, reduced-in-One or without a Principle of Sufficient Philosophy). Under these conditions it is possible to proceed to an inaugural abstraction of Philosophy rather than of Plato and his particular doctrine. However, does Philosophy exist outside of Plato or Hegel? No, certainly not, but only an initial and maximal abstraction, that of philosophizability, is necessary to give its full range and force in order to make this circle which passes for all circles or systems, and which envelops them or which is enveloped by them.

The Idea of an absolute transcendence, including a Platonist one, has three limitations, the first two of which are philosophical, the third non-philosophical: 1. Overmastery cannot be defined by transcendence alone (so simply posited or objectified), since

218

it is a blend with immanence; 2. it is auto-encompassing, which limits in an internal way its own objectivity (auto-limitation); this is what ends in the maximal abstraction of the doctrinal content of the philosophies and clears it of the Idea of philosophizability; 3. this philosophizability cannot be objectified from the start in an external or operative way. Even considered as auto-encompassing, it must be reduced already in-Real and declared hallucinatory, or else it is positing it operatively, not only as transcendence but with the help of an operative transcendence that remains at the exterior of thought and entrusts thought to transcendence, and all by leaving to mastery something of its own hallucination, a belief that lies at the root of "semblance." Platonic gnosis is far too dualistic and too grounded in heteronomy to think the discourse of immanence in a truly immanent way, if only in-the-last-instance. Like philosophy, and maybe even more than philosophy, gnosis forms its own proportion in immanence, and it devotes itself to the excess of transcendence, to an intimidating and hyperbolic moral nature. Hence the interest of current gnosis for the older works of non-philosophy where the thinking was more cutting-edge, more dualistic, and the nuances less discernible.

That being said, this doctrine of non-religious gnosis is of course a possible type of non-philosophy, in the functional sense, but it does not correspond, as has been sufficiently shown, to the main intentions of non-philosophy. Its starting axioms do not allow it to thematize in a truly immanent way the usage of this type of language. Responding to a question on his usage of language and its possibility, Saint Michel said, I take concepts and I wring their necks. To what extent does gnosis not slice through these concepts and make their heads roll into occidental darkness? Is a non barbarous hatred possible? Why not convert hatred into rage? For us, revolted by philosophy or the Irreconcilable, we are the choice between hatred and rage, between hatred and struggle (not at all quietist "indifference").

The Struggle with the Gnostic Angel:
1. Affectivity and Inspiration

The Angel as a symptom of Platonism and orientalism in philosophical gnosis would be a second example (besides Rebellion) of the non-philosophical interpretation of a gnostic theme. We will not examine here the richness and complexity of the Angel as a figure of the mundus imaginalis in oriental philosophy, but only one of its aspects and what it can symbolize. What sense can non-philosophy, for its part, give it?

The Angel appears, alongside other things, amongst the figures of philosophical sensibility, those which we may call "transcendental" in a larger sense. We must include figures that are sometimes more anonymous and inhuman. Aristotle, who was somewhat of an empiricist, attributes wonder to the philosopher because it is an affect which directs the being in his Being. Plato, philosopher of transcendence, attributes mania, divine inspiration, to the poet rather than to the philosopher and to the philosopher its inferior form, namely demonological and oracular inspiration. Descartes, Christian philosopher, attributes to the philosopher admiration before the perfect being and all-powerful nature of God. Bergson, philosopher of the mystical élan, creative emotion. Hegel, bacchanalian drunkenness which crosses through death and drives the most determined to nothingness. Nietzsche, drunkenness and the joy of going through Dionysian dismemberment and tragic pain. Kant, who limited Platonic digressions out of "respect," and who had the tendency to withdraw from this fairly general agreement for fanaticism and the neighboring affects amongst the other philosophers.

The instance of the Angel is a repeat of Platonic mania; it brings back together every inspiration, whether they are brilliant, poetic or popular, the idea which falls or which comes, as fanatic progenitor of the Idea. Does the Angel come then to theory as God comes to the idea (Levinas)? But recent gnostic theoreticism is a quasi-Platonic Idea; instead it concerns an inversion of Levinas' formula. The Angel comes to theory but in reality this is the

220

thought-Angel, a Platonism which comes, if not to God, at least to the Rebel. In addition this function of the Angel serves as mediation between the theory-subject and the World or thought. It upsets the continuity of causality, what is this "coming to" [*venir à*], what is its possibility? Its function is religious and does not seem to enter into a "scientific" kind of project in so far as non-philosophy has an aspect of science.

Now what about sensibility from the non-philosophical perspective? Once again a global inversion of perspective imposes itself according to the new basis of Man-in-person, not even counting that this accepts treating the problem as affectivity rather than simply sensibility, even ontologically speaking. Non-philosophy distinguishes a triad within philosophy, that of affect as effect or result, of affection as operation, of affectivity as an aggregate unifying these two terms and doomed to a Principle of Affective Sufficiency. Non-philosophy then reorganizes it through a distinction that must break with the triune and unitary conception where affect and affection are conditioned one to the other inside affectivity. Here we find this other "logic" that we call unilateral which is, 1. the affect positing the unitary correlation as axiom or abstract in an axiomatic way, in particular of every relation with an affection, the Affected-without-affection or the future (as the Lived is without-life); 2. affectivity is that total and sufficient correlation; 3. affection is a subject-existent-affective, *a priori* clone or phenomena of … for … affectivity. The Affected-without-affection is an affect-lived-in-the-last-Humaneity, which does not go without saying for philosophy which substitutes for it Being, God, Angel, a Demon, a god like Apollo or Dionysus, etc., or at best a Transcendental Ego. It does not precede affectivity, which would be absurd, but it is separated from it and has primacy over it. On the other hand affection now determined by the Affected lived in an immanent way is the radical beginning, being the subject, not of … but for the understanding [*intelligence*] of affectivity. Neither a melancholy occidental genius, nor an oriental genius of exaltation, but the Affected as strictly universal human gift of affection....

Whether we are talking about the Angel, or about any other philosophical affect, as we have said, it arises from the Principle of Sufficient Affectivity, which must be isolated and manifested as suspended by non-philosophy. From this perspective three operations are necessary in order to deepen the reduction of the Angel: 1. Platonic fanaticism [*enthouisasme*] is reducible at the same time as it is generalizable as a test of the Auto-encompassing or of Philosophizability whose grasp by and of the subject is by definition enthusiastic [enthousiasmante], more than in a merely psychological sense; 2. This fanaticism, either the Angel or the People, is itself lived-in-Man and it is sufficiency raised and manifested as such; 3. Fanaticism is not at all destroyed or even revealed in its sufficiency of all-affectivity, for the Angel is in-Man but it is still not determined in-the-last-Humaneity. The Angel must be determined as first affection, as radical beginning not of … but for … sufficient fanaticism. It is under these conditions that the philosophico-Platonic generality of the Angel is reduced and included from now on as subject-existent-Angel.

Another idea of the People is now possible. The people, like the Angel, no longer designate anything here except the subject-existent-People, conforming to this pressure which wants the subject to be a non-quantitative multitude in the way that Man is One-in-One, a designation which is also no longer qualitative but determines the philosophical relation of these two characters. Existing-in-a-multitude is the law of the subject just as being-given-in-One is that of Man. The People are the affect-subject that is exactly possible in this context and under these constraints still called for in the non-angelic term of "Angel."

From the perspective of this non-philosophical reduction, non-religious gnosis (which attributes to the Angel a non-thetic Transcendence) still assumes the Angel as auto-affection because mania or inspiration here appears exterior and transcendent in the religious sense of the term, which is not the case for us who see there the effect of philosophical transcendence or philosophizability. From the perspective of non-philosophy, inspiration is real as well but does not concern the choice of materials to be treated, which, as such, are seized and inscribed in the form of philosophizability. Inspiration is not something different from the auto-encompassing impulse, inspiration and expiration of universal philosophizability. Gnosis has evidently been replaced by the Angel making it that form-philosophy or that which also gives it in-One or without-givenness. As a Platonic doctrinal decision it must substitute the inspiration understood in exteriority for this immanence of being-given. Gnosis assumes an external affection by the world in its people, if it adds itself to determination-in-the-last-instance, and this is because the World has not first been posited in-One. This "doctrinal" Angel is at least the symptom of transcendence or an absolute position of the World and of the refusal of non-philosophy's initial conditions of the first axiom, that of the radical Immanent. The first axiom of non-philosophy does not provide an absolute position (auto-position) of the World (of mastery) but its radical position, which is a completely different matter.

But if the Angel is the affect of the World itself in its people and as a people-World, then it must be reduced in its in-itself-absoluteness. As gnosis refuses this possibility it then represents for gnosis another possibility, coming from the World, offered by it, that of the weapon to struggle against it, but which must be "oriented" by the Rebel-subject. Gnosis attributes a "transcendental dialysis" [*dialyse transcendental*] to the Angel which thus separates itself from the Mastery with which it can confuse itself and of which it detaches itself when it comes to theory and allows itself to be oriented by it. It has a tendency to make instances objective and to attribute the dualysis to the Angel alone whereas for non-philosophy dualysis is the set of two operations.

We will defend the thesis of the being-immanent of philosophizability as a World-affect, of philosophical fanaticism, or of the World as an affect-without-affection in-the-last-Humaneity. The World as pure philosophizability is de-angelized or a de-Platonized Angel. The Angel of the World has not come to theory but a theory (of the Angel) must come [*venir*], future, to the Angel and in this sense itself must happen [*advenir*] in its non-philosophical theory. It must then be understood as auto-mania, angelic, or a maniacal distance closed in on itself, and can thus become the object of a unified theory of philosophy and the Angel.

The case for saying that the Angel falls from heaven comes from the "oriental" gnostics in the East. It is true that Heaven is typical of these kinds of surprises and we even allow for miraculous descents and arrivals. The pure transcendental Rebel has no function apart from marking the place of rebellion and something of the rank and date of the Angel inserting it into the apparatus, while finally Man-in-person intervenes even less in regards to mastery than within non-philosophy. It is a miraculous risk if the Angel comes to theory or if the People make of themselves a Rebel. And what does the Rebel make of this popular or angelic diction? The problem is always that of the suture, here of Man and the People, constant within philosophy, which resolves it by the over- of over-mastery.

Struggle... 2: The Antithesis of the Angel – Cruci-fiction

But the symbolic signification of the Angel is still more profound for the relations of non-philosophy to Christianity and gnosis. These last two form a contradiction around the Angel, for there is a religious antithesis of the Angel which goes on to decide the kind of combat with the Angel that can haunt non-philosophy.

Let us assume by simplifying, though, through a plausible hypothesis, that in Christianity the Angel serves as a simple messenger and has no other function, above all no constitutive function in the relations of God and man, and so Christ is sufficient to exhaust the problem of their relation. Let us equally assume that gnosis uses the Angel as the messenger of Christ but this time the message is constitutive (as gnosis or knowledge itself) of man's salvation and suffices to assure it that consequently Christ has not suffered on the cross, no more than man has in imitating the experience of his crucifixion. The Angel is in this sense that religious persona who separates Christianity and gnosis. Either the Cross or the Angel....

The struggle with the Angel may take on a possible double meaning: one from Christianity and the other from gnosis. The first refuses the gnostic thesis of the uniquely divine character of Christ that symbolizes the Angel, Christ being "the Angel of Angels." The antithesis naturally moves itself into the element of religious transcendence; that, more nuanced, of non-philosophy, which stops simply opposing itself to angelism as well as to its contrary, an opposite that we logically call "crucifiability" or, even better, the cruciformity of Christ and every man. Neither deiform [*déiforme*] Christ nor cruciform Christ.... This is a pragmatic in-the-last-Humaneity of angelic deiformity and of christic cru-ciformity, their unified theory such that it no longer reconstitutes a philosophical system, with its sides (bilaterally or bifacially), Christian and gnostic in various measures (Hegel, Nietzsche, Deleuze, and the ambiguity of the theme of the death of God), but constitutes instead a Stranger-subject with Christian and angelic aspects (unilateral or unifacial). The ultimate term here of the transformative work of non-philosophy is what we can call the *a priori* or Christo-angelic phenomenon, unified and unilateralized identically in-the-last-Humaneity. Save Christ from a sufficient cruciformity, save the Angel from a deiformity that is also completely sufficient. Extract from the Cross its persecutory power and attribute it to the World such that it supposes itself in-itself, persecuting straight away the christo-angelic subject, but also extracting from the Angel its power of salvation and attributing it to this subject and saving it from sufficient crucifixion. The subject alone must be saved; salvation ceases to be this symmetrical act of sufficient creation, the relative autonomy of the World signifies the limitation of redemption of the Stranger-Subject alone. The World is less good than Christianity imagines it but better than gnosis imagines it, and yet it is not a question of environment and of the right measure of Other-than ... good and Other-than ... bad.

This is our non-Docetism, something like our cruci-fiction.

Theory of the Crime-World:
Victimization and Victimizability

It is difficult to resume the differend of non-philosophy and Neo-platonic gnosis without a word from Kant: Plato the father of every digression in philosophy.... The formula is so worthy of that old philistine, although he was a pietist and not very divine when he confined God to a simple postulate of reason and feared fanaticism. And in any case gnosis assumes this digression with panache. But since Plato, the world – the dreadful World – nevertheless changed, evil has earned its pedigree by becoming, if we can put it this way, "popular," amongst other things we have gained consciousness of its "radicality" and "banality," and this consciousness has at least intensified this radicality and banality. The victims as well, those whom Platonic gnosis has not loved and whom Plato hastened to embalm and idealize in the figure of the philosopher Socrates who, as said in passing, thought according to an oracle and a demon, proof that he is a character "just looking" for philosophers. But what does the spectacular death of a wise Greek man matter in the theater of existence when compared to the murder and extermination of unknown victims in the state of a multitude, murdered in the name of their human identity? And from the spectacular victim to the unknown victim it is not a question of quantity. The victims should have earned recognition, failing to be recognized by philosophy, and they should at least be honored by thought. If the World enriches itself with the consciousness of evil merely to subvert the conscience, it does not appear too extravagant that we set the Platonic clock back to the hour of the crime-World, that in particular we reevaluate the relation which gnosis has placed implicitly between philosophy and the category of the mortiferous, a connection in relation to which Platonism has an awkward or insufficient position. Non-religious gnosis understands mastery less as a sufficient philosophy or specularity (one would moreover have to say auto-specularity), which like Law mortifies through the World and Obedience to the subject (all these terms are quite religious and say nothing in any case about the structure of philosophy). The expression of the dead Law [*Loi mortifère*] suggests a transcendence of the religious rather than the philosophical type but the epekeina-physical dimension (which often serves it as a support) cannot be isolated in an abstract manner like the rest of philosophy. And the World can certainly bring the hour of justice, the Great Midday, but not the Just as Future-in-person.

Transcendence is mortiferous, but death cannot remain anonymous under the threat of confusing itself with a simple destruction and must be put in relation to the victim as one of the first ways of naming Man. Humans have this primacy over the rest of the Beings of the World, of being victimizable by definition as they are philosophizable, and globally for the same reason that in-the-last-Humaneity it is humans who philosophize humans and men who kill men. This signifies that the thought-world does not only kill humans case by case, nor even en masse, all of which would want to ground the universal victimization of-the-last-instance on the positive historical fact of genocide and political or ethnic matters; of course these are inseparable from philosophizability but also of course too narrow to explain the necessity and contingency of crime. The mechanism of "victimizability," if we can still put it this way, is different although not separable from the criminal facts through which it passes and spreads itself out but which raise victimization to the level of a philosophical concept.

The thought-world proceeds by way of an alienating belief that touches every human being, in knowing that their persecution or their murder, always local and particular, is accepted as being crime par excellence and reflects itself spontaneously as a dimension of the World, form-crime or crime-World. Yet we put forth that the belief in absolute All-crime is precisely what prevents justice from being delivered to the victims. Why? Of course, this would not be meant in the sense in which this belief would be a simple illusion of victims themselves exaggerating their unhappiness in a hyperbolic way, but because this belief in all-crime, an effective and material belief like the imaginary, dissolves in revisionist generalities and sometimes even more, the individual victim's potency of real Humaneity, his radical human identity. In the absolute all-crime, the persecuted identify themselves in the crime and back themselves into a circle with their persecutor or prepare themselves to return to the scene and switch roles. This is why philosophizability reduplicates the empirical crime into an ideal crime, and this couple constitutes the effectiveness of the crime, which envelops within it a future persecutor. Crime is not what we believe it is initially, it is a concept and as a concept it oversees itself. And in the same way the victim oversees himself as a persecutor to come or as one in progress. Furthermore, we consider that true crimes, along with complete crimes and those which have drawn all their consequences, are those which transform the persecuted into persecutors. Every concept assumes a general element in the variable dimensions that make indeterminate (within transcendence, political or religious) the identity of the victim, crime and the criminal (human identity in-the-last-instance rather than the historical, ethnic, or political instance). One destroys nature and therefore man through man's biological aspect, but one kills them and persecutes them because of what they are as men. It is under this last rubric that they are known as "victims." A truth and a thought must be given to this term "victim," truly presupposed universals, and we must stop defining the term through examples, or even through an exemplary but always particular crime through which it refers to some particular content rather than to a structural trait and a formal power of the World. Philosophy can demand an exemplary and foundational crime, that of Parmenides and Socrates, for example, the psychoanalysis of the Father's murder, or the Jewish people in the singularity of the Shoah. A particular crime (and coming from historical explanations that are always possible) can be lived as empirically absolute, an effect of an infinite, hyperbolic and unfathomable intention, exemplary in the unilateral destruction of humanity. But once outside of history and its neighboring parameters, as non-philosophy, there is nothing more exemplary of crime than the death penalty. It is not intelligible for Man that if this lived experience is a preliminary object for a supplementary philosophical interpretation to then assume that philosophy and non-philosophy have for their final end to render the World intelligible.

Thus the unitary ternary of crime, criminal, and innocent (or exceptional victim) is undone. In reality crime does not happen in thirds, or even three/fourths (if we include the justice which closes the system), but in a more restrained (non-) circle, that of unilateral dualities between the Victim-in-person (Man-in-person) and the circle of all-crime unilaterally alloying a criminal and a victim, with the intermediary dualities of the subject-existent-Just (being Justice determined in-the-last-Humaneity) with these two poles.

However, this schema lacks a final piece. We have prohibited every recourse to historical phenomena under the title of foundational cause or elective victim of crime, yet it is evident that the decision of persecution must take on a theoretical status, albeit one without abstraction. It is impossible to pass over this without saying more, without saying a non-philosophical word or two regarding the millions of murdered or persecuted left by history and so abandoning them to what may be a new form of generality. There is not Man-in-person on one side giving its identity to the victims and a thought-world or crime-form on the other side which would be a pure objective and independent form, which would drive a gnosis Platonically indifferent to Man. The concrete victim matters, man in-world as a symptom of Man-in-person qua victimizable in-the-last-instance or Victim-in-person. If we name Man-in-Man as such it is because the occasion gives us certain victims which have their symptomatic value with regard to Humaneity (and not humanity). Which ones, though?

How is the subject the weakest and most susceptible to being persecuted by the World? The subject whose weakness and powerlessness, (the role of negative or insufficient condition) calls in some way (in any case from the World's point of view) for persecution and victimization? The Angel is by definition, as subject determined-in-the-last-Humaneity, the victimizable subject.

Whereas the figure of the Angel serves to demonstrate the divine or superhuman character of man, it no longer serves the human subject, thus persecuted and victimized in-the-last-Humaneity. Human kind is precisely the persecutor and enemy of the Angel as subject.

These victims have been killed and persecuted with fire and by fiat in the gnostic cause of identity, of its radical and unilateral affirmation. But whose identity are we talking about, if indeed every man is rightly reclaiming it and refusing it? Identity alone, far from every identification, can be posited as an ultimatum to philosophy and religion, identity demanded and postulated as true but without-truth and not sufficient for the truth, as force-(of)-identity, indisputable and necessary, that no philosophical or religious decision can validate, verify, or even falsify. This identity of gnostic essence, this heretical decision is determinate but not foundational; it is its inverse novelty. Impossible but real identity, unintelligible even after philosophical explanations and good will. The last identity, that after which there will be nothing else, not even nothingness, above all not difference, comes to the subject from the depths of messianicity which forms humans. Even the World has a destiny; it is in the hands of the inversives rather than the subversives.

These victims, which we will call symptomatic rather than exemplary, have not had the chance to be idealized and ingratiated in a philosophical monument, not even with a camp literature, with a memory in either case. Even the earth in which they have been buried and lost cannot serve as their memory. Socrates was not subject to burial in a foreign land, the Jews reduced to ashes have undergone the degrading but final memory of the mass grave where they were persecuted – they were buried in a criminal earth. Our Socrates, for the non-philosophers, is the Unknown Heretic, the Unmanned Angel which no earth can identify and which comes with Man from nowhere. His tomb is not empty like that of the historical Christ; it is our memory which is empty of his and every tomb. Heretics are not a people dispersed to the four

230

corners of the Earth but a people without-World, of a diaspora before every place. Only the heretics who have been spewed out from their earth and heaven, who are buried in an earth of exile or who have had to disinhabit their heaven and have been cast into hell, only they find grace in the eyes of Man who first loved them.

Giving Death: The Last Responsibility

It is not clear that the Platonic form of gnosis, in so far as it is reinserted into religion, takes humans seriously when it classifies them into two categories, those who fear death and those who do not. The old Greek problem of whether to fear or not fear death is typical of the ideal-world of wisdom and the fundamentally happy man (or happy by his destination) who is capable of heroism. We now have another problem, more crucial, to be settled without recourse to the auto-justificatory transcendence of the polis. This is murdered man by "himself;" this is the fact of giving death, not of receiving it from an exterior evil genius, and of giving it still when we receive it. This is man as victim not by destiny, mostly unaccountable, or even author of an error still unknown to himself, but a victim according to himself, murdered in-the-last-instance according to Man. For humans, receiving death is first and foremost giving it in the sense where giving is not an operation but the being-revealed of death in-the-last-Humaneity. The wise Greek man is only a suicide of the polis and philosophy, but we now know, this is our conjuncture, that man is a suicide of humanity, if only so in-the-last-Humaneity. He is responsible for his suicide but it is not his in-the-last-instance. Also, in crime and not only in rebellion, Man-in-person only self-authorizes itself in the occasion limited by the World, of means and ends that the World provides it with. This is not giving meaning to death (whether that meaning be anthropological or as consciousness), it is the lived-without-life for death, received in addition, and which gives it and makes it human in an ultimate way. It is given-in-lived-experience even when it is received, so that "giving death" is an ambiguous formula, and the murderer only gives death on the condition of taking it and transmitting it, but this is how he gives death. The Murderer himself "gives" death precisely as a human. Can giving death in this sense perhaps allow for us to rethink euthanasia as a gift of death in the name of the last Humaneity? The victim must leave the vengeful circle of life and death and determine it more exactly.

There is also another way of treating, in-the-last-immanence, the problem of man without throwing the final responsibility onto the World. The difference between non-philosophy and non-religious gnosis is visible here, mastery and death are human in-the-last-instance even when they come from transcendence, but the transcendence it comes from must already be defeated or uncrowned of its pretension, for death is already vanquished, not by Life but by the Lived-without-life. This is the whole problem of what we call "mastery," the problem of its internal structure and not only the more or less violent synonyms that we give it. Mastery cannot simply be declared "absolute," we will not confuse its declaration of absoluteness or confuse its pretension with its real state or its being-given-in-Real more exactly.

Appended Notes on Non-Philosophical Gnosis and Non-Religious Gnosis

It is important to avoid confusing non-religious gnosis and what non-philosophy does in its usage of gnosis. The former hijacks the non-philosophical apparatus and ends up criticizing it. It concerns knowing if gnosis utilizes non-philosophy as a model that is still at bottom philosophical, or if non-philosophy utilizes gnosis as simple materials.

Can we graft gnosis, which is not a philosophy, onto the non-philosophical discovery of the Real? Maybe, but non-philosophy has a specific rigor because it treats philosophical language in a univocal way, including that of the Real. Can we understand under this term (the Real) also Soul or Materials understood with a religious accent or in a religious context? It is possible if the Real is indifferent, which undoubtedly it is, but the term "real" is not,

232

and is engaged by philosophy which through the term itself is the master. This gnosis thus supposes any vocabulary whatsoever and is above all not necessarily that of philosophy or in any case haphazardly philosophizable, it can play the role of a symptom for the discourse on the Real. There is also in this indifference to the vocabulary of decision a disavowed mastery, poorly controlled and guided by religion. In reality the words "soul" and "material" give rise again to a fetishism of grammar, as every religion wants it. The same difference exists between non-religion and non-philosophy as between theology and philosophy, the same way of proceeding on the part of religion and theology. Non-philosophy recognizes the power of philosophy, which non-religion does not do in innocently making use of this power. This is the usual procedure of capture by theology, by way of a transcendence that even sees immanence but yet refuses to give effective primacy to it, primacy of effect and practice.

Non-philosophy holds to a certain account of the history of philosophy which as a history of philosophy, above all of the contemporary kind, exposes and demonstrates the tricks of the master-philosopher. Those of Kant, for example, with his distinction of two forms of the transcendental, within the analytic of truth and in the Transcendental Dialectic. Gnosis uses this last transcendent concept of the transcendental, not the reformed transcendental in the sense of immanence and specifically the Kantian sense. Those of Derrida and the paleonymic strains or textual chains, which transmit the symptom, against the ruptures within structuralism or occasionally in Foucault. Finally, those of psychoanalysis that suggest the infinite ruses of the Master and cannot be reduced to Lacan's (certainly fundamental) tripod. Non-philosophy could be the psychoanalysis of mastery and rebellion, but finally adapted to these objects, not merely a simple transferal of its "meta-psychological" concepts to philosophy. It must be a non-philosophy, not a meta-philosophy.

When gnosis is tacked onto non-philosophy, it is no longer able to be treated by that which it attempts in its way to absorb.

This type of system by syncretism is historically inevitable, as the force of philosophical and religious resistance is "natural" and constitutive. But if suffices to know that these neo-blendings - overplatonizations (Saint Gilles) or overhusserlizations (Saint Michel), etc. - of the practice of unified theory, in being given a distorted image, can still be used or are open to being reworked.

The allegedly Platonic or gnostic "radicalization" is the involuntary falsification of the radical's or immanent's practice. Need we be reminded that according to non-philosophy it is the radical that radicalizes, and it is not radicalization that would create in some idealist way the radical? The radical's forced synthesis with Platonism or gnosis, not as simple materials but as doctrine, does not function in a coherent way but adds the religious suture to the philosophical suture, it is a supplementary construction. What can be coherent as the non-philosophical is a unified theory of philosophy and gnosis, which goes through the mediation of philosophizability and abandons, one way or another, its status as limited doctrinal position in order to become simple material.

Non-religious gnosis wants to accumulate rigor and the cutting edge. Non-religious rigor is found in non-philosophy from which the non-religious borrows the discovery of the immanent Real inthe-last-instance. But the cutting edge, which the non-religious strongly imposes on it in order to rectify and intensify non-philosophy, is thought to be found in Platonic and gnostic transcendence, through the religious element in which these two doctrines bathe, and generally through the pathos of division, albeit called in-immanence. Thus either non-philosophy does not have universal validity (which the non-religious reclaims since it was not integrated with either Platonism, gnosis, or Maoism) or else here we find a contradictory montage which consists in adding to non-philosophy those entities that double it and whose only utility is to bring it back to the bosom of philosophy, since this gnosis has cast its own concept of mastery onto a larger object which is the philosophy that it understands as sufficient specularity and which is in reality sufficient auto-specularity.

This usage of gnosis diminishes the interest in non-philosophy to the "discovery" of the human or immanent Real. It immediately interrupts analysis in order to impose a Platonic apparatus on this Real (for reasons it believes to be sound). What makes this suspicious is that gnosis speaks of radical immanence in the spirit of transcendence or from the Platonic type of the One. As the rest of the argumentation, namely non-philosophy as such, is limited by this point of view or still raises disguised mastery, and as we have assumed that both theoretical propositions are coherent in their order, we must conclude that non-religion and non-philosophy do not understand the same thing under the name of the Real, of Man-in-person, of One-in-One or of non-consistency, only having in common a vocabulary arranged in approximately the same order.

The image of non-philosophy distorted in the glazed over Great Mirror of logic (the pure transcendental Rebel) leads to an unbelievable imbroglio. It allows for all the definitions of philosophy given by non-philosophy to return against it. This is retaliation in the place of inversion. Gnosis contradictorily accuses non-philosophy of being a theoreticism (just as non-philosophy made the same charge against philosophy) and at the same time of being a "practice" as non-philosophy would equally have itself be. Unilateral identity, in the clone, of theory and practice is disarticulated into two opposing poles, theoreticism and practice, an absolutely sure sign of a return to the philosophical repressed.

The general argument of indifference to "equivalent" doctrinal positions must be nuanced. On the one hand, already from the side of materials, or philosophy, for itself or in-itself, the indifference is neither to the structures nor to the objects incarnating these structures. On the other hand, regarding the contingency of the materials, it must not be confused with a general or nihilistic indifference, or with that of an empty form. The real-transcendental operation on these materials cannot be indifference of a philosophical order, a mode of transcendence. Every indifference has its source in the Real as being-separated or Other-than....

But mastery, bringing about the Real (which it can do and necessarily does by virtue of its being-given-in-Real and by its structure), is known by it within cloning, an operation in which the Real gives it and its radical identity as well as its own struggle or indifference, which is now transcendental and in-the-last-instance. They want to be able to affect materials and even the pretension or the demand of the material to the core. Real indifference, the spirit of struggle or the Other-than … passes through a transcendental state where it "charges" itself with responsibility for the materials and now exercises itself directly on them. The One-in-One is immediately invested within the transcendental instance that it contributes in constituting, carrying it towards the materials that it affects. The root of this indifference is real but it concerns its transcendental form, thus in relation to positions and doctrines. The point of view of these positions is indifferent to the Real or does not affect it but therefore is itself the force of transformation of these positions. To such an extent that the Stranger-subject cannot have the same indifference as the Real except on the condition of adapting it to these positions, being drawn from an *a priori* experience-understanding.

Struggle is the real condition of rebellion, but it must be effectuated in a unilateral "relation" to mastery in order to acquire a transcendental character and to affect mastery in its structural support. The transcendental cannot be a double of the Real, but it must be penetrated by an immanent struggle or alterity proper to the Real.

Real indifference is radical and in any case does not define itself except by its power of determination. It is real alterity, the spirit of struggle that the transcendental actualizes or brings into existence. The argument about the indifference of non-philosophy goes against gnosis which is itself indifferent to the utilized language. In the same way that the Sékommça turns against religious evidence, the "fact" of the Real turns against the Rebel and the Angel.[4]

---

4. *Sékommça* is a contraction of the common French expression *c'estcommeça* meaning literally "it is like that" and was developed at length by Guy Lardreau and Christian Jambet in

Platonism and purism go together on the most abstract or most "ontological" plane, whichever it is. The purism of the pure Rebel or the Angel believed capable of bringing down mastery (and reproaching non-philosophy for its alleged empirical taste for various regions of mastery) and all the masters (reproaching non-philosophy once again for its alleged refusal to consider the diversity of transcendences). It is therefore useless to repeat to what extent this call to purity and purification, to the hatred of the World as well as of philosophy, has a troubling heritage if it is interpreted ideologically. Just as non-philosophy is neither Greek nor Jewish in its principles, as we have already said, it is neither occidental nor oriental in the sense that these terms are not only historical or geographical but also geo-philo-political. How can one still have recourse to these oppositions, that of an Orient as bearer of light and an Occident veiled in shadows?

To oppose the Orient as a generalized form of thought and the Occident as a restricted or restrictive form of it is to assume that the second transcendence, epekeina-physical, is its excellent and generalized form, and that the Occident essentially lives through meta-physical transcendence as the case would tend to prove (this is a symptom) of Saint Michel's grounding phenomenology upon the critique of "phenomenological distance" and ontology alone, forgetting that other distance – the transcendence of the One. However, the nearly exclusive promotion of the transcendence of the One and its "oriental" confusion with religion seems also to be a completely arbitrary decision, a refusal to consider the multidimensional complexity of the philosophical apparatus. Setting it aside within the materials, already placing itself in the posture of a unified theory, refusing to unilaterally choose and thus to engage itself in a war that is at first sight a fratricide. The choice of oriental philosophy is in the end a choice for religion against philosophy and obviously against the spirit of non-philosophy. Generalizing the philosophical, must we not, no doubt, still go

their *L'Ange* as a mode of ideological naturalism or the idea that how the world is organized is done so necessarily. Gilles Grelet has taken up this concept and expanded upon it in his own work. – T.N.

forth in that operation like the philosophers themselves, on the basis of an initial intra-philosophical choice. The transcendence in epekeina can at most give place to an abstract or hyperphilosophical generalization but not through a formalization of philosophy adequate to its complexity. Philosophy is too serious an affair to be left to the philosophers alone....

If oriental philosophy has developed the aspect of epekeina-physics and occidental philosophy the two aspects of meta- and epekeina-physics, but above all the first side, then is it the first that envelops the second or the inverse? Which is an excrescence of the complete concept of philosophy? The occidental explores all the dimensions but the epekeina superficially in a weak blend, it remains more empirical than religious, sober in its unfulfilled desire for some mystique. It forms a negative or hollowed place for the divine. The oriental, on the contrary, fosters a positive meeting with religion in which it attempts to absorb philosophy, which it does not cease to sober up in the form of negative theology that takes itself directly into the Logos with which the Occident feels itself to be on equal footing. It falls to non-philosophy not to reduce its material to one of these two dimensions nor even to their weak blend, but to think this blend as philosophizability or Auto-encompassing, to be the unified theory of the Orient and the Occident from this point of view.

Against the Angel's abstract epekeinaphysical conception of rebellion, we advance a transcendental and an *a priori* discipline which takes its object out of the blendings of mastery and rebellion. There is rebellion, philosophical discourse and only it in the least assures us so, illusion or not, and even assures us that the Master has exhausted all his tricks, meaning their detail. From this perspective it is necessary to give primacy (but not exclusivity) to philosophical discourse over a discourse that is too massively religious, in as much as philosophy aims to mask mastery and disguise it under a liberating outside. There is rebellion, is this the response to *quid facti*? What is its right or its pretension to matter for reality, the World or History; is this the question *quid juris*?

In the ways that they are required, both are as little Kantian as possible here. Non-philosophy is also a matter of letters and maintains its rigor in being the least "taken in" by philosophy and its swelling ideologies. Yet we posit its question in this quasi Kantian way, without giving anything constitutive of Kantianism to non-philosophy, or we metaphysically deduce rebellion. Non-religious gnosis seems to be a metaphysical rather than a transcendental deduction of rebellion.

The deduction of an absolute and pure Rebel is only possible if the immanent Real has made a transcendent usage of it. On the other hand, how can an immanent usage of the Real not throw us into mastery or transcendence from the start, turning us to language and requiring us to look for weapons in philosophy? Radical or practiced immanence (this is one of the senses of "radical," or else it is an absolute immanence) implies an unreserved vow to language since immanence gives us nothing of thought or nothing of the World. The forced hand of philosophical Logos is the only means for helping to uni-verse the mastery whose contours it outlines. Religion, spontaneous or stowed away in the lone epekeina-physical dimension of philosophy, is a certain particular "oriental" decoupage of this endlessly vague body but which is ruled by philosophy. It is necessary to posit immanence through the means of immanence, and as it has no such means, to use the transcendence of philosophical language, but first reduced through radical human immanence. Not by a transcendental reduction of philosophy, meaning still second and exterior, but the real "reduction" must be immanent, brought by Man or the One-in-One. On this basis all the work comes from the Rebel-subject.

Man-in-person, while immanence through and through, announces itself to the World as future. Not as "transcendent," for this would be an interpretation still in terms of alterity proper to mastery. A transcendence is positive and productive, it is sufficient, which is never the case with Man. In reality, the content of this alterity of Man is not rejected or excluded but the very spirit of struggle, the simple but necessary possibility of rebellion as future or "Other-than." This is the force of uni-laterality, the proper acting of Humaneity's non-action when mastery is no longer ignored, but given even before being taken into account and introduced into the global calculation. This is one of the constant and major confusions surrounding non-philosophy, unilaterality reduced to transcendence, the Other-than … reduced to the Other-of…. Gnosis posits the Immanent Radical as alterity in place of positing it in an immanent way as uni-laterality – these are the wages of Platonism. The transcendental essence of the Rebel includes a moment of the spirit of struggle which does not distinguish it from Man but designs it as unilation of mastery. It is clear that the transcendence/immanence dyad is still in philosophical usage and that it must be understood as Immanent-in-person and Other-than … transcendence (which is never in its way simple). In other words, immanence and transcendence no longer here form a dyad but a unilateral duality.

Gnosis defines materialism by the last instance (unlike Dialectical Materialism which is a kind of idealism and empiricism). But not by adding the theses of practice as Marx demanded with regard to Feuerbach, instead just as theoreticism without practice or what tries to be the "destruction of practice" (Saint Gilles). This contemplative materialism is highly paradoxical, even if non-philosophy seems to allow this kind of game (Real = Soul = Matter). It comes to the same thing as the formula of materialism as "not-all," a formula that is still sufficient. Non-philosophy defines the last instance as structured in a unilateral duality, which is true practice and must not be understood as empirical or historical. It is the One (-not-) all and certainly not the One-All as Deleuze, being a good Spinozist, believed it to be.

Who thinks, what is the subject of thought? It has never been said that the transcendental moment (the spirit of struggle assumed by the Rebel-subject) was that of thought, since the transcendental is a function of the Real and thus it cannot think. The subject is the transcendental identity or the formed clone 1. of essence or of the transcendental and 2. of philosophical content

240

transformed under the real-transcendental conditions of essence. Transformed in what sense? In the sense that it has lost the unity of the system, now replaced by the identity of the Real. Yet if we remove the unity of the system, we change everything, the dyad of particular contrary terms that were inseparable from the unity of the system. This content transformed by the real arrival of the transcendental is necessarily a new kind of *a priori*, this time being an *a priori* for philosophy. Thus the subject is, by way of its transcendental essence, non-thought. Thought can only come from mastery but transformed as *a priori* content of the subject. As we have not isolated the transcendental moment of effective experience, it does not need the Angel, or else it is another name for philosophy, its religious name. Mastery must happen there where the Real is and it can only be served by materials out of which the cloned subject emerges from the Real. Does gnosis really want to say something else when it says that the Angel must come to theory? No, except that the point of departure is religious and that this introduces an excessive and unintelligible or "irrational" transcendence in relation to that of philosophy. This is why the formula "enter into theory" or "come to theory" sounds like "enter into religion" or "enter into gnosis." In this way gnosis allows for a margin of play, of refusal, or will in the Angel or in the people. Such room for maneuvering goes hand in hand with the ideal of theoreticism and contemplation that is inseparable from the Platonic break or chorismos. Non-philosophy leaves this margin of refusal to the resistance of mastery; this is the sense of practice as well.

Non-religious gnosis cuts and only forms a cutting edge, while non-philosophy prepares itself in struggle and only makes struggle. For the gnostic maxim, worthy of a saint but only really worthy of Saint-Just, say anything provided that it cuts, we oppose the maxim, struggle rather than vanquish. Struggle as Man-in-person rather than cutting like the philosopher. Provided that what cuts? A maxim like this loves the effect and the result, to conquer, to take or break open the head, the head that is not regarded for by the means. In particular, this kind of statement signals a disinterest for victims without encountering any resistance. This repulsion is possible, sometimes even desirable in certain cases, but it belongs too much to philosophy not to be worrisome.

Non-philosophy has posited the problem of rebellion at the heights of philosophical mastery, we accept this formula. But without forgetting that it is not a question of placing non-philosophy higher than … of rising just to the level of philosophy which gathers together every possible height. Does this also mean that religion, under its philosophico-oriental form, is higher than philosophy and dominates it? Man-in-person is neither the Most-High nor the Most-Low, but that which determines a subject starting from their religious balance. It is true that non-philosophy can seem like an attempt to take another thought higher than philosophy, but by eliminating for itself this height or that heroism, not by rivaling it in height as a religion would have it. This is the same way that it carries itself "to the heights" of religion and gnosis without ever coming to an "All-gnostic." This is why it has no more or less value than philosophy. Neither higher, nor lower, it clones this thought and makes justice (in-the-last-instance) of this injustice. Making justice of … this is completely the double sense of non-philosophy.

Philosophy allows for a specification of its most abstract forms. Philosophical Decision is not a formal system but it is relatively capable of being formalized, and not generalized as claimed in the content of an empiricist interpretation. But however capable it is of being formalized, it allows for a certain empirical concreteness.

The phenomenal content of the Rebel is formed from the materials of mastery and rebellion in their blended origins, but in this new state having lost their combinatory principle and in having received another which transforms them profoundly in the form of an *a priori*, being the non-rebelling Identity (of) itself. As a matter of course this *a priori* is the identity-form of … for … the materials of mastery and forms the last concrete content of Rebellion, but this time phenomenal or in-Humaneity.

The pure Rebel of gnosis can pass at best for what non-philosophy calls the Other-than … or the spirit of struggle, but this is not transcendental except in the context of the Rebel-subject, thus of a double causality and not only derived from the Real but from mastery as well to which it would have made an allusion without it playing a more consistent role. Decidedly, all difference is a result of Platonism and is located within the type of some last relation to mastery or to the World. The neo-gnostic Rebel has something of the jealous Rebel (Jewish gnosis) and the hateful rebel (Platonizing gnosis), while the non-philosophical Rebel is something of a … "Marxist," it labors and transforms mastery. It is not the transcendental representative of the Real near to mastery. The Real is never represented or representable but acts directly, which is to say transcendentally through the spirit of struggle, from All-mastery rather than near it. The re-introduction of representation in this sequence is not accidental or a case of an inadequate word, it is Platonism and gnosis which proliferates their entities. We are unable to resist evoking the critique of the theory of Forms in the first part of the *Parmenides* and above all the argument of the Third Man. The pure transcendental Rebel doubles the Real, the Angel in his way doubles the Rebel, but must there not also be a second rebel, a transcendental-repeat in order to bring about the suture with the Angel, is that suture not effective or effectuated from the very start, a first time by the being-given-in-One of overmastery, a second time by cloning, namely the being-given-in-One-in-the-last-instance? We could say that this supposes a solvable problem, to which we reply that such supposing as solvable is not assuming that it is resolved, gnosis and philosophy in any case assume it unable to be resolved, and finally that this radical solution is that of immanence, not that of transcendence or religion which can only resolve it in an arbitrary way by a violent and vicious decision. But is not radical identity a form of the vicious circle? If one wants it so, except that here there is not any alternative. Radical identity is independent from the vicious circle, not opposed to it, and has already reduced it. The new duality is minimal and unilateral if we

243

measure it via the distinctions of model/copy or ability/act, which are always somewhat bilateral; in any case, it is weakened.

The radical changes nothing in the absolute or leaves it to its illusion that it lives for itself, which is its absolute life. But the radical permits the emergence of the non-worldly clone of the World and what knows the absolute as a hallucination. In gnosis, we may ask ourselves if the radical is not also absolute, if immanence is not also ultimately objectified, if unilaterality is still not that of Platonic transcendence, if Non-Thetic Transcendence is not still understood in a transcendent way.

The radicality of the in-different Real (this is not a definition) lets the two sides of every philosophy (the dyad) manifest themselves, while the Platonic absolute has a tendency to absorb them in a single side which is no longer unilaterality through immanence but the One-All. Jealousy or hatred of that which is (this is always the choice) inside the dyad, of one side opposed to the other and privileged as All, this is philosophical injustice. Radicality excludes the All for its account and is happy to think it through axioms and explain it by theorems.

A kind of balance is established between the Real and mastery. Non-philosophy gives nothing to the Real and much to mastery which occasions the transcendental. Gnosis gives little to mastery, which needs the supplement of the Angel in order to fill out its causality, and so, very probably, gives too much to the Real, as always in philosophy. And what is it that we can give too much of with regards to the real? It is obviously transcendence. Does not gnosis re-introduce here a certain hypostatic process which cloning had eliminated?

A transcendental without an *a priori*, without a more or less formal understanding to which it is correlated, is hardly imaginable, except in returning towards a hazy and mystical concept of the transcendental under the influence of Plato. The Stranger-subject of non-philosophy possesses a concrete content pulled from the blend of mastery and rebellion, which is intimately conditioned during the cloning by its transcendental essence. In regards to this *a priori* of the Rebel, an *a priori* for mastery, we have nothing to say, but this is the transcendental that determines it here via its identity and its alterity (Other-than …). The *a priori* itself, is the result thus transformed by the occasional prompting exercised by philosophical mastery. It concerns an *a priori* for philosophical mastery, not of an *a priori* for physico-mathematical knowledge as in Kantian knowledge. This *a priori* is the appearance or the phenomenon "of" (for) mastery such that it constitutes the Stranger-subject. The Angel holds in a useless and supernumerary way, but inevitably, the place of that *a priori*, as if metaphysics determined the transcendental (in the philosophical way). How would the Angel or the People not incessantly be threatened by the return to mastery? And the transcendental having finally been vanquished, how would it not remain too distant to save them from the empiricism of mastery?

"Mastery" is defeated in two moments: the first time, simply as overmastery or rather as a pretension to the Real, certainly brought to the edge by the One of the system or epekeina-physics. The second time as a structure supporting this sufficiency and it is there that the transcendental One of overmastery, which is finally taken into account, is substituted for the transcendental-real Identity that at once imposes the transformation of mastery and rebellion, the two terms of the dyad. The non-philosophical transcendental is the Real functionally claiming to be of the auto-encompassing philosophy-form, not an object or an intra-philosophical understanding or a practice, that applies to the thought (-world) and can only come from the Real.

All non-philosophy is made in order to resolve, among other things, by cloning, the aporia (Marxist in particular) of a transcendental subject at once susceptible to alienation in mastery, thus of thought, and capable without contradiction of disalienating itself. Philosophy oscillates between an effective but definitively alienated subject and an inalienable but ineffective subject. The solution to this aporia of every philosophy is the unilateral disjunction of Man and the Stranger-subject, of the real and the transcendental.

245

This is the Real effectuated by philosophy, but the Real distinguishes itself from it. Cloning permits that neither the Real nor the transcendental are cut in two, either as each of them or the one to the other, as if the transcendental was shared between the Real and the empirical.

The gnosis that struggles with and against non-philosophy is a "materialism" but that signifies at most that it speaks in a transcendent way about matter and not in an immanent way in-the-last-matter. As if in a similar manner non-philosophy were a "realism" because it centers everything on the "Real." Generally, certain non-philosophers give themselves an overly narrow and limited list of adversaries like idealism, spiritualism, phenomenology, "sufficient specularity," and so appeal to materialism.

The transcendental does not compromise the real or alienate it within the experience of mastery, but it can be absolutely indifferent to it since it can effect the Real (being given-in-One and not being an absolutely exterior instance) which, at once, as transcendental, draws on an *a priori* which is transformed by experience. The force of the transcendental transforms the appeal of the Real through the materials by an *a priori* for this material.

"Worldly material is transcendent." This formula is too general and equivocal. The World is constituted by transcendence, moreover complicated, in the sense that it is its fabric or its substance. But it is not itself transcendent to.... Transcendent to what? To itself, auto-transcendent, but not transcendent to the Real. The Real is Other-than ... which moves the World away such as already given in-Real, but this is not a new transcendence or a form of what is the substance of the World. It is moved, rather held at a radical distance by the Real itself which makes it fall or lapse but on its own mode of immanence, not on a mode of transcendence. If we say "the World is transcendent," we make transcendence a universal adjective, an essence which applies again to the transcendence which forms the World. This statement is typically Platonic; it leads to an argument which we can call the Third

Transcendence, and in fact generalizes transcendence in the relations between other terms.

A terrible indifference to the World would allow non-philosophy to be too empirical or to give too much to the World in the form of a practice, or still more, "a theoretical domination of the world, a practice of domination" (Saint Gilles). This is an error in the interpretation of the scientific formula of "theoretical domination," to which gnosis opposes the "weakness of thought."

The transcendental no longer forms the knot between opposing instances, and it was barely made in Kant where it is the unity which returns out of metaphysical duality, so that every knot is always re-knotted as much as untangled. But cloning achieves the clearing away of every exterior or topological knot and even the triadic or philosophical knotting of Kant. Cloning is the identity which remains what it is even when it unilaterally "knots" (a half-knot?) transcendence, which is the substance of the World. Refusing to treat immanence in an immanent way, gnosis is condemned, as is every Platonism and Lacanianism, to the transcendent knotting of some instance in place of cloning. More exactly we superpose or add knotting to immanence rather than cloning, which would result from the radicality of immanence. The Real of gnosis or of Plato is too transcendent to give the World. It is necessary to choose between knotting and cloning. Non-philosophy is more Spinozist and Marxist than gnosis, which is more Platonist. It posits that the One is in-One and that the World is necessarily given in-One. That which we call unlearned knowing or the vision-in-One is unknown for non-religious gnosis, which makes of the One an inert or transcendent rather than a phenomenon, "a last instance" without the dashes that assure us of its cloned identity. The One can only be called a "necessary condition" in relation to the World by giving it, and by a negative necessity, moreover, not sufficient so that philosophizability is taken into account and more than just mentioned. It is then only mentioned or reduced to its being-given-in-One, no longer active as an occasion.

In non-philosophy, the Angel may be confused with an *a priori* layer of the force-(of)-thought or of the subject and would come to practice, thus to the Master rather than the theory-nothing-but-theory. But the Stranger-subject has a transcendental essence which, even as *a priori*, is still radically distinct from the Master.

(Non-) religious gnosis is a system of place holding [*lieuten-ance*], of representation, of an intermediary or interim between a first term that is original or represents nothing and the Others (Real, Subject or Theory or Man, Christ and Angel or People). Why not a "vicar?"

Gnosis disassociates the Real and the pure transcendental subject of thought. Therefore they do not think and thought must be occasional twice. In one case the subject is pure transcendental without thought, in the other the subject is also transcendental or has for an essence the transcendental. What is this thought which has no essence and this subject which is weakness or absence of thought? It is the history of the blind and the paralytic. The double occasionality of mastery and its efficacy of thought according to the Real and the Subject comes from the transcendental distinction of the Real and from the transcendental. Non-philosophy assumes thought as occasional only once, because it does not distinguish the Real and the transcendental, except precisely when speaking of that occasion.

Gnosis opposes the establishment of the Rebel-Subject (or pure transcendental) within the Real to the cloning of the Stranger-Subject. We do not see what this establishment corresponds to except that it represents the Real near transcendence, which is thus an occasion but a weak one. It is a transcendent interpretation of the Determination-in-the-Last-Instance. Even the transcendental does not come to represent the Real here. At bottom gnosis assumes that the World intervenes in absolute exteriority in relation to the Real, hence the transcendental which is simple dignity in relation to the World. As non-philosophy assumes that the World is already in-One when it finally becomes self-manifest, the "passive" necessity of the One or the Other-than …, the negative

248

struggle is still real and not transcendental, and it has no need of thought as a transcendental. Gnosis posits Mastery in exteriority or refuses to see that the Real, which certainly does not think, is capable of "giving" or "manifesting" thought. In reality what is lacking in gnosis is the beginning, the position of the problem, the right comprehension of the presupposed-real-of-thought, which is a whole, certainly unilateral or in-One but a whole or a duality. The in-One gives the One and also thought without having to create it or engender it by a procession. Platonism and materialism place a primary exteriority of transcendence between the presupposed and thought. Gnosis gives itself the World in a dogmatic way as an occasion, not comprehending the occasionality of the World in an immanent way, not bringing about the genesis of occasionality. This is why we insist here on an immanence which is unable to be treated Platonistically or Platonically but practically by immanence itself. All the rest follows....

The instance of the gnostic or pure transcendental will not be blended with thought or alterity, in contrast to the non-philosophical transcendental. It is a "descent" of "the Real into reality and for it" (Saint Gilles). How does one explain this descent, which is not a participation in reality, except by an unrepentant Platonism? The transcendental needs an occasion but it does not imply a descent. Not only the Real but the transcendental remains separated. Yet within non-philosophy the transcendental also is not blended with the alterity of the World, cloning is precisely not a blending. It is the thought which identifies itself in the Real-as-transcendental but the Real remains separated from thought.

Real, Theory or Transcendental, thought or Angel or Non-Thetic Transcendence, we recover here a triad which corresponds to the One, to Being or the Intelligible, to the Soul of the Neoplatonists, with affective changes to the term "soul." This Neoplatonizing interpretation of non-philosophy goes against its sense as well as its modern, scientific and universal *aspects.* Only the "discovery" of the Real as immanent saves gnosis from Neoplatonism.

Only the Stranger-subject is by definition possessed by the passion of heresy, not exactly Man-in-Man, of which we can only say that Man-in-Man is Heresy-in-person, the presupposed of heresy anyway, which is not itself heretical. Heresy, which does not invent itself, is a force, not a forcing, that at best discovers itself and invents itself on this basis.

Is it about "compromising with the World" or "composing" with it as non-religion believes non-philosophy does? Making an exchange or trade-off with it? By what synthesis? Do not confuse the unifacial struggle of the Stranger with the transaction or the face to face of decisions…. The Stranger is the ultimate determination in action of every economy, general or not. Even hatred of the World has its limits; it is still about saving the World from the World.

To give it more justice it is necessary to distinguish between the World which is the global Adversary (with for example the spontaneous decline of philosophy which does not stop indeterminably falling into it) and the two fronts on which non-philosophy struggles, which are the banks of the World: the Friends-Adversaries.

The ultra-Platonist principle of non-religious gnosis: to love theory and to hate practice, to come to theory or turn away from practice. The principle of non-philosophy: theory and practice are identical in-the-last-Humaneity. This is the alpha and omega of the non-Feuerbachian theses.

Non-religious gnosis is a possible interpretation of non-philosophy in its second stage, where the primacy of science in the Real goes hand in hand with a transcendence that is partially reciprocal for the Real and philosophy, where the latter is still not really given-in-One, where real indifference is poorly distinguished from transcendental indifference, and immanent cloning is theoretically nonexistent.

Non-philosophy affirms a "secularity" by principle, as universal as it can be or as philosophy can be. It refuses conspicuous religious adherences in thought, and even the ruse of non-religion, which non-philosophy has the means to unmask and to analyze.

Univocal Publishing
123 North 3rd Street, #202
Minneapolis, MN 55401
www.univocalpublishing.com

ISBN 9781937561055

Jason Wagner, Drew S. Burk
(Editors)
This work was composed in Garamond.
All materials were printed and bound
in October 2012 at Univocal's atelier
in Minneapolis, USA.

The paper is Mohawk Via, Pure White Linen.
The letterpress cover was printed
on Strathmore Premium Wove, Mist Gray.
Both are archival quality and acid-free